CONSTRUCTING CHANGE

Studies in Critical Social Sciences Book Series

Haymarket Books is proud to be working with Brill Academic Publishers (www.brill.nl) to republish the *Studies in Critical Social Sciences* book series in paperback editions. This peer-reviewed book series offers insights into our current reality by exploring the content and consequences of power relationships under capitalism, and by considering the spaces of opposition and resistance to these changes that have been defining our new age. Our full catalog of *SCSS* volumes can be viewed at https://www.haymarketbooks .org/series_collections/4-studies-in-critical-social-sciences.

New Scholarship in Political Economy Book Series

CONSTRUCTING CHANGE

A Political Economy of Housing and Electricity Provision in Turkey

EZGI B. ÜNSAL

Haymarket Books
Chicago, IL

First published in 2021 by Brill Academic Publishers, The Netherlands
© 2021 Koninklijke Brill NV, Leiden, The Netherlands

Published in paperback in 2022 by
Haymarket Books
P.O. Box 180165
Chicago, IL 60618
773-583-7884
www.haymarketbooks.org

ISBN: 978-1-64259-775-2

Distributed to the trade in the US through Consortium Book Sales and
Distribution (www.cbsd.com) and internationally through Ingram Publisher
Services International (www.ingramcontent.com).

This book was published with the generous support of Lannan Foundation and
Wallace Action Fund.

Special discounts are available for bulk purchases by organizations and
institutions. Please call 773-583-7884 or email info@haymarketbooks.org for more
information.

Cover design by Jamie Kerry and Ragina Johnson.

Printed in the United States.

10 9 8 7 6 5 4 3 2 1

Library of Congress Cataloging-in-Publication data is available.

Contents

Preface   IX
Acknowledgements   XII
List of Figures and Tables   XIV

1 **What Is This Book About? General Introduction and Methodology**   1
  1   Objectives and Contribution   1
  2   Methodology and the Structure of Analysis   13
      2.1   *Systematic Dialectics and Hegelian Heritage*   16
      2.2   *Marx's Materialism and the Incorporation of Empirical Material into Theory*   17
      2.3   *Essence and the Process of Change*   20
      2.4   *Levels of Abstraction: Tendencies and Countertendencies*   23
      2.5   *The Value of Labour Power*   29
      2.6   *The Systems of Provision (SOP) Approach to Social Reproduction*   33
  3   Conclusion   37

2 **A Literature Survey on Financialisation**   39
  1   Introduction   39
  2   Financialisation as an Object of Study: The Rise of Finance and Its Impacts on the Economy   41
      2.1   *Cambridge Theories of Distribution*   42
      2.2   *How Do the Cambridge Theories of Distribution Relate to Financialisation?*   45
      2.3   *Empirical Analyses on Firm-level: Decreasing Real Investment, Slowing Down of Accumulation*   48
      2.4   *Empirical Analysis on Aggregate Level: The Impacts of Worsening Income Distribution, Determination of Different Accumulation Regimes*   50
      2.5   *Emphasis upon Increasing Levels of Debt and Securitisation*   53
      2.6   *Asset Price Inflation Approach and 'Forced' Indebtedness*   55
      2.7   *Conclusion*   57
  3   Financialisation as a Reference Point for Periodisation   58
      3.1   *Annales School and Recurrent Financialisation*   60
      3.2   *Financialisation as Coupon Pool: Social Accountancy and Cultural Economy Approach*   60

3.3   *Finance-led Accumulation Regime as an Alternative to Fordist*
        Regime: French Regulation School   63
3.4   *Varieties of Capitalism (VoC) Approach*   66
3.5   *Tri-partite Class Regime and the Crisis of Neoliberalism:*
        Duménil and Lévy   68
3.6   *Financial Expropriation Approach: Lapavitsas and Dos*
        Santos   70
3.7   *The Increasing Presence of Interest-bearing Capital*   71
4   Conclusion   76

3   **Financialisation in Developing and Emerging Economies**   78
1   Introduction   78
2   Historical Development of Financialisation in Developing
     Countries   81
     2.1   *Reserve Accumulation Strategy and the Narrowing Down of the*
             Policy Scope   86
     2.2   *Crowding-out of Investment and Changes in Firm and*
             Institutional Behaviour   91
3   Conclusion   93

4   **The Political Economy of Turkey since 1980**
    Towards Differentiated Global Integration   95
1   Introduction   95
2   1980s and 1990s: Capital Account Liberalisation, Export Boom and
     Public Indebtedness   100
3   Political Economy of Transition: The Differentiated Impacts of the
     2001 Crisis   104
4   After 2001: Restructuring of the Banking Sector   110
5   After 2001: Household Indebtedness   120
6   After 2001: Capital Restructuring?   125
7   Conclusion   131

5   **The Political Economy of Electricity Provision in Turkey**   134
1   Introduction   134
2   Privatisation of Electricity Provision: Rhetoric and Experiences
     around the World   138
     2.1   *Scholarship on Privatisation of Electricity Provision: How and*
             What to Regulate?   143
3   Energy Sector Outlook in Turkey   146
4   Historical Background and Institutional Framework for Electricity
     Provision in Turkey   149

    4.1   *Privatisation Process I: Policy Design and Price Regulation* 152

    4.2   *Privatisation Process II: Addressing Losses and Theft and Other Problems in Implementation* 160

5   The Case of Hydroelectric Power Plants (HEPPs) in Turkey: How They Are Built and Financed 166

    5.1   *Ilisu Dam: A HEPP Project* 172

    5.2   *Coruh Development Plan* 173

6   What Role to the Finance? 176

    6.1   *Firm Financing: An Investigation of Corporate Balance Sheets in the Electricity Industry* 180

7   Conclusion 188

6 The Political Economy of Housing Provision in Turkey 191

1   Introduction 191

2   Production Matters in a Comparative Context: Housing Provision in Britain 195

3   Production upon Landed Property: Marx's Agricultural Rent Theory 200

    3.1   *Rent in Urban Settings* 205

4   The Dynamics of Housing Production in Turkey: A Construction Boom Facilitated through State Institutions 210

    4.1   *A History of Housing Provision in Turkey within the Context of Urbanisation* 214

    4.2   *The Rise of a State Institution in the Transition towards Market-based Provision: TOKI (Housing Development Administration)* 218

5   An Empirical Investigation of the Construction Sector Firms' Financial Statements 225

6   The Dynamics of Housing Consumption in Turkey 232

    6.1   *Housing Consumption: Who Consumes How Much?* 237

7   Conclusion 239

7 Conclusion 244

1   Introduction 244

2   Main Findings and Contribution 244

3   Further Issues and Concluding Remarks 251

Bibliography 255

Index 276

Preface

This book provides a political economy of electricity and housing provision in Turkey. While doing so, it also sheds light on the evolution of the Turkish economy from the early 1980s to its current state.

It is argued that the world economy has been financialising rapidly since the 1980s. Although there is not a single definition of financialisation upon which everyone agrees, it can be broadly and loosely defined as the increasing dominance of financial motives, activities, actors and interests over the real economy with possible destabilising repercussions, as one of the defining features of the contemporary world economy. This book argues that although the Turkish economy was also characterised by the undeniable increase in the volume and importance of financial transactions across different sectors which increased macroeconomic volatility, it also experienced significant increase in its productive capacities. The electricity and housing industries are chosen to show how that strategy played out in reality.

The financialisation literature has given specific importance to the growth of the real estate markets as one of the telling signs of increasing speculative activities across the economies. This book reveals the contribution of the growth of the construction sector to unproductive accumulation through real estate speculation in Turkey, however extremely limited, given the size and depth of the financial markets in the country. However, by explaining how the state-ownership in the land market could facilitate a housing supply boom, the book discusses that the upward pressure on asset prices due to increasing demand was not immediately disruptive for the Turkish housing market. On the aggregate level, it is argued that the growth of the housing industry contributes to unproductive accumulation due to the industry's structural inability to move towards high productivity given its cyclical, short-term nature and labour-intensive production techniques theoretically. In Turkey, on the other hand, the firms operating within the housing industry had strong interlinkages with the energy sector, as most of them had investments in the electricity generation segment with a long-term, capital-intensive character, which contributed to the stability of the housing market and the economy. By emphasising the importance of these contextual elements, the book explores how the outcomes of financial expansion in Turkey especially since the early 2000s have been considerably different than the outcomes in developed economies, which inform the majority of discussions on financialisation often around its destabilising impacts on production, growth and distribution.

However, it is undeniable that the financial expansion process revealed some similar underlying tendencies across the board, such as the commodification of social provision. In order to focus on such common tendencies instead of diverse outcomes, the book shifts its focus away from the contradictory macroeconomic trends, towards investigating the increasing scope and depth of the commodity relations across the economy. Once the focus is placed on the changing nature of commodity relations themselves instead of their impacts on the aggregate economy, the significance of the energy and construction sectors for the Turkish economy is also more clearly understood.

These sectors are crucial for the Turkish economy not only because their share in the aggregate economy is growing, but also because their products reproduce the workforce as they are indispensable for the survival of the society. In that sense, the empirical investigation of these sectors does not only reveal how the financial expansion process simultaneously leads to increased production and systemic volatility, but also how the changing organisational relations within them determine the way in which the workforce is reproduced. In the case of Turkey, such reproduction increasingly depends on the market, which is accepted as a common feature of financialisation across the board.

The book has two distinct but inter-related purposes. The primary, and the more obvious, purpose is to provide a nuanced narrative of the evolution of the contemporary Turkish economy in light of the housing and electricity industries since the 1980s, without portraying it either as a success story in its own right or a doomed economy without any hope for redemption. The second, overarching purpose is to show how two seemingly opposite trends of increasing productive capacities and financialisation can coexist alongside one another, by telling the narrative of the Turkish economy. It is true that many of the studies of contemporary economics do not place much value on the contingent narrative details of real-life economic phenomenon, as long as those details do not lead to neat cause and effect links as informed by the theory. This book also suggests that a different way of theorising is possible, in which the contextual details are not the noise, but rather indispensable parts of the whole. In fact, this methodological consideration is the underlying narrative thread of this book, which binds its different parts together.

As the book is based on my PhD thesis completed at SOAS, University of London, Economics Department in 2018, it is possible for the reader to detect an ongoing conversation with the scholars and practitioners within the economics profession. In that sense, the book aims at reaching out to readers who are interested in the evolution of the contemporary Turkish economy and also those who are interested in the discussion and application of different methodologies within economics. As economics has established itself as

a social science with an exclusive use of the formal analytical method especially since the 1950s, contextual empirical studies are occupying less and less
space within the profession as opposed to top-down approaches making use
of collective data. Adopting a contextual approach and emphasising its necessity alongside other methods, this book is designed to communicate with the
general audience without a professional training in economics, but also those
who are familiar with such methodological and theoretical discussions within
economics.

Since the completion of my thesis in 2018, the Turkish economy has entered
a new, volatile macroeconomic path triggered by the sudden devaluation of
the Turkish Lira in mid-2018 and deepened by the global Covid-19 pandemic
in 2020. At the time of writing this book in 2020, the Covid-19 pandemic is
still ongoing, with possible unforeseeable long-term effects. Therefore, I have
chosen not to discuss this period in the book at length, and instead focus on
the previous long-term path, which paved the way for the current state of
the economy. Throughout the book, the reader should remember that most
of the empirical work conducted is related to the pre-Covid-19 Turkish economy. However, given the structural approach adopted, we can safely claim that
many of the trends identified here will continue to prevail after 2020.

The findings contribute to the literature on the financialisation of social
provision and the political economy of Turkey, by confirming that social provision sectors are increasingly under the influence of finance, making these
sectors prone to volatility while contributing to their growth at the same time.

Acknowledgements

This book is based on my PhD research conducted at SOAS, University of London. The thesis itself has been a product of a difficult, yet the most valuable learning process in my life so far. Many people helped me throughout. First and foremost, I am more than grateful to my thesis supervisor Ben Fine, who has always been very generous with his time, patience and knowledge beyond worldly limits.

I am thankful to Jeff Powell and Ismail Erturk for reading the thesis so thoroughly and providing insightful comments. I am thankful to Costas Lapavitsas, who encouraged me to start the PhD and provided support and supervision during my first year. Alfredo Saad-Filho was immensely helpful throughout. I couldn't have started this PhD without the encouragement and support of Onur Yildirim from METU. He provided great academic and personal support during my years at METU and believed that I could be happy at SOAS.

It was true that SOAS Economics Department was a facilitating and welcoming environment, and I am grateful to so many of its members. Ourania Dimakou provided encompassing guidance, and became a source of inspiration with her kindness, intelligence and humour. Elif Karacimen was another source of inspiration, who patiently read my work during the early stages of the PhD. I am thankful to Bruno Bonizzi for his friendship and academic support, I always felt very lucky to have known a truly reliable friend and colleague like him. Simon Dikau has been a great friend; I will miss our long weekend lunch breaks and museum visits.

Besides being a member of my department, I felt lucky to be a part of the wider SOAS community. Since the day we met, Franziska Fay has always been by my side throughout this journey. Nithya Natarajan, Mehroosh Tak and Zoe Goodman gave me great support during the final year, this book could not have been completed without them. Shreya Sinha, Aditya Ramesh, Pinar Cakiroglu, Serap Sarıtas, Francesco Formichella, Lorena Lombardozzi, Sara Stevano, Jo Tomkinson, Ayse Arslan, Victoria Stadheim, Amrisha Uriep, Lea Bou Khater, Eurydice Fotopolou and many others helped me in different ways throughout.

I am thankful to the theory and life discussions with Christian Koutny, who patiently listened to many details of this book. I've been so lucky to have a caring friend like Mersiye Bora, whose unconditional friendship is one of the most solid, reassuring things in my life. Ozge Unsal is also my rock. Fatmanur Sari helped with the name of the book. Anastasia Apostolou has listened to every single detail of my life and I'm grateful for the insights she provided which have changed me deeply for the better.

Finally, I would like to thank my family, my sister and friend Bensu Unsal, and my mom and dad. This book is dedicated to them, who gave me so much without expecting anything in return.

Figures and Tables

Figures

1   Share of electricity generation and construction sector credits in total domestic credits   2
2   Disaggregation of total debts in Turkey   5
3   Exports of goods and services in Turkey (% of GDP)   97
4   Gross fixed capital formation in Turkey (% of GDP)   98
5   External debt stock (% of GNI)   99
6   Disaggregation of total debts in Turkey according to sectors   112
7   Total loans issued by domestic banks in Turkey (according to currency types)   112
8   The share of foreign exchange liabilities in total liabilities of financial sector   113
9   Financial sector FX position in Turkey   114
10   Turkish financial sector loans maturity structure (% of total financial sector loans)   115
11   Short-term external debt stock by borrower   115
12   Short-term external debt stock by borrower (% of total short-term external private debt)   116
13   Total credit liabilities in Turkey (flow – million USD)   117
14   Turkish non-financial corporations credit liabilities maturity structure (% of total credits)   117
15   Credits given to SMEs by domestic banks in Turkey (million USD)   118
16   Current account deficit financing items in Turkey   119
17   Credit types issued by domestic banks in Turkey as a ratio of total credits   122
18   Credit types issued by domestic banks in Turkey as a ratio of GDP   122
19   Disaggregated consumer credits in Turkey (nominal, billion TRY)   123
20   Disaggregated consumer credits (% of total consumer credits)   123
21   Disaggregated consumer credits (% of GDP)   124
22   Turkish non-financial corporations' total FX liabilities   126
23   The historical institutional structure of electricity provision in Turkey   150
24   The share of the public sector in electricity segments (2001-2014)   153
25   Public sector (TETAS) electricity trade   156
26   TETAS average wholesale electricity prices   157
27   Electricity sector openness ratio and free consumer limits through time   158
28   Electric power transmission and distribution losses (% of total output)   160
29   TEIAS investment program costs and actual costs   163

30   Domestic electricity prices according to sectors   165
31   Sample hydroelectric power plant model   169
32   The share of electricity generated by HEPPs (including a dam) in
       Turkey (%)   171
33   The shares of different types of electricity generation facilities in total industry
       investments   171
34   Coruh Development Plan   174
35   Comparison of textiles, electricity and construction industries according to
       their shares in total domestic credits   178
36   Credits given to electricity and construction industries (share of total
       credit)   178
37   The breakdown of total cash loans given to electricity generation, natural gas
       and hydraulic resources industry according to maturity and currency type   179
38   The breakdown of domestic credits given to electricity generation, natural gas
       and hydraulic resources industry according to maturity and loan type   179
39   Total amount of foreign credits obtained by the energy sector (billion $)   180
40   Electricity firms' liability structure   183
41   The share of shareholders' equity in total electricity firm liabilities   184
42   The share of bank loans in total electricity firm liabilities   184
43   Electricity firms trade accounts   185
44   The composition of assets according to durability (electricity industry)   185
45   The share of total financial assets in total assets (electricity industry)   186
46   The share of total short-term financial assets in total assets (electricity
       industry)   186
47   The breakdown of marketable securities item according to types (electricity
       industry)   187
48   The share of tangible fixed assets in total assets (electricity industry)   187
49   Annual building construction permits issued in Turkey   194
50   Comparison of construction sector growth and real GDP growth in Turkey   212
51   Domestic bank credits given to construction sector in Turkey   213
52   Credits held by construction sector firms   227
53   Construction sector firms short-term and long-term bank credits as a share of
       total liabilities   228
54   Construction sector firms liability structure   228
55   Construction sector firms asset structure (share of total assets)   229
56   Share of land, buildings and plant, machinery and equipment items in total
       assets   229
57   Housing credits as a share of total household credits and number of housing
       loan borrowers as a share of total loan borrowers in Turkey   234
58   Real credit growth in housing in 2015 (annual percentage change)   234

59   Residential property price index (2017=100)   235
60   Price-to-rent ratio in housing (2015: index 2010=100)   236
61   The amount of credits given to households below median income level (as a
      share of total household credits)   239

Tables

1   Comparison of selected economic performance criteria in middle income
      countries   8
2   The development of installed capacity for electricity in Turkey   148
3   Privatisation of electricity industry timeline   151
4   Loss-theft aim ratios of selected regional distribution-retail companies   162
5   Actors and tender values in electricity distribution-retail segments   164
6   Fixed and variable cost characteristics of various electricity generation
      technologies   167
7   CBRT company account statistics, electricity generation, natural gas and
      hydraulic resources industry   182
8   Strassmann's findings regarding the relationship between construction and
      economic development   211
9   Fixed capital investments made by different sectors   213
10   Selected revenue-sharing projects of TOKI according to tender values   222
11   CBRT company account statistics construction sector firms   226
12   Construction seasonally and calendar adjusted turnover index   230
13   Construction seasonally and calendar adjusted production index   231
14   Construction total hours worked and gross wages and salaries indices   231
15   Percentage of household credit borrowers according to income groups   238
16   Amount of credits issued according to income groups (million TRY)   240
17   Number of loans issued according to income groups (million TRY)   241

CHAPTER 1

What Is This Book About? General Introduction and Methodology

1   Objectives and Contribution

This book is based on my PhD research conducted from 2013 to 2018, which started as an attempt to understand the developments within the energy and construction sectors in Turkey, which have continued to be primary drivers of accumulation since the early 2000s. During the course of my studies, the Turkish economy has changed very rapidly, along with the rest of the world. However, most of the trends this book discusses, such as financialisation and marketisation of social provision have prevailed, even deepened. As the book is primarily focused on the pace and direction of change, the research stays as relevant as it was in 2013, if not more.

Since the early 2000s, the rapid growth of these sectors drew considerable attention. Among total project finance credits, energy sector projects have received 42% in December 2019, while the share of infrastructure and real estate and infrastructure has been 30% and 10%, respectively.[1] The increase in the share of energy project credits was rapid especially until 2016, increasing from 8.2% of GDP in December 2015 to 8.9% of GDP in June 2016. The success of these three sectors with strong inter-linkages in attracting credits in comparison to other sectors is striking, especially considering that the aggregate share of all other sectors in total project credits was 18% in December 2019, including traditionally powerful industries such as textiles of which credit share was around 4%, decreasing from 13% in 2000.[2] In June 2020, electricity generation sector received 6.8% of all credits, while the share of construction was 8.3% in the same period (see Figure 1).

The fast growth of these sectors was significant, not least because such transition has also been a primary source of social and political conflict and acquired a symbolic value in representing the fast pace of change the Republic has experienced since the election of the AKP government in 2002. At a time

---

1   Disaggregated biannual project finance statistics have started to be collected by The Banks Association of Turkey (BAT) from December 2014 (www.tbb.org.tr).

2   Banking Regulation and Supervision Agency (BRSA) Interactive Monthly Bulletin (http://ebulten.bddk.org.tr).

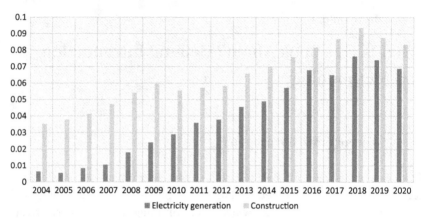

FIGURE 1   Share of electricity generation and construction sector credits in total domestic credits

when the global direction of change had been associated with decreasing productive investment in the core economies, change in Turkey was mostly associated with rapid urban transformation, facilitated through a wide spectrum of construction projects, from residential houses to giant slum regenerations, roads, airports and bridges. The construction boom did not remain limited to the urban arena as it was highly related to the growth in the energy sector too, as 919 hydroelectric and 565 thermal power plants had been issued licences for electricity generation from 2003 to 2017.

This book argues that from 2001 to 2017, the expansion of these two sectors also reflected a wider organisational transformation of the economy, which was not limited to a secular boom in financial or consumption incomes. Indeed, these developments were in line with a relatively optimistic growth pattern with an inflation rate of 7.5 per cent in 2015, 2.5 percentage points above the target, in a period when many of the countries in the region, especially many East European countries such as Hungary and Poland, fell into a deflationary spiral (IMF, 2015). The Turkish economy operated within a relative stable macroeconomic climate from 2001 to 2017. Although the economy has entered a new volatile phase since 2018 triggered by the devaluation of Turkish Lira in the international markets, which has lost almost 50% of its value against dollar in a year, the book will primarily focus on the previous long-term path. This choice is made in order to explain the specific role played by the energy and construction sectors in the accumulation pattern, which is only fully understood in the long-term, but also to investigate the development of the sectors themselves without significant external shocks.

Rodrik (2009) showed that especially during 2000-2008, GDP per capita and GDP per worker improved significantly, the annual rate of growth of GDP per worker increasing from below 0.025% during 1990-2000 to above 0.035% during 2000-2008. Gross fixed capital formation stayed at an annual average of 25.2% (with an annual growth rate of 7%) and 28.2% (with an annual growth rate of 3.4%) as a share of GDP during 2001-2008 and 2009-2016, respectively. This was promising and slightly above the world average of 24.6%, although not comparable to the fastest growing economies such as China, for which gross capital formation level was well above 45% of its GDP during 2010-2016.[3]

On the other hand, other aggregate performance criteria were not as promising, especially considering that such relative success was achieved at the expense of a growing current account deficit and were not translated as improvements in employment. Unemployment stayed persistently high above the 10-12% band during the entire post-2001 period. These aspects raised concerns whether the growth path in Turkey, sustained through incoming short-term capital flows following the gradual capital market opening since 1980s, was robust and sustainable in terms of contributing to employment and leading to significant structural change (Demir, 2009a; Onaran, 2006; Onaran and Stockhammer, 2005; Onis, 2006; Yeldan, 2006; Yenturk, 1999). These concerns were further supported by the rapidly declining growth rates since 2018, which decreased from 7.4% in 2017 to 2.8% in 2018 and 0.9% in 2019.

In this light, the book also tries to locate the developments within energy and construction sectors within a systemic narrative that would also contribute to the understanding of the workings of the Turkish economy in particular, as a constituent part of the world economy. Among many other possible avenues, it was the thrust of the financialisation literature that provided the most systemic and critical insights into the issues at hand, especially with respect to the global developments taking place in financial markets and their impacts in general, and their 'transmission' through financial liberalisation in developing countries in particular.

As Karacimen (2014) argues, one of the first telling signs of the financialisation of the Turkish economy is the financial deepening through an expansion of financial services to a broader base of population. In line with global trends, there was an increasing orientation towards financial activities in the country, which led to the establishment of secondary asset markets in housing as well as electricity, combined with a boom in consumption credits rising as a

---

3   World Bank National Accounts Data (http://data.worldbank.org). Also see Table 1 for a comparison of select macroeconomic performance criteria of different middle-income countries.

share of GDP from 1.8% in 2002 to 18.7% in 2012, within which the share of personal loans increased from 4.7% in 2002 to 33.5% in 2012 (Karacimen, 2014). For the financialisation literature, there is usually a link between the growing consumer indebtedness and declining productive investment levels in economies, as the growing consumption is an important indication for the economy's attempt to boost aggregate demand in the face of a structural ability to facilitate long-term productive investment (Dymski, 2010; Lapavitsas, 2013; Toporowski, 2009).

Within that framework, the growth of the real estate sector has a specific importance as one of the pillars of a consumption-driven aggregate demand structure, which in turns contributes to the macroeconomic fragility given its proneness to generate rapid boom-bust cycles as seen in the 2008 crisis (Bernanke and Gertler, 2000; Borio and Lowe, 2002; Dymski, 2010; Montgomerie and Büdenbender, 2015; Wray, 2008). As Bernanke and Gertler (2000) argued, however, the relevance of the housing markets for economists, and of the asset markets in general, stayed limited to the extent they signal underlying inflationary forces. The financialisation literature has a unique approach to the housing studies in the sense that it extends the relevance of the asset markets through establishing theoretical links between inflationary (speculative) asset markets and financial and macroeconomic instability. Through a systemic lens, the financialisation literature does not only investigate the possible destabilising impacts of the underlying inflationary forces within the housing markets, but also explores how the development of speculative housing markets through the promotion of individual consumption affects the composition of aggregate demand in favour of consumption during a period of declining productive investment levels and stagnant growth.

However, given that the financialisation literature examines the impacts of inflationary asset markets primarily on a macroeconomic level, it has its limitations. This is especially visible in investigating the Turkish case, where the inflationary processes in the asset markets were accompanied by a substantial increase in credits expended for productive investment, resulting in an expansion of total loans given to non-financial corporations, especially after 2010. As Figure 2 demonstrates, though increasing rapidly since 2010, household indebtedness in Turkey stayed comparatively low compared to indebtedness levels in the non-financial and financial sectors.

Indeed, the growth in the non-financial corporations segment was rapid since the 1990s, as its share in the GDP increased from 65 per cent in 1990 to 83 per cent in 2006, while the share of the public sector halved from 35 per cent to 16 per cent in the same period. Rodrik (2009) claims that the importance of such growth was that it signalled an economy-wide technical change,

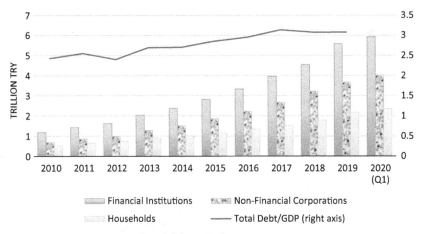

FIGURE 2   Disaggregation of total debts in Turkey

as evident in the increase of the share of plant, machinery and equipment in private gross fixed capital formation, which almost doubled from 32.5 per cent in 1989 to 70.4 per cent in 2006. However, especially since 2010, it is argued that most of the new investments were made in non-productive sectors such as construction, which is seen as a short-term strategy with serious limitations for future growth (Orhangazi, 2020).

Within this macroeconomic outlook, this book will investigate the specific role of the construction and energy sectors, which grew simultaneously during 2002-2017 in Turkey. As the investigation of the real estate markets gained a significant importance within the financialisation literature, the book benefits from its insights immensely, in terms of acknowledging the systemic nature of the issue. However, it also diverges from that literature in terms of its methodological focus, as the majority of financialisation studies use a primarily macroeconomic lens.

If we are to adopt a macroeconomic focus, the real estate asset markets in Turkey are not meaningfully important given their size. In Turkey, the value of mortgage loans as a share of GDP did not even reach 1 per cent prior to the Mortgage Law in 2007, and it did not exceed 7 per cent even as late as 2017.[4] However, irrespective of such relative macroeconomic insignificance, the increasing trend in individual housing consumption has been striking especially since the reorganisation of the market through a state institution

---

4   BAT (The Banks Association of Turkey) consumer and housing credits statistics (www.tbb. org.tr).

named TOKI (Housing Development Administration) between 2002-2004 and the enactment of Mortgage Law in 2007. In order to detect how a speculative housing market is formed under such conditions, the book abandons the conventional macroeconomic focus and instead takes a closer look into the workings of the housing markets themselves.

Once that approach was adopted and research proceeded, some discrepancies became more evident between what was observed in Turkey and the postures of the financialisation literature due to such methodological difference. One problematic conclusion of that conventional macroeconomic focus is the geographical bias towards core economies. As one of the primary financialisation hypotheses suggests a global orientation of the non-financial sector towards financial activities, the macroeconomic focus leads many to investigate whether this results in lower levels of physical investment, hence to stagnant or fragile growth (Tori and Onaran, 2015). However, as the size and the depth of financial markets in developing economies are not comparable to the core economies as exemplified above, such shift usually cannot be empirically observed on a macro level, although they are going through substantial changes themselves.

A second problematic feature of the literature is that it builds upon a dichotomous understanding of the interests of 'finance' as a whole (including a variety of actors, motives with conflicting interests) as opposed to the real economy. Indeed, there is a certain stream within the literature, combining the Varieties of Capitalism (VoC) approach with the analytical focus of financialisation studies. This approach acknowledges that different institutional settings play a role in the emergence of accumulation systems if, for example, the interests of 'financial rentiers' are conducive to production as long as ownership structures allow for a collusion of financial and productive activities with a close association of big banks and businesses in coordinated (export-led) as opposed to liberal (consumption-led) economies, or if financial centres with a stronger national or regional orientation have been successful in combining the two areas of activity (Engelen et al., 2010b; Gabor and Ban, 2013; Hall and Soskice, 2001).

The VoC approach has been valuable in terms of rejecting a 'convergence' hypothesis with respect to the impacts of finance on different macroeconomic configurations and emphasising differentiated comparative performance. In the case of Turkey, which is far from being unique, the links between the big banks and businesses in Turkey have been traditionally strong since the early days of the Republic. After the restructuring of the financial system following the 2001 crisis which eliminated many small risky banks, this structure was even strengthened, contributing to an accumulation system in which the characteristics of both comparative systems were present. While a decline in gross savings was followed by a consumption boom and increasing unemployment in the post-2001 period, export performance of manufacturing sector also improved. Although such improvement could not result in the diversion of gains into private savings through a capacity for strategic labour coordination, which determines the ultimate success of export-led economies according to Gabor and Ban (2013), the two trends (financial and export orientation) existed simultaneously in Turkey. The book examines these trends without attempting to detect whether one predominates over the other, but rather putting the emphasis on the ways in which the financial system relates to the broader society, more nuanced in the actual operation of economies than a structural separation between those that lend and those that borrow money (Ashman and Fine, 2013).

A third problem with the literature on financialisation has been identified as the presence of dichotomous understanding of the state existing as an independent body with clear and unchanging objectives as opposed to those of businesses. Again, it should be noted that the literature acknowledges that the impacts of globalised competition on welfare expenditures would be mixed, depending whether competition will lead to a shift from delivering of public goods to public inputs or increased social expenditures in order to compensate for increased social risks (Hall and Soskice, 2001; Onaran and Boesch, 2014; Rodrik, 1998). Nevertheless, it is important to also acknowledge that these two trends have been going hand-in-hand in many countries, irrespective of which one dominates. Public expenditure as a ratio of GDP increased substantially after 1990 in Turkey; general government consumption increasing from 12% of GDP in 2000 to almost 15% in 2018, as Table 1 below shows. Meanwhile, the period also witnessed intensified privatisation experiences, electricity being among many of these such as telecommunications and mining, far from suggesting a clear pattern for the state's involvement in the delivery of public goods.

Here it is necessary to add that the existing empirical literature on financialisation does not sharply contrast with the arguments of this book, and the possible avenues for finance to facilitate output are acknowledged especially within the context of developing countries (Gabor, 2010; Stockhammer and Onaran, 2013). Nevertheless, the financialisation literature does theoretically favour the crowding-out of investment hypothesis with an emphasis on how unproductive channels of lending has been conducive to consumption-induced demand or how comparative advantage was achieved in many countries through export competitiveness based on wage suppression instead of structural change.

TABLE 1   Comparison of selected economic performance criteria in middle income countries

% of GDP	General government Final consumption		Gross capital formation		Exports of goods and services		Imports of goods and services		Gross savings	
	2000	2018	2000	2018	2000	2018	2000	2018	2000	2018
Turkey	12	14.8	18	29.6	20	29.5	23	30.6	18	27
Latin American	15	16.5	20	18.7	19	23.1	20	23.4	17	16.8
Lower middle income	11	11.7	22	28.3	27	25.8	26	31.5	25	26.5
Upper middle income	16	16.3	26	30.8	27	25.2	23	23.8	28	31.4
High income	17	17.8	24	22.1	26	32	26	30.8	24	23.1

SOURCE: WORLD BANK NATIONAL ACCOUNTS DATABANK

These observations led to a search for an alternative systemic explanation, as the main thrusts of the financialisation literature alone could not account for the developments within the energy and construction sectors in Turkey or identify the wider organisational developments around them. Despite the problems identified, the financialisation literature has been incredibly helpful to connect what has been going on in core economies with respect to the emergence of "secondary" circuits of capital as in the proliferation of complex derivative financial assets and activities as well as rising inequality and segregation in consumption, which the literature has succeeded in highlighting and bringing together; meanwhile the developments in transition economies such as Turkey have been increasing production going hand-in-hand with these developments.

To reflect these multifaceted processes, instead of breaking with the tradition of financialisation, the book places the focus on the *increasing scope and depth of commodity relations across the economy,* shifting the focus away from the macroeconomic issues of growth, stability and investment as discussed above. As change comes in many forms and ways, so do its consequences. In the context of developing economies, the increasing importance of finance as a whole is not easily observable as the financial markets are not deep and broad enough to support extensive asset markets. They are, nevertheless changing, first of all, with respect to the global developments of the financial markets themselves. The literature on financialisation of developing economies has been interested in investigating such a transition facilitated through the changes in the core, by focusing also on the impacts of intensifying capital flows on the domestic exchange and interest rates which further affect the real economy determinants (Bonizzi, 2013; Kaltenbrunner, 2011; Kaltenbrunner and Painceira, 2015; Painceira, 2009; Powell, 2013). However, this book argues that the developing economies have been experiencing change not only as a transmission mechanism from the core, but also domestically in their own right, which is visible in the *increasing scope and depth of commodity relations* across the economy.

This understanding is in line with a particular context-specific methodology and a ground theory in economic history, which is unfortunately no longer accepted widely within the mainstream economics discipline but discussed broadly within its heterodox schools of thought. On the basis of this ground theory, which keeps the focus primarily on the ways in which accumulation proceeds, financialisation is conceptualised ın accordance with the layered formation of the accumulation process: consisting of tendencies, countertendencies, as well as contingencies; operating on different levels of abstraction and interacting with one another. In that respect, financialisation is concerned not only with the heavier presence of finance and its corresponding impacts on distribution, aggregate demand and/or investment and growth, but how the economies evolve with respect to these structural as well as contingent forces, and identifying the areas of potential change where conflicting forces interact with each other (Fine, 2013). The potential for change is for example manifested through the risks that are associated with the securitisation process: that once money is advanced to make more money in expectation of interest and there is an obligation to repay, it can take on a market life of its own, i.e. securities and derivate assets emerge which bear no relation to the original value of the debt/stock. The detrimental impacts of this process on the real economy were seen in the collapse of the housing asset bubble in the USA in 2008.

Building upon the macro-level insights of financialisation studies, this book investigates the processes of financialisation locally, through the investigation of increasing depth and scope of commodity relations in and around provision goods (housing and electricity in particular), while also placing it within a global context. The choice of provision goods as the location to look for this

dynamic related to another crucial consideration of this book that is not discussed by the financialisation literature per se, but is the reflection of a ground
theory mentioned above.

This understanding concerns the impacts of financialisation on the *value of
labour power,* which is not discussed by the financialisation literature directly,
but is an important consideration of the particular understanding of financialisation conceptualised in this book. The value of labour power is defined as the
collection of provision goods which are necessary for the workforce's survival,
and the money wages that can buy these goods. Therefore, their production
processes concern not only the sectors themselves, but the reproduction of
the workforce itself. Conceptualised by Fine and Leopold (1993), the systems
of provision approach investigates how the provision goods are produced and
consumed as the commodity relations deepen within an economy. This book
adopts this commodity-specific approach in analysing the construction and
energy sectors.

From that perspective, the analysis of the energy and construction sectors has two simultaneous concerns: first, how the workforce is reproduced
through the wage goods of electricity and housing in Turkey; and, second, how
this process is in tandem with the broader commodity production processes of
the economy. In that sense, it has a specific methodological lens which makes
such investigation a crucial part of the analysis. The second half of this chapter
is devoted to the discussion of these methodological concerns fully, in order to
locate the following chapters in a more grounded theoretical framework.

As a result, this book is both highly abstract, with respect to the methodological and theoretical discussions, which will be pursued in Chapters 1 and 2,
and highly concrete with respect to the conduct of individual empirical studies
in Chapters 5 and 6. The conceptual framework on financialisation and the
value of labour power has been indispensable for investigating the empirical
studies with respect to their national and global context more fully, as well
as framing them in a theoretical context. On the other hand, the individual
political economy analyses of electricity and housing help us understand what
is happening around these commodities in Turkey, which is a good exercise in
examining change with respect to *how it is occurring.* The book seeks to hold its
separate pieces together through this methodological thread.

This introduction aside, this chapter consists of another section on methodology and the structure of analysis, investigating the different methodologies
employed in Marxian political economy and explaining the specific interpretation adopted in this book with respect to its relevance for the determination of the value of labour power and its place in the systems of provision
approach. Starting with the widely-accepted interpretation named *systematic*

dialectics, it discusses how the interpretation adopted in this book differs from systematic dialectics with respect to Marx's materialism that brings a historical and empirical aspect to the analysis, on the basis of the concept of essence, unfolding within a layered formation of causal structures, consisting of tendencies and countertendencies and contingencies, interacting with each other at all times. It then describes the different ways in which the value of labour power can be determined. Drawing upon this, the last section describes how the systems of provision approach is interested in revealing the ways in which the value of power is lowered through commodification of provision goods, together with increasing (and changing) living standards differentiated within and across income groups.

Chapter 2 will provide *a literature review on financialisation* with respect to the concerns raised, and the definition given above. On the basis of the methodological principles laid out in Chapter 1, it identifies two distinct methods for approaching financialisation and gives its own definition. By theorising financialisation along a continuum of increasing commodity relations leading to the restructuring of the circuits of interest-bearing capital in overall accumulation, the book suggests that many definitions of financialisation with predetermined impacts on the overall accumulation patterns may or may not be present depending on the specific development trajectories, especially located within an uneven global context, which will be discussed in Chapter 3 on *financialisation in developing and emerging economies.*

The emphasis of the financialisation in developing and emerging economies literature has been on the negative impacts of financial deepening through capital account liberalisation and the entrance of foreign actors on the scope of domestic policy options, together with widening opportunities for speculative activities such as carry-trade. The dependent nature of the integration of developing countries and the importance of uneven international relations are also emphasised.

Locating Turkey in a comparative context, Chapter 4 will provide *a political economy of Turkey since the 1980s.* It is widely acknowledged in the literature that the gradual capital account liberalisation since the early 1980s gave rise to a secular increase in the net primary arbitrage gains, especially over dollar-denominated assets, the annual average uncovered interest arbitrage (UIA) gains reaching 10, 19 and 40 per cent during 1989-1994, 1995-2001 and 2002-2007, respectively (Onis and Senses, 2009). However, this book argues that the financial deepening during the 1980s and 1990s *also* benefited the restructuring of industrial capital in the following period, visible in the shift from low-technology to higher-technology industries and productive techniques within manufacturing sector in the post-2001 crisis period.

Specifically, Chapter 4 discusses how manufacturing firms could channel appreciated currency into capital deepening, while fiscal expansion contributed to aggregate demand during a period when the private demand was not so strong. 2001 crisis and the subsequent financial sector restructuring process with the help of the IMF have constituted a historical turning point through its differentiated impacts on different actors in the economy. The crisis contributed to capital deepening through favouring internationally competitive large conglomerates with tight relations to the financial sector, over smaller enterprises, as their access to credit decreased significantly after the elimination of small and riskier banks during the financial sector restructuring.

In short, Chapter 4 emphasises that through reinforcing the existing oligopolistic structure and protecting industrial mark-up rates, the policy practices that are readily associated with financialised accumulation, such as labour market and financial deregulation, were beneficial for both financial and industrial restructuring in Turkey. This aspect shows divergence from what is underlined by the financialisation literature with respect to the developments in the core, which suggests a crowding-out impact of the financial interests, with these developing at the expense of productive investment, or leading to an export boom through wage squeeze without significant structural change.

Chapter 5 will move on to the first core empirical study of the book on *electricity provision in Turkey*. Together with the commodification process of electricity facilitated through gradual privatisation since the early 1980s, the restructuring process discussed in the previous chapter has been most relevant for the electricity system, as the increasing levels of productive investment mostly benefited the generation segment associated with high economies of scale, through accelerated construction of hydroelectric and thermal plants. The relevance of the finding that there was considerable increase in the productive capacity of this sector is discussed in relation to the theoretical framework adopted in this book and the financialisation of nature literature.

The sixth chapter is dedicated to the political economy of *housing provision in Turkey*. Housing markets are mostly discussed in the context of mature capitalist economies with respect to the possible impacts of increasing dependence on owner-occupation and corresponding increase in housing demand on overall accumulation through speculative price appreciations. Within the Turkish context, especially the path followed by the housing industry differed significantly from the developed country cases, where the housing sectors acquired an output-restricting character upon increasing consumption demand. In contrast, the housing industry in Turkey was characterised with a supply boom especially after the restructuring of a state institution, Housing Development

Administration (TOKI), between 2002-2004, increasing the annual building permits from just over 40,000 in 2002 to over 140,000 in in 2014 (TURKSTAT). The reasons behind this phenomenon will be discussed in Chapter 6, especially in reference to the productive characteristics of the housing industry in general and the importance of the social relations surrounding landed property, by locating Turkey in a comparative context.

It is argued that some productive characteristics of housebuilding industry can be conducive to the emergence of speculative housing markets, in case the natural division due to different risk/return characteristics between capital-intensive land development and labour-intensive housebuilding industries are obstructed by the limited availability of land (Ball, 1983). By drawing upon Marx's theory of agricultural rent, this book argues that the intervention of landed property might give rise to a speculative structure without this being necessarily reflected as output restriction and globalised price appreciations. In Turkey, both localised and sectoral level rent revenues facilitated through the state could be appropriated as capital gains by all the actors in the sector, although this process did not threaten overall accumulation as the consumer base as well as risk diversification of financial institutions stayed limited, and the supply boom prevented the sharp price increases. Moreover, the intersectoral linkages with the energy sector protected profitability for especially larger firms, which could continue operating within a highly competitive industry.

Chapter 7 concludes by outlining possible new research areas and emphasising that the findings further support the underlining methodology adopted in the book which implies that the analysis of provision systems, as well as financialisation, is context-specific and the focus is analytically situated on the entirety of organisational relations including the economic, social and historical dimensions.

2 Methodology and the Structure of Analysis

The methodology adopted in this book is along the lines of a certain reading of Marxian political economy. As is general knowledge, Marx's methodology has long been a subject of contested debates and there are many, sometimes conflicting interpretations. This chapter will not provide a comprehensive literature survey of such differences in interpretation as it is beyond the scope of this book. Some methodological aspects in different traditions will be selectively presented, however, throughout the chapter to clarify some disputed issues and their relevance for the methodology adopted.

The modern reader who is familiar with the contemporary economic theory might question the relevance of an extensive methodology discussion in a book about the political economy of construction and energy sectors in Turkey. The discussions on methodology exist not only because locating the following empirical chapters in a theoretical context is necessary. There is another important reason for the decision to include this part. Today, methodological debate is mostly absent in the economics profession, a science which has more or less accomplished to present itself as the only 'positive' social science especially since the 1950s and overcame all confusions concerning its method (Blaug, 2003; Fine and Dimakou, 2016). As the book favours a more contextual understanding of the economy instead of a positivistic approach, this chapter outlines how a contextual understanding is not necessarily in conflict with ground theories, but it can be conceptualised theoretically. Although this issue is discussed within the Marxian political economy context in that book, my purpose is less to prove that this way of understanding is the one and only way, but more to show it is *a* legitimate way among many other possible avenues. If this book has any methodological claims, it is in fact precisely the emphasis on the existence of such plurality in the ways of seeing the world, of which debate has long been absent in the economics profession. It is also this methodological claim which binds the otherwise separate chapters of the book together.

The methodological reading adopted in this book follows from Ilyenkov's (1977) outline of Marx's dialectical logic, along the lines of the interpretation presented by Fine and Harris (1979) and Fine (1982a) and later by Saad-Filho (2002). This interpretation is first based upon that Marx's political economy concerning capitalism takes its departure from a more general understanding of human nature as fundamentally social and relational, i.e. not existing in isolation from its social surroundings. As this issue has been discussed widely, such as in the debates on Marx's transition from his earlier works to 'mature' works, it relates to his materialistic understanding of history.

Briefly, it depends on the understanding of human beings with different, usually conflicting motives. As history has not existed since the beginning of time, it is determined by the contradictory interactions of human beings with nature, with their productive instincts and with their fellow human beings. There are three basic contradictions that lie behind the dynamics of history (Milonakis, 1997). First, there is the contradiction between nature and human beings, giving rise to the act of production and productive forces, as human beings transform nature with their productive forces. In this sense, capitalism is a mode of production. This relationship is mediated through the relations between human beings in the production process giving rise to production relations. In the capitalist mode of production, production relations take the form of class relations between wage-labour with no access to their means of production and capitalists who own the means of production. Methodologically speaking, this helps us explain why Marx's analysis begins with class, rather than the individual. As Milonakis (1997) claims, there is also a third contradiction between productive forces and production relations depending on the outcomes of the first two, which defines the actual developmental course of history. While the relationship between human beings and nature leads to the development of productive forces, the relationship between classes leads to class conflict and the relationship between these two explains the existence of certain trajectories of development.

It is important to emphasise that Marx's analysis of capitalism in the three volumes of Capital is to provide a critique of capitalism based upon its understanding as a historical reality, which not only serves as a conditioning environment to humans, but also is conditioned by them. In that regard, political economy is not studied in isolation from history, but is an integral part of history. This is not to suggest a purely historical, inductive take on political economy but rather to accept that the laws of political economy work under the laws of motion of history *in general* as a product of collective human development. Along with his understanding of historical movement in general, there is another a priori consideration that the capitalist economy is a systemically integrated whole that is both logically prior to, and greater than the sum of its parts. The analysis starts from this given whole, which is the capitalist economy as the simple abstract, as a mirror image of the concrete reality of capitalism. Then it proceeds towards the concrete material processes on the basis of an essence that is determined by this whole in order to reconstruct the concrete material in thought. So far, these aspects of Marx's philosophy are not specific to his analysis of capitalism but will be discussed very briefly in the next section to clarify some issues which are relevant for the purposes of this book.

The aim of this chapter is to locate the following chapters on such an understanding of Marx's method and his analysis of capitalism, first, on the basis of two overarching themes and then to move on to other closely related theoretical issues that are a primary consequence of his method, such as the conceptualisation of the value of labour power. The first theme concerns the dynamic change. The second concerns the incorporation of the empirical material into the theory. On the basis of these, the levels of abstraction and the tendencies and countertendencies of capitalism are discussed. Lastly, the notion of value of labour power is discussed.

2.1   *Systematic Dialectics and Hegelian Heritage*

As suggested above, Marx's method first assumes there is a given totality and then aims at explaining this through its internal connections. The procedure based on the reconstruction of the concrete as a unity in thought with its own internal connections is accepted as the Hegelian heritage in Marx's method. For Chris Arthur (1998, 2002) for example, Marx's method follows Hegel's closely in the sense that they both attempted to treat a pre-given whole in which the categories are ordered strictly logically. As Hegel claims there is no historical ordering of his categories, Marx's conceptual development also is also not historical, although this has later been misrepresented by Engels. Chris Arthur (1998) claims that Engels' misrepresentation gave the theory a historical content reducing the purpose of abstraction to disentangle the pure logical forms from historical contingencies. Such reading of Marx's method along with Hegelian principles named by Arthur as *new dialectic,* also referred to as systematic dialectic in general, has been prominent among some scholars such as Murray (1988), Moseley (1993), Shamsavari (1991) and Smith (1998). The systematic dialectics is based on the principle of the organisation of a system of categories in a definite sequence, deriving one concept from another purely logically.

The first principle of the new dialectics is that the capitalist economy is a given whole with internal consistency, as stated above. Its reconstruction in thought requires abstraction, not on the basis of common attributes in things in order to derive concepts for categorisation, but rather on the basis of the essence which is the actual universal cause of the whole. The ordering of the concepts follows from more simple and abstract concepts containing the essence towards more complex and concrete concepts on the basis of the contradictions in simpler concepts. As the concepts become more concrete and refined, the analysis is also reproduced at more concrete levels of abstraction. This movement, however, does not resolve contradictions in the simple categories. As Shamsavari (1991, p. 42) notes, "the fixed opposition between simple and complex is reproduced rather than solved" and therefore simple categories and the contradictions within them continue to exist alongside the more complex categories. It is such existence of the contradictions that make the movement from the more abstract to the more concrete necessary and also sufficient for the derivation of the capitalist economy in thought as a system with internal consistency.

On the basis of this consideration, the dialectic of value consists of three steps as in all dialectic movement (Arthur, 2002). First, the commodity appears as the initial concept introduced in the first chapter in Capital. The contradiction within it (use value as opposed to value) necessitates the introduction of money which moves the analysis to a more concrete level of abstraction. Later, the contradiction within money (quantity as opposed to quality) necessitates the introduction of the concept of capital. Capital represents the disclosure of the system by returning back to itself (money creating more money). It is only when the system discloses by returning to its starting point, a system is complete and therefore can be analysed systematically (Smith, 2003). This way of ordering of the categories according to levels abstraction also underlie the internal causal structure in terms of direction (from more abstract to the more concrete), although a contradiction cannot be reduced to a unilinear causality where cause and effect are ontologically independent entities.

Systematic dialectics offers a comprehensive interpretation of Marx's method on the basis of development of more complex concepts with the help of contradictions in simpler versions of the same concepts. Although such movement of thought is helpful in terms of determining the direction of causal structure, it can be misleading as it is based upon an idealistic understanding of the concrete reality in which the movement between different levels of abstraction is done seamlessly with no regard to historical reality. This book is based on a reading of Marx that differs from Hegelian systematic dialectics, especially in light of the incorporation of the historical. The next section will focus upon how it differs and why such difference matters.

2.2 Marx's Materialism and the Incorporation of Empirical Material into Theory

As is well known, Marx rejects idealism in his very own famous words "ideal is nothing else than the material world reflected by the human mind and translated into forms of thought." The nature of the ideal and its place in Marx's theory is a far-reaching philosophical issue that cannot be discussed in great detail here. Nevertheless, this section will provide a brief summary in order to discuss the issue which can clarify some methodological concerns such as the relationship between the empirical/historical content and the theory.

The rejection of idealism does not imply that the starting point of a conceptual framework is the empirical reality as in induction, but rather to indicate that the ideal concepts existing in the human consciousness are based upon reflections of the material world. The conceptual procedure still moves from the ideal (abstract) towards the material (concrete), but it has a material basis in the sense that the ideal itself is just a reflection of the material. The ideal is understood on the basis of first, there is a priori consideration that thought, and its concepts are distinct from the objects of the real world that are under the analysis. Second, human beings use their intellectual capacities in order to transform themselves and the external world through the means of thinking.

The first is an ontological distinction. This means, the distance between a concept and its real-life correspondence is independent of the level of complexity of the issue that is being conceptualised. Therefore, it cannot be wiped away by means of refinement of the concept, although a more refined concept might represent the complexity in a brighter light. As such, this does not contradict with an idealistic understanding of the world, but this needs more elaboration.

In Hegel, idealism takes an objective form where all subjects and objects exist in an encompassing whole. While human beings (subjects) try to make sense of themselves and the real world, their thinking is first directed towards the objects in their surroundings. If thought in the broadest sense of the word is a capacity that creates knowledge in many forms, thinking first creates forms of thoughts (concepts) about things observed in nature as in contemplation, perception or imagination. This means that until the thought form itself appears, thinking can only make sense of things that already comes with a form of thought (concept). The thought form itself appears only in the course of thinking about thinking (thought) itself, which is the real source of all thinking. This nature of thought form gives it a peculiarly distinctive feature as pointed out by Ilyenkov (1977, p. 112):

> But before man began to think about thought, he had already to think, though still not realising the logical schemas and categories within which this thinking took place, but already embodying them in the form of the concrete statements and concepts of science, engineering, morals, and so on. Thought was thus realised at first as activity in all the diversity of its outward manifestations. The thought-form here was 'sunk' into the material of concrete thoughts, sense images, and ideas, was 'sublated' in them, and was therefore counterposed to conscious thinking as the form of external reality.

In other words, thinking cannot be developed fully until the thinking subjects had already thought before with the help of concepts given in contemplation and imagination. This forms the basis of Hegel's differentiation of simple-abstract universality (concepts given in contemplation) from the universal concept which is the actual origin of all concepts. For Hegel, the purpose of thinking is to achieve these universals, therefore a real abstraction is not done to categorise objects according to their common attributes, but rather to find the essential determinations in objects (particulars) from which the actual particulars emerge. This refers to *essence* in Marx's philosophy on the basis of which abstraction proceeds.

Another important consideration to understand the ideal in Marx is that human beings transform the world and themselves through the means of their thinking. Referring back to Hegel and what has been discussed above, thinking first starts as an activity that is directed towards everything else which later moves towards itself. Subjectively, when thinking is first directed towards everything else but itself, thought can only mirror reality given in the forms that are already within consciousness. But thinking has an active side to it that human beings think and act on their thoughts without necessary correspondence in their subjective consciousness. Therefore, thought reveals itself not only in logic and its concepts, but also in what it creates in the external world through objective activity.

So far, such conceptualising of thinking as a joint product of conscious and unconscious elements which are reflected in objective activity, referred by Marx as the investigation of the 'active side' of human thinking, does not contradict Hegel's philosophy. Fundamentally, all thoughts mirror reality and are ideal in the sense that the gap between the thought and reality cannot be fully eliminated. For Marx however, the nature of the ideal is material as all ideal (logical) forms mirror images of universal forms of reality outside thought, reflected in human consciousness. As Balibar (1995, p. 24) claims, Marx's materialism has nothing to do with the matter, but he uses the term materialism in order to position itself as opposed to idealism "in which the world is an object of contemplation which seeks to perceive its coherence and its meaning thereby to impose an order on it." In idealism, concrete is merely a manifestation of the abstract. For Marx, the representation of the order of the world is done by referring to the activity of the subject which constitutes both the order and its representation. In other words, there are mediations in the manifestation of the abstract as the concrete as such a process is only possible in the activity of the subject.

The act of realising thought in objective activity in the forms of things and events outside consciousness makes thinking a real productive process, as the objects within consciousness can only be altered through the continuous incorporation of unconscious elements which can reflect back as objective activity. It also underpins the specific importance of collective forms of human creation and production in Marx's philosophy in relation to human consciousness, the latter being a product of the former. Thought (thinking) is first accepted as the ideal component of the real activity of social people transforming both external nature and themselves by their labour (Ilyenkov, 1977 p. 2). The ideal is the subjective image of objective reality, i.e., reflection of the external world in the forms of man's activity, in the forms of his consciousness and will.

Through an investigation of the active side of thinking, which is reflected in the *whole inorganic body of man* that includes the aggregate historical process of human production, Marxist methodology can move from being an analysis of subjective ideal forms towards being an analysis that is concerned with the substance of such ideal forms as part of an objective reality. For example, in the context of the capitalist economy, the concept of price is ideal in the sense that it already exists in the consciousness of all operating agents. This does not mean that price as an ideal form does not have real existence. Prices exist not only in the minds of operating agents, but they are first, a subjective reflection of an objective reality, namely values as abstract human labour. Prices are not merely reflections of values, however, as values only appear in their ideal form in exchange and the determination of future value relations is mediated not only through the values themselves, but also through their corresponding prices.

Upon such considerations, Marx's materialism is helpful in understanding why it is not possible to restrict scientific method to a pre-given set of rules as offered by the systematic dialectic method. In Marx, logic and history are inseparable not to imply that the empirical material constitutes a natural starting point as in induction, but rather to imply that the empirical material is a part of the theory which makes the method irreducible to a set of logical rules. This issue is also closely related with understanding the process of change which will be discussed in the next section through the concept of essence.

2.3   *Essence and the Process of Change*

As capitalism is a dynamic system, its nature is best understood with concepts that are sufficient to reflect and discuss change. It was argued in the previous section that Marxist methodology is interested in examining consciousness not fixed in the form of knowledge, but also in its expanded manifestations. This allows it to move from mirroring reality towards reconstructing reality in thought. Such process also represents a movement from a static reflection of reality towards a dynamic reconstruction where things are not only represented in their present state, but in continuous change, i.e., in their becoming. This is a distinctive feature of Marxist methodology that has important implications for the development of theory and research design and is a direct implication of the dialectical as opposed to the formal logic employed.

As Ollman (2003, p. 64) points out by quoting James Coleman (1968), there is an interesting status of the concept of change within formal logic:

> The concept of change in science is a special one ... It is based on a comparison, or difference between two sense impressions, and simultaneously a comparison of the times at which the sense impressions occurred.

That is because due to the principle of contradiction in formal logic, "the concept of change must, as any concept, itself reflect a state of an object at a point in time." This indicates, change can only be conceptualised as more or less static comparisons between two different states of objects/conditions reflected at two different points in time. Because the theory is not interested in the process of change itself, change becomes a matter of empirical observation, which can only be examined after one object/condition has turned into another object/condition. This is also the method of examining change in contemporary mainstream economics. Because the logical schema does not allow the incorporation of the process of change as the beginning of a thing in consciousness, the real world that is always changing is represented with some facts external to the theory against which the theory can be tested for validity. This is observed for example the division of variables in economics into those that are exogenous and endogenous the latter being determined by the former (Milonakis and Fine, 2009). While the explanation is done through the help of external factors (exogenous), exogenous factors themselves stay unexplained by the theory.

Marx's analysis, however, is interested in the actual process of change itself. There is a systemic priority of movement over moment, as things do not simply exist and undergo change, but the transient movements are also part of their nature not less than their momentary existence (Ollman, 2003). This makes the theory adequate for grasping not only what things are, but also how things are changing and what they are changing into (i.e their becoming things). Marx's most important main abstractions about capitalism such as value, commodity, capital etc. incorporate processes (as well as relations) *in themselves* as part of their intrinsic nature. This is to suggest that things are presented in their organic continuation between as well as through their past, present and future states. For example, capital is in itself a process and relation. This indicates that capital is not an empty concept to be filled with empirical observation, but rather the path in which capital became (i.e. how it emerged historically as well as logically) is also a part of the concept of capital itself. This point will be further elaborated with a discussion of *essence* and how Marxist methodology is based upon the usage of abstraction with the help of such essence.

Briefly, it is possible to talk about different ways of abstractions, the most common being the abstraction on the basis of common empirical attributes.

In this way of abstraction, the observer/theorist creates a subjective structure of categorisation depending on the attributes of his/her choice. Economic categories such as employment, supply, trade are based on such method of abstraction. For Marx, the purpose of abstraction is not to categorise empirically common attributes, but rather to find the actual source of movement of things on the basis of their essence with both logical and historical determinations. It means, the structure of categorisation does not only exist in the mind of the theorist based on a conceptual derivation. It depends on real abstraction reconstructing reality in thought (i.e. disclose concrete universals) on the basis of their essence.

In general, essence can be described as the most general feature of the particulars. The definition of general is important, as it does not refer to most common or observable feature, but rather the feature that determines the particulars both logically and historically. It is logical, as it allows for the reconstruction of the concrete particulars as a totality in thought. For Reuten (2003, p. 43), essence is fundamentally logical as it is "the interconnection of all the moments necessary for the reproduction of the object of inquiry."

It is also historical, as it is the actual source from which all particulars emerge. The essence appears as a single particular with a tendency to become general and develops from itself (Ilyenkov, 1977, p. 232). It means, essence does not exist separately devoid of any form which is then later manifested in other particulars as a form. It always exists with a form, form being the mode of existence rather than the manifestation of essence (Saad-Filho, 2002). To give an example, in Marx's analysis of capitalism, abstract labour is the essence of value. Does the generality of essence mean that abstract labour refers to the existence of human labour in all exchange relations? In the real world, labour always exists with a form, as concrete labour such as wall painting, tailoring, mining and so on. If we abstract from these concrete labours, we end up with a type of abstract labour that is a common element in all labours, which is the capacity to work, labour devoid of any form. However, although such abstraction is the first step for determining the essence, it is incomplete in the sense that it is ahistorical hence is not sufficient to explain why the abstract labour is the essence of value which is exclusive to capitalism. Abstract labour is also historical in the sense that it is also where value actually comes from. As Saad-Filho (2002, p. 12) argues,

> The claim that abstract labour is the substance of value is based upon three premises. First [...] labour is a transhistorical condition for social and economic reproduction. Second, abstract labour is the typically capitalist form of labour, and it predominates over concrete labour. Third,

value (or commodity) relations are the general form of human intercourse under capitalism, and in this mode of production value relations mediate social and economic reproduction. Capitalism developed historically through the generalisation of value relations, among them the monopoly of the means of production by a class of capitalists, the diffusion of commodity production through wage labour, the growth of commodity exchange, and the subordination of production by the profit motive. These value relations have established historically the predominance of abstract labour; conversely, the diffusion of abstract labour reinforces the commodification of human relations and production for profit.

This paragraph summarizes how Marx's analysis can develop through the determination of the essence. Because capitalism developed historically through subordinating individual production to the profit motive through the emergence of wage labour and commodity production by capitalists, abstract labour has emerged as an essence with a tendency to develop from itself, self-expand, leading towards further dominance of abstract labour over concrete labours. Because essence is historical as well as logical, it emerges at a certain historical time, determining the particulars coming *after* itself. This reflects the passage of historical time from past to present and future not as an empirical observation external to the theory, but within the theory itself. Upon this principle, the relationship between future and present can be conceptualised as different from the relationship between present and past, making the analysis dynamic, which is a crucial aspect of Marxist methodology that is absent in the case of static analyses (Fine, 1982b).

So far, this chapter provided some methodological guidelines for a general understanding of Marx's theory concerning the general laws of motion of history which are not specific to capitalism as a particular mode of production. The next section will discuss the laws of motion that are specific to capitalism on the basis of tendencies and countertendencies.

2.4   *Levels of Abstraction: Tendencies and Countertendencies*

What the previous sections attempted to clarify is the fact that Marxist methodology is not based upon pure conceptual development in which each time a more refined and complex concept introduced for the same phenomena, earlier simple ones are replaced. On the contrary, simple and complex concepts referring to same phenomena necessarily exist alongside each other in Marxist analysis. In fact, the direction of movement is determined by the interaction of corresponding forces operating simultaneously at different levels of abstraction.

In the context of the capitalist economy, the world economy is considered to be a pre-given whole, constituted by the coincidence of production, exchange and distribution as the different moments of the same whole. Although all moments are essential, production is accepted to be more determining. From the practical side of things, this can be explained by production being a pre-condition for moments of exchange and distribution. At a deeper level, the primacy of productive forces and relations in human development play a role. On the basis of this, the capitalist economy is defined by the continual production and appropriation of value through the cycle of production, exchange and distribution. Referring back to wider methodological issues discussed in the previous section, value is accepted as a concrete universal based on the essence of abstract labour. It means that it is an integrated, self-expanding system. Marx shows value as self-expansion with the circuit of capital (M-C-M') where money value in the beginning of the production process produces some surplus value and comes out of the production process as more money value. Marx's analysis in Capital is interested in reconstructing such reality at increasingly more concrete and complex levels.

While the entirety of all relationships of value are always context-specific, and as such irreducible to systemic level analysis, there are some structural forces determined by the relationships that are systemic at certain levels of abstraction. In principle, while a relationship that is most abstract, stemming from production and affecting the whole system is referred as a tendency (such as the law of the tendency of profits to fall), other structural relationships that work in opposition to tendencies at more concrete and complex levels are called countertendencies (all phenomena in exchange and distribution). The structure of abstraction allows for the system to be analysed not as a mere aggregation but as a totality in which what holds true from the view of individual capitalist does not hold from the view of all capitalists in competition, not only as an empirical observation, but as a theoretical necessity. Carchedi (2008) differentiates three types of tendencies in which a tendency can either dominate and operate at all times, operate cyclically or cannot dominate at all. This book is based on the notion that the tendencies and countertendencies operate simultaneously *at all times,* irrespective of what is observed empirically. Tendencies and countertendencies always interact with each other, but not at the expense of each other. There are also empirical contingencies interacting with the tendencies and countertendencies.[5]

---

5   As Fracchia and Ryan (1992) suggest, a contingency possesses truth by virtue of its historical reality, hence is not simply an 'error' that is left behind unexplained by the abstract conceptual analysis (cited in Saad-Filho, 2002, p.117).

For example, although a contested topic of which discussion requires a much wider space than this, the law of the tendency of law of profits to fall can be shown as an example for a systemic level tendency. It concerns the production of value, implying that given competition and exchange, labour is continuously replaced with machinery, organic composition of capital rises for the overall level of economy leading to a fall in the profits. This seems to be in contradiction with the more concrete analyses of value, where the replacement of labour with machinery leads an increase in the profit rates because technological advancement decreases the unit production costs, given that profits are determined by the total size of the capital regardless of its composition. This issue needs further elaboration as it relates directly to the changing interpretations of value at different levels of analysis.

As pointed out by many, there are two different approaches to value in Marx. While the first can be named as the embedded (simple) labour approach, the second can be referred to as the reproduction (real cost) approach (Saad-Filho, 1997). In the simple labour approach, value is referred as the total abstract labour embodied in the commodity, including the past labours of inputs. In the reproduction approach, value is measured by the labour time necessary to reproduce the commodity, in other words, real costs of production in value terms. For Perelman (1999), rather than being confusion, both definitions hold true and the difference between them represents an important shift in the analysis from static to dynamic interpretation of value, although the differentiation between the two is not limited to this. Perelman (1999) argues that in the first chapters of Volume I of Capital, Marx assumes a simple reproduction scheme for the economy, meaning a static, or at least proportionally expanding economy with all inputs retaining their initial characteristics. This has important implications for the interpretation of value analysis as a whole, as in the static case, the commodities are assumed to exchange at prices proportional to their underlying labour values. In the case of simple values, value measurement takes place presuming that we can measure the previous inputs of abstract labour and calculate the transfer from inputs to outputs occurs irrespective of the depreciation of the capital goods. For example, if a machine lasts ten years, we can assume that one-tenth of its embodied value is transferred to commodities produced in a given year (Perelman, 1999).

Later, the analysis necessarily moves towards expanded production, where the economy is growing exponentially with the help of technical innovation in production, and this move is also represented by the shift in the definition of value from simple values to reproduction values (although Perelman notes that Marx introduces reproduction values even before his dynamic analysis). In the case of a dynamic economy with technical change, the impact of new technology also has an impact on input values, their real costs reflecting not their underlying embodied labour times, but rather their current reproduction in value terms. This introduces certain complications to the analysis, leading some to reject the existence of objective values altogether as it is not possible to know the real costs of inputs in terms of their reproduction values in the present period and the capitalists can only know the costs of capital goods at the time they are purchased.

It is important to note that the difference between these two definitions of value is not simply a shift from static simple reproduction to expanded reproduction but a necessary interpretation of value at distinct levels of abstraction due to the requirement of the subject matter at hand. As widely known, while the analysis moves from the pre-occupation with production in Volume I of Capital towards exchange and distribution in Volume II and III, the analysis gets more concrete because production and exchange and distribution are accepted as integral moments of a totality, situated at different levels of abstraction. At the most abstract level of production, the circuit of capital can be referred to *in general*, abstracted from the different individual capitals competing in exchange. At such an abstract level, the primary relation is the one between capital and labour, therefore it is possible to talk about the existence of simple, embodied values as labour is abstracted from the individual concrete labours.[6] Distinct from labour and capital's share from the revenues as wages and profits, the relationship between the two at this level refers to a qualitative relationship where values are socially produced as a whole by labour through exploitation, surplus value is accumulated and capital relation is reproduced.

At a more concrete level, it is shown that how such accumulation and reproduction is sustained through the intervention of money and competition. In Volume II, exchange issues are discussed to show how economic reproduction is simultaneously a balance between value magnitudes and a balance between use values across the sectors of means of production and means of consumption (Fine and Milonakis, 2009, p. 64). While the primary relation between capital and labour disrupts the balance towards a single production process, the balance between value magnitudes and use values is maintained through the social capacity of use values to command money through exchange on

---

6 For the process of abstraction of labour from concrete labours, see Saad-Filho (1997). It takes place through the processes of normalisation, synchronisation and homogenisation. Individual concrete labours are first normalised across those producing the same commodity. Second, they are synchronised across those produced the same commodity in the past or with different technologies. Third, they are homogenised across other types of labour as the commodity is equalised with money (Saad-Filho, 1997).

this level. Volume III moves on to the analysis of distribution and how surplus value takes the form of profits, wages and rent in total distribution of income. In exchange and distribution then, value relation moves away from the primary division between capital and labour while the exchange and distribution relations obscure this relationship, and capital exists as the sum of individual capitals in competition. The existence of individual capitals produced by individual concrete labours means that values also do exist not independently, but rather as a part of the social whole. This is also why the 'transformation' process of values into prices of production takes place – to refer to individual firm or sectoral level values (prices of production) as distinct from social aggregate values. Countertendencies exist at this level of capitals in competition working in contradiction with the tendencies. In principle, tendencies are more determining than the countertendencies as they are more abstract and the product of the system in general.

Within this context, it can be argued that the LTRPF operates at the level of capital in general and is concerned with the mass of surplus value produced and whether it can be accumulated through time. Briefly summarised, first there is the consideration that technical progress leads to the replacement of labour with capital goods and the ratio of constant capital to variable capital (c/v) in value terms increases over time.[7] This indicates as accumulation proceeds, less total surplus value is produced and embedded in the commodities, leading to a fall in the profits.

At the level of capitals in competition, however, the intervention of money points out to the consideration of a different dynamic. At this level, there is tendency for capital to be equally rewarded according to the size of capital advanced, while productivity levels vary according to the level of technical progress in each sector. The incompatibility between these is mediated through the movement of capital in and out of sectors with the help of the money and credit system, allowing prices of production to be established for profitability to move towards equalisation. In that regard, prices of production as dynamic individual reproduction values systematically diverge from simple, embedded values. As an empirical reality, in the capitalist mode of production, capitalists receive an average rate of profit regardless of the ratio of constant to variable capital. Average prices (capitalist prices of production) systematically diverge from values as a result of the way value is produced (by wage labour) and is distributed (according to the capital advanced) which is made possible by the free mobility of capital and labour between sectors and occupations as while

---

7   See Saad-Filho (2002) and Fine and Saad-Filho (2010).

capital moves from less profitable to more profitable sectors, labour moves from less productive to more productive sectors (Milonakis, 1995).

This aspect of the theory has led to many criticisms including the famous critique of Okishio for example, where he shows that given Marx's interpretation of dynamic reproduction values as prices of production, unlike what is suggested by the LTRPF, the introduction of new techniques will actually lead profit rates to go up as the unit cost of output will decrease. From the perspective of the simultaneous movement of tendencies and countertendencies, however, while the Okishio critique focuses on the effects of the introduction of the new techniques on unit costs and profit rates, it ignores that unit costs are necessarily reduced by replacing people with more productive machines, which is of primary importance for the sustainability of accumulation (Fine, 1982b, p. 119). Decreasing unit costs and decreasing production of the surplus value go hand in hand and the focus of the analysis concerning LTRPF is not to determine whether profits actually fall after the interaction of the law as such and the counteracting tendencies, but rather to find out whether these two influences can continue to co-exist as accumulation proceeds.

The analysis is, therefore, interested in these double aspects of capital accumulation, which is both productivity-enhancing and labour-reducing in a self-disruptive manner that could be sustained through the systematic expansion of the capital relation towards new areas of social life.[8] Capitalism tends to expand the realm of commodity production so that the capital relation can afford the expansion of each tendency. This is sustained by the stock for accumulation made available by the concentration of capital ownership either through the reinvestment of profits, or through the merging of capitals, which is called as centralisation. Surely, this is a simplistic summary of the extensive debates surrounding the transformation problem and the related issues, but it is included to emphasise how the tendencies and countertendencies refer to the changing interpretations of the value relations according to different levels of abstraction. Because the causal structure is designed in conjunction with the levels of abstraction in Marxist analysis, the abstract structure itself is explanatory in terms of giving an idea about the possible movements of value for each category of capitalist economy, with respect to the corresponding location of the concept within a layered formation.

Let us consider the same issue from the angle of labour in order to determine the movements within the category of employment, for example. As

---

8   This will be explained more in detail in the section on the systems of provision approach in the second half of this chapter and its relation to financialisation in Chapter 2.

summarised above, the most abstract level is the level of production where the relations of value are primarily concerned with the division between capital and labour and its reproduction. The tendency for aggregate division of labour then involves the reproduction of this relation towards the movement of individual productions towards a single production process reducing the minimum necessary labour time required for the reproduction of the aggregate relationship, at the expense of the social division of labour within the production process.

The countertendency, on the other hand, takes the competition between individual capitalists into account within an existing labour process. Therefore, the social division of labour concerns the development of distinct production methods with varying productivity levels as a result of the competition to reduce the necessary labour time to produce certain commodities compared to rivals. Specialisation and co-operation of labour are among these methods contributing to the productivity levels within the workplace. Then, the observation of tendencies and countertendencies in the context of employment implies that while the former is directed towards de-skilling of the labour and the creation of more simple jobs, the latter is concerned with the increasing specialisation, co-operation of labour within the production process that results in the increased requirement for skilled labour. Because the expansion of the capital relation is at the same time labour-reducing and productivity-enhancing, each has different implications for the category of employment.

A Marxian analysis of employment is therefore, again, not concerned primarily with the development of one tendency over another, but rather with the compatibility of these two tendencies together through the self-expansion of capital relation. This is only accomplished through the simultaneous existence of simple, abstract concepts along with more complex and concrete ones within the theory itself as an important feature of Marx's methodology. The next section will discuss tendencies and countertendencies in the context of value of labour power, which is a concept that has a primary importance for the purposes of this book.

2.5   The Value of Labour Power

As with other commodities, this value [of labour power] was then further determined by the cost of production. But what is the cost of production ... of the worker, i.e. the cost of producing or reproducing the worker himself? This question unconsciously substituted itself in Political Economy for the original one; for the search after the cost of production of labour as such turned in a circle and

never left the spot. What economists therefore call value of labour,
is in fact the value of labour-power, as it exists in the personality
of the worker, which is as different from its function, labour, as a
machine is from the work it performs.

MARX, 1981, p. 678

In his analysis of capitalist production, Marx distinguished between labour
power as a commodity, which is the capacity of labourers to produce, and the
labour activity itself as the actual act of producing certain commodities during a production process. Such differentiation is of crucial importance for the
whole structure of the analysis and the theory of exploitation, as the usage
of labour power as a commodity is actually where surplus value comes from,
due to the non-corresponding relationship between the payment made for the
commodity of labour power at the beginning of the production process and
the actual value produced by the labour by the end of it. Therefore, the definition of the value of labour power distinct from the act of labour is an important issue for Marx with many important and direct implications, for example
for the theory of exploitation. Its determination, however, has been subject to
debate as with many other concepts in Marxist political economy.

Broadly, there are two distinct ways of determining the value of labour
power. The first is the product of the classical approach to the labour theory
of value, where labour values are assumed to be proportional to embodied
labour times in commodities. Hence, the value of labour power is also determined by the labour time embodied in the commodity of labour power itself,
which is equal to the total labour time embodied in the use values that are
necessary for the reproduction of the labourer, such as clothing, food, shelter
and so on (fixed bundle approach). In some later interpretations, where values
are not necessarily accepted as proportional to embodied labour, but rather
as the aggregate monetary equivalence to reproduce the commodities, value
of labour power is determined differently. For example, see the definition of
value of labour power from Foley (1986, pp. 35–36) below:

> The capitalist buys the worker's capacity to produce for a certain sum of
> money – the wage, which is the price of labour power. [...] Money is a
> form of value; thus we can regard the money paid in wages as the equiva-
> lent of a part of the social labour time expended by the society. The value
> of labour power in this sense is the labour time equivalent of the wage:
> $w^* = mw$
>
> where w^* is the value of labour-power, the number of hours of social
> labour a worker receives in exchange for an hour of his labour-power; m

is the value of money;[9] and w is the money wage, the amount of money the worker receives for an hour of labour-power.

In this interpretation, the value of labour power is not determined through the embodied labour in the commodities consumed by labourers, but rather through the monetary equivalence of such value, which is represented by the workers' wages given its unit value component in money. Developed by Foley (1986, 1982) and Duménil (1983) simultaneously, this approach to labour theory of value has been named as *New Interpretation* (*NI*) that has been prominent among many other scholars including Mohun (1994), Lipietz (1982), Moseley (2015), who also adopted approaches along similar lines with the NI – despite some differences especially with respect to the treatment of constant and variable capital, as Moseley (2015) argues.

The core argument of the NI is that given the value of money as monetary expression of total labour time performed within a certain production process, and given the value of labour power as money wages in value terms, Marx's labour theory of value can be summarised as "the expenditure of living labour in production adds money value to the inputs in production' because money value of the net output equals total living labour following the aggregate equality between total profits and total surplus value".[10] The NI accepts that because money can be used an immediate expression of abstract labour, the economy can be conceptualised as a 'single system', where values and prices do not exist as two different sets of relations, but rather as a single price system governed by the values. In Foley and Duménil's (2008, p. 5) own words:

> [I]n the traditional approaches, two sets of prices are considered, one proportional to values (embodied labour times), and the other equalizing profit rates (a dual system), when only one price system prevails in real-world capitalism (a single system).

---

9   The value of money (also represented by λm or MEL) is the quantity of labour represented by one unit of money – the standard of price that translates a certain amount of money commodity into monetary units (Foley, 1986, p. 25). In other words, the value of money is 'the ratio of the net domestic product at current prices to the living productive labour expended in an economy over a period of time' (Foley, 1986).

10 Following from that, "the paid and unpaid portions of the total expended labour are definitionally equal to the wage and gross profit share in the net domestic product. As a result, the rate of exploitation measured as the ratio of the gross profit share in national income to the wage share in national income coincides with the corresponding ratio expressed in labour-time equivalents." (Foley, 1986, p. 19).

This new definition to the value of labour power is also accepted to bring a 'solution' to the famous transformation problem between the values and prices of production by introducing a single system. In this single system, transformation procedure seems to be unnecessary, because the purpose of simple value analysis is assigned as the aggregate determination of the level of exploitation, to be replaced in more concrete analyses with a more refined value analysis (prices of production).

The NI has certain important implications for the value theory, concerning the issues mentioned above: aggregate determinations such as exploitation as well as the relationship between values and prices. This chapter cannot provide a detailed treatment of NI, as it is only interested in its definition of the value of labour power, although this definition is in direct relationship with its treatment of other issues mentioned.[11] The NI approach to the value of labour power could be named as the *value form approach*, which is in direct opposition with the fixed bundle interpretation. The value form approach introduces an ex-post identification of the workers' share of wages from income with the value of labour power, after the production takes place and income is distributed. This is different from the fixed bundle approach where the value of labour power is determined ex-ante by the total quantity of the labour values in the commodities necessary for the survival of the labourers. Obviously, these are very different conceptualisations of which implications are sharply revealed, for example, in the relation between the value of labour power and productivity increase (Fine et al., 2004). In the fixed bundle case, if the value of labour power as a bundle of use values remains unchanged, increased productivity means the value of labour power decreases, because production of the bundle is less costly. On the other hand, money wages approach indicates that as the productivity increases, the value of labour power increases as the money wages can command more (cheaper) use values.

Based upon the methodological preoccupations summarised so far, this chapter argues that the value of the labour power is *both* determined by the commodities consumed as well as the money wages at distinct levels of abstraction. From the perspective of tendencies and countertendencies, the contradictory implications of both determinations of the value of labour power implies a tendency to reduce the value of labour power by cheapening of the products (less value embedded) and the counter-tendency that enables workers to buy more subsistence goods with their money wages. The value of labour power is a simple abstract concept, a quantity of value, of which

---

11   See Fine et al. (2004) and Moseley (2000) for a detailed critique of NI.

determinations as a quantity of fixed bundle of goods or a quantity of money is not direct, but rather mediated through the relationship between values and prices.

Conceptualised in this way, the value of labour power is not only concerned with how much workers get, but also how and what they get with their money wages. As a quantity, the value of labour power is determined at the *beginning* of each production process, concerning not only the shifting balance of forces between capital and labour, but also the relation of money wages to economic and social reproduction, of which the customary standard of living is one component (Fine et al., 2004). This issue is absent in the value form approach as the value represented by wages bears no relation to the value of the commodities consumed, given that prices and values diverge from one another. The customary standard of living is referred to in the fixed bundle approach, emphasising the role of moral and historical elements in the determination of the value of labour power, implying that the standard of workers' sustainability is not entirely capitalistically determined. The impact of moral and historical elements could be possibly seen for example in the impacts of the extent of domestic labour through family and kinship relations on social and economic reproduction, or, and increasingly, state provision. This refers to a use value analysis for the value of labour power, which is the indispensable half of an analysis of capitalist accumulation that concerns a simultaneous production of use values and values, while the former being subordinated by the latter as the accumulation proceeds. The next section will discuss systems of provision approach to the value of labour power to discuss these issues in greater detail.

2.6   *The Systems of Provision (SOP) Approach to Social Reproduction*
The systems of provision approach to social reproduction was first developed by Fine and Leopold (1993) in *The World of Consumption,* to provide an alternative to consumption studies which was an emerging field of research during the period. Its approach to consumption is concerned with the dynamics of the capitalist accumulation summarised above, which involves a simultaneous production of use values and values. In that sense, it is used in this book to understand the composition of the value of labour power through the consumption of provision goods as use values, as well as to investigate the value relations in and around these sectors. Although this may sound like an entirely theoretical preoccupation, as Weeks (1983, pp. 219-220) suggests, there is a very practical side to this exploration:

> The process of reproduction in capitalist economy is the circuit of capital. Fundamental to understanding of this circuit is the two-fold nature

of commodities, for the reproduction involves both the reproduction of value relations and the reproduction of material wealth. That is, capital must be reproduced both in money form and material form. On the material side, labour-power and means of production must be reunited in each successive circuit. On the value side, capital turns into money in order that it be exchanged against use values and assume its productive role. Marx's analysis of circulation was precisely the study of this opposition and interaction of the abstract (value) and concrete (use value). This approach is not an obscure theoretical one, but a quite practical one: since value must have a material form (be objectified in a commodity), the real nature of circulation requires that we consider both the circulation of value and circulation of use values.

Therefore, the systems of provision approach is concerned with the ways in which this double circulation occurs, which is neither addressed by value form nor by the fixed bundle approach to the value of labour power. If the value of labour power is solely determined by the money wages, the analysis of the extent to which sustainability is determined through non-market elements is lost. In the fixed bundle approach, this is referred as the moral and historical element in workers' sustainability implying that it is not entirely capitalistically determined, and how each good is produced and consumed differentially within and across different countries is determining in setting the standards for use value production. In other words, whether these goods are provided by the state, within the family or through the market, will determine what workers buy with their money wages to sustain themselves.

In approaching the value of labour power then, the issue is not only how much workers can consume on average, but also with the determination of final consumption standards that differs within and across different income groups as well as countries. From the perspective of tendencies and countertendencies, the process of the emergence of consumption standards for wage goods is in direct relations with the value relation, in line with the accumulation process itself, suggesting while certain customary consumption norms are left out by a single production process, new norms are continually established as production processes also move towards increased specialisation and refinement of the final consumption products. In other words, while value production processes lead towards the homogenisation of the production of different use values as commodities, such as housing and electricity analysed in this book, this process is far from linear as different customary standards for the consumption of use values will also emerge due to individualised consumption patterns. Weeks (1979, p. 278) explains this phenomenon as following:

Accumulation is a process of qualitative change, in which the means of production are revolutionized and capital is redistributed. In the earliest moments of expansionary process, individual capitals cannot attract labour power at more or less constant wages, because of the size of the reserve army. But as the reserve army contracts, rising wages become the mechanism by which the existing labour power is redistributed (centralized) toward more effective capitals. In a capitalist economy, based as it is on free wage labour, rising wages are the only mechanism available to capital to make the division of society's labour power among branches of industry conform to the changing pattern of production within and between branches of industry. To affect this redistribution, rising wages must accompany the rapid expansion of capital. This reflects the unique role of the means of subsistence under capitalism. Under feudalism, the subsistence needs of the masses are merely the means by which labour power is reproduced. Under capitalism, subsistence needs take the wage form and serve not only to reproduce labour power, but also to regulate its social division.

In other words, it suggests that how subsistence needs are satisfied under capitalism does not refer to an arbitrary process but is itself a direct result of how the value of labour power is reproduced as a commodity, which also regulates its social division in the abstract. This is not to suggest a total subordination of consumption by production. On the contrary, it refers to how final consumption is increasingly removed from the consumption of means of production in capitalist mode of production, proportional to the extent that living labour is expelled from the production process.

This point requires further elaboration, as it refers to one of the most distinguishing characteristics of capitalist commodity production from other modes of simple commodity production. Under the capitalist mode of production, there is a distinction between the production of means of production and the production of the value of labour power, as while the former is incorporated within the value relation, the latter is left for the workers' final consumption. For Fine and Leopold (1993), this refers not only to a qualitative, but also a quantitative difference, as the buying and selling of means of production tend to dominate the process of circulation quantitatively, even if the majority of net income is consumed through wages. More significantly, this is only satisfied because:

Final consumption involves the exit of its value from continuing circulation, its role is no longer defined by the internal logic of capital and its laws. Instead, it has a simple an undifferentiated relation to economic agents as purchasers.

FINE AND LEOPOLD, 1993, p. 262

This indicates, unlike other modes of production, such as feudalism in which the reproduction of labour power has to be maintained through the ruling class' direct expenditure and as such not differentiated from the production of means of production, under capitalism, no stereotypical pattern of final consumption is guaranteed, giving rise to increased differentiation of consumption standards, while the value of labour power is reduced through the intensified use of machinery in the production of these commodities.

Meanwhile, the extent of the discrepancy between these two simultaneous processes is proportional to the social division of labour as the accumulation proceeds. There are two aspects to this distribution: first capital flows to branches where the rate of profit is higher, and second, centralisation proper removes the labour from low-wage capitals (Weeks, 1979).

On the basis of these, the systems of provision approach to social reproduction has two underlying theoretical premises. First, in line with the widening discrepancy between the production of use values and values, and the domination of the latter over the former, final consumption and productive consumption become more distinct, the former being increasingly individualised. Second, although the increasing scope of value relations leads to an inversion of the logic of value and define exchange relations for consumption purely as horizontal relations between use values -"x of commodity X exchanges for y of commodity Y" (Fine and Leopold, 1993, p. 266)- they also embody the underlining productive determinants together with the cultural and historical norms which governs who consumes what. In other words, the specific sectoral developments such as the levels of technical progress as well as wider national development trajectories will be determining for the analysis of individual wage goods.

In light of these considerations, this book adopts a systems of provision approach to social reproduction; first, in order to understand how specific use values of electricity and housing is produced and consumed in Turkey. As suggested, this aspect is concerned with heterogeneous production processes and hence should be analysed accordingly, reflecting the specific characteristics of each good as well as country (namely, taking the moral and historical elements into account in determining the value of labour power). Second, however, use value production also refers to a value production process, the implications and dynamics of which can be used to understand wider processes in and around provision goods. The value implications might be relevant, for example, the literature on financialisation that examines the destabilising impacts of the rising asset price inflation in financial markets in close affinity with the usage of such assets as a source of wealth by the households due to an individual-ised private consumption culture around housing, pension funds and so on (Toporowski, 2009, 2000). The individualised private consumption culture is also relevant for the increasing levels of consumption indebtedness, irrespec-tive of alternative views on the possible impacts of such increasing consumer debt levels (Barba and Pivetti, 2009; Lapavitsas, 2013). More importantly, it refers to how an intensified commodification of wage goods, reinforced by financialisation, reduces the value embedded in the wage commodities, hence the value of labour power in the abstract.

In that sense, the systems of provision approach to electricity and housing in Turkey is also interested in identifying a common underlying causal factor in the production of these goods, which is the transition towards market-based provision forms alongside increasing differentiation in the ways in which such transition occurs. This is relevant for a transition to a financialised accumula-tion pattern, as the regular revenues on the basis of the existence of a broad base of customers might lead to increased financial gains and an emergence of secondary circuits of capital, depending on the availability of credit, spe-cific consumption culture as well as how the sectors function in general, with respect to the improvements in productive investment together with techni-cal progress and/or economies of scale. The next chapter will provide litera-ture survey for financialisation in order to connect these wide-ranging issues through the dominant literature on the issues relating to the latter aim of the book, described above.

3   Conclusion

This chapter provided a general introduction for the book, against a back-ground of study and the identification of problematic issues in the existing literature. As explained, the book does not challenge the findings of the exist-ing literature on financialisation, instead, it offers a deeper perspective that incorporates issues that have not been addressed by the literature directly, but is a result of an understanding that connects the concept of financialisation to the grand theories of capitalist accumulation, in line with the methodo-logical principles of Marxian political economy. More specifically, it shifts the attention away from the impacts of financialisation on aggregate categories of circulation such as investment, wage/profit share etc, towards a more direct investigation of capitalist accumulation as the simultaneous production of use values and values in general, and the production of the commodity of labour power both as a use value and value in particular, through an empirical investigation of electricity and housing systems in Turkey.

There are two reasons for the particular choice of the commodities electricity and housing in Turkey. The first is contingent, as the fast development of the construction and energy sectors since the 2000s have been determining for the overall pattern of accumulation, as mentioned. Second, and from a more theoretical perspective, as these commodities constitute the value of labour power (necessary for the labourers' survival) in light of the considerations above, their investigation across the chain of activities from production to final consumption directly refers to how the value of labour power is determined specifically, in line with the cultural and historical practices, but also reflecting the overall development trajectories of the particular economies. It is argued that the final consumption goods are increasingly produced as commodities as the accumulation proceeds, referring to a lowering of the value of labour power in the abstract. This argument is explained through a methodological discussion on the different conceptualisations of the value of labour power in general, and the conceptualisation of the systems of provision approach in particular. In that sense, the increasing commodification goes hand-in-hand with increased differentiation of consumption patterns, far from suggesting a uniformed process across and within countries, income groups and different wage goods.

This discussion so far does not specifically address the process of financialisation, which is one of the primary concepts against which the change in the Turkish economy has been discussed recently. After providing a general literature survey on financialisation, the next chapter will discuss how the commodification of wage goods is one of the fundamental pillars of the financialised accumulation patterns.

CHAPTER 2

A Literature Survey on Financialisation

1   Introduction

This chapter explores the concept of financialisation with the help of an inter-disciplinary literature survey covering the contributions from urban sociology, geography and primarily heterodox schools of thought within economics, namely the contributions from French Regulation School, Post-Keynesian, New-Keynesian and Kaleckian economics as well as Marxian political econ-omy. After a brief discussion of the selected theoretical views on financialisa-tion, it gives its own definition as the increasing presence of interest-bearing capital as the material base of the current phase of capitalism, based on the methodological principles outlined in the previous chapter. Then, it moves the analysis to its investigation in developing and emerging countries, to be dis-cussed in the following chapter.

The literature on financialisation is extensive and the most widely accepted broad definition has come from Epstein (2005), as "the increasing role of finan-cial motives, financial markets, financial actors and financial institutions in the operation of the domestic and international economies." As an empirical phe-nomenon, the growth of the financial sector and the increasing importance of the financial activities have been well documented and measured, primar-ily using the US data; Palley (2013) finds the US financial sector's (including finance, insurance and real estate) output as a share of GDP increased from 15 per cent in 1973 to 20.4 per cent in 2005. During the same period, the financial sector's debt to total debt increased from 9.7 per cent to 31.5 per cent, while total credit as a share of GDP also increased three times.

The literature is, however, more interested in the impacts of these on the workings of the economy than the secular expansion of the financial sector itself and the corresponding proliferation of financial activities and assets. The most evident and devastating impact is considered to be on growth, as it is assumed that the increasing rates of financial profit led to a crowding-out effect on productive investment. As Palley (2013) notes, the increase in the credits given by the US economy was not manifested as the increases in pro-ductive investment, as the gross fixed investment spending as a share of GDP decreased from 19.2 per cent in 1979 to 16.5 per cent in 2005.

As the concept gained wider application since the 2008 global financial cri-sis, it has been argued by some, such as Christophers (2015) and Michell and

Toporowski (2014), that financialisation became a buzzword to explain any development taking place within and around the financial markets, and therefore lost most of its analytical legitimacy and explanatory power as a theoretical concept. There are two aspects to this. The first concerns, as Michell and Toporowski (2014) argue, whether there is coherence and rigour within theorisation on financialisation with respect to the financial processes that goes beyond the evidence for increased financial activity and turnover. The second is about, as raised by Christophers (2015), irrespective of the internal coherence, rigour or sophistication of these explanations, whether financialisation as a concept can contribute to the understanding of the contemporary capitalist economies in general, especially given its nebulous character in expanding itself far and wide.

These concerns are far-reaching and legitimate, also relating to the wider methodological issues surrounding the concept, which is why the literature is surveyed through the lens of these two concerns. As Sawyer (2013) distinguishes, despite too many different answers, there are basically two primary ways of answering the question of what financialisation is. The first is to view financialisation as an object of study in the broad terms of evolution of the financial sector and the increasing importance of finance in general. For that, there is no single definition of financialisation, as it can take many different forms across time and place (Sawyer, 2013). This way of conceptualisation is aimed towards understanding the causal mechanisms through which the intensified financial orientation can affect the firms and the economy, which is accepted to be historical in terms of its emergence but is not theorised as such (employing the categories of supply and demand analysis). The products of this methodological choice are outlined in the first half of the chapter, the majority of which came from the Post-Keynesian school of thought.

The second methodological choice is more historical, which is to view financialisation as the present phase of capitalism (or its material basis), coinciding broadly with neoliberalism since the late 1970s and early 1980s. Although it is not possible to draw a clear line between these two approaches, the choice between them underlines some important methodological differences that cut across disciplinary divides, especially in terms of the arbitrary divide between historical and abstract analysis, as briefly discussed in the previous chapter. If financialisation can be explained solely through the categories of supply and demand, what role is history to serve more than as a background? If, however, it is used to periodise with respect to real historical time, what distinguishes it from a historical account of chronology? If it implies a structural sequentiality, what parameters are selectively used to determine the phases? Does it imply that the parameters that are left behind, such as the parameters that account for national diversity, play a minor role for the global trajectory of capitalism? If no structural succession of events is assumed, on the other hand, what determines the coherence of various historical trajectories given the wide scope of contemporary national diversity? Although these questions are far broader than the scope of this book and will not be answered as such, this chapter will address some of them cursorily through drawing a distinction between the two methods for approaching financialisation.

With these considerations, this chapter provides a selective literature survey on financialisation, in light of the methodological distinction between different ways of conceptualisation, outlined by Sawyer (2013). As the book aims at reaching readers without a formal training in economics as well as those within the profession, some technical discussions are left out of the book, while some well-known discussions to the insiders, such as the Cambridge discussions of capital, are explained in detail.

Once the different approaches are discussed, the book gives its own definition of financialisation as the increasing presence of interest-bearing capital which the material basis of the current stage of capitalism, to which a transition towards market-based provision of wage goods is conducive. The first section discusses the first stream of literature that approaches financialisation as an object of study broadly associated with the rise of finance and the theoretical and empirical implications of this phenomenon. Within this tradition are the Post-Keynesian/Kaleckian, circuitist and some Marxian approaches to financialisation. The second section discusses the definitions of urban sociologists and human geographers, the French Regulation School, Varieties of Capitalism (VoC) approach, and some other Marxian interpretations, including the approach adopted in this book, which define financialisation historically as the current phase of capitalism. The third section concludes by pointing towards the distinction between the two approaches, favouring the latter in terms of shifting the emphasis away from the mechanical cause and effect structures and towards the process of change itself.

2   Financialisation as an Object of Study: The Rise of Finance and Its
        Impacts on the Economy

This section will discuss how financialisation can be approached broadly as an object of study with respect to the rise of finance and its impacts on the rest of the economy since the early/mid-1980s. Within this tradition, the Post-Keynesian/Kaleckian literature and some Marxist interpretations on financialisation addressed the majority of empirical processes, such as the increasing importance of shareholder value mostly associated with its impacts on real investment levels and slowing down of accumulation, as well as the increasing household indebtedness and its implications for aggregate demand and inequality. As these studies bring together a set of otherwise unrelated observations, such as inequality and growth, the next section will give a brief introduction to Cambridge theories of distribution, which can lay out the fundamental building blocks for the later studies on financialisation.

2.1   Cambridge Theories of Distribution

Cambridge theories of distribution emerged as a distinct school of thought in response to dissatisfaction with the orthodox macroeconomic theories of distribution in the post-World War II period. The pioneers Kaldor, Kalecki, and Robinson, developed an alternative theory of distribution within the capitalist economy in line with Keynesian principles, suggesting that distribution matters in terms of having an impact on aggregate demand hence total output levels through the mechanisms of saving/consumption functions. Although Keynes himself was not preoccupied with distribution but rather with the impacts of investment on aggregate levels of output, the pioneering works of Kaldor, Kalecki and Robinson have been considered to be along Keynesian lines because of their emphasis on investment and saving functions, with the logical priority of investment over saving (in other words, investment determining savings rather than vice versa).

The first and most important assumption that characterises the pioneers' work is that the economy operates according to the principle of scarcity of demand, rather than scarcity of supply. In that sense, there is a logical priority of demand over supply and this partially explains the importance given by Post-Keynesian macroeconomic analyses to business cycles to investigate the impacts of demand-driven fluctuations on accumulation. On the product side, the national output is disaggregated into consumption and investment $(Y = C + S, I = S = sp\,P + sw\,W)$, while the expenditure side is disaggregated into wages and profits $(Y = W + P)$. It is assumed that the capitalists have a higher propensity to save (sp) than workers (sw). These equations hold for all levels of profits and wages, hence the aggregate output itself is determined by the balance between savings and investment and by the multiplier (Kregel, 1978).

Harcourt (2006) notes that Kaldor (1955) called his work Keynesian for three reasons:

1)   He located the origins of his theory in Keynes' analogy of the widow's cruse: The economy was structured in a way that the more profit-receivers spent, the more profits they received. Because profit receivers as a class can always decide what to spend on investment, but never the

amount of profits they are going to receive, the causation always follows from investment towards profits (and therefore the more they invest, the more they receive as profits.)

2)   The first aspect implies that capitalist investment is determining for the economy in terms of aggregate output (income) and hence employment. In an economy, an exogenous planned investment (subject to animal spirits) determines income and distribution which further determines saving to respond to planned investment.

3)   Although Keynes himself was rather interested in the total level of activity and income determined by investment, the Keynesian multiplier can only be applied for that purpose in the short run, with changes in income bringing planned investment and planned saving into equality, because money wages are sticky in the short period. In the long run, however, the multiplier is applied to income distribution rather than directly on output, assuming prices are more flexible than money wages and the propensity to save out of profits is greater than the propensity to save out of wages.

In Kaldor's model, the budget constraint of a firm plays an important role in determining the macroeconomic rate of profit, for a given accumulation. Through the 'valuation ratio' (i.e. the ratio of the market value of the securities held by the public to the value of stock of capital goods, which is very similar to later what is known as Tobin's q ratio), he provides a link between the financial value of the firms and wealth of households in his distribution theory (Lavoie and Godley, 2001).

Later, Kaldor incorporates the functional relationships of distribution into his theory of growth that implies the actual progress rate of an economy is dependent on the portion of the income saved, the growth of labour productivity and growth rate of population, none of which is an independent variable, but rather interact with one another (Kaldor, 1957). By looking at the empirical constancies over long periods of historical time,[1] he finds that while the capital/output ratio remains roughly constant, *capital per worker grows over time,* therefore technical progress is endogenous in capitalist accumulation.

---

1   These are the share of national income between capital and labour, the rate of growth of the capital stock per worker, the rate of growth of output per worker, the capital/output ratio and the rate of return on investment. Kaldor observes these constancies by looking at the US and UK statistics over long periods of time. For example, for the United Kingdom, the share of wages has shown only small variations around the level of 40% of national income in the period 1840-1950 (Kaldor, 1957).

In Kalecki's distribution model, on the other hand, there is also an investment function (that is absent from Kaldor's model, determined by 'animal spirits'), depending on the profit and saving levels of the firm, therefore on the mark-up (monopolistic firms imposing a mark-up level over their average costs to be reflected in final prices) levels. On the supply side, the economy is determined by the degree of monopoly, which is accepted as one of the primary factors in determining the price levels and therefore corresponding saving and output levels. In the Kaleckian model, firms are not price takers, but rather they have the ability to determine the margin of prices over costs, reflecting the degree of monopoly. Given the firms' decisions over the level of prices relative to average costs, the equilibrium level of employment and expected profits would both be determined with the latter triggering the investment decisions by firms that would, in turn, determine the division of national income between wages and profits (Harcourt, 2006).

In that sense, the Kaleckian model displaces the Kaldor's emphasis from the impacts of long-term distribution trends towards short-term cyclical movements that are influential on the long-term trends (Carvalho, 1984). In such theorisation, higher mark-up levels and higher monopolisation has negative impacts on output levels as lesser amount of savings (hence investment in the long run) at the end of period is enough to match the desired levels of planned investment in the next period, with higher retained earnings from sales from the previous period.

The contribution of Cambridge is to claim that the economy is restricted by aggregate demand, and to go one step further than the classical Keynesian analysis to claim that investment determines output and employment, through the share of income between profits and wages. In the long run, this has impacts on the accumulation rate, as investment and saving levels are adjusted to changes in the short-run aggregate demand level, which is assumed to have an analytical priority over supply. On the supply side, the economy is restricted by the degree of monopolisation, as firms are able to set mark-up levels over the competitive market prices given their output restricting capacities. If a certain economy or sector is characterised by a high degree of monopolisation, this implies lesser amount of output produced (or in other words, higher profits returns and hence a lesser amount of savings necessary to match the current levels of investment).

This theorisation differs from the orthodox theory in which the distribution of income is determined by the price at which the individual agent can sell and the economy is primarily governed by the supply side productivity improvements (Kregel, 1978). In the orthodox theory, as Kregel (1978, p. 38) argues, there is no 'macro' theory of distribution as "[a]ssuming initial factor endowments are equal, if the supplies of factor services can adjust to the differences in relative factor prices, then personal income will be equal – unless there are market imperfections and significant differences in innate skills. Thus, because the skills are distributed randomly across the population, income will also be random, or at least statistically randomly distributed." Moreover, the demand for a factor is seen as ultimately deriving from the factors' contribution to output at the margin of production (from its marginal productivity), including the price of an additional unit of labour being equal to its marginal productivity, given there is full employment in labour markets. Post-Keynesian theory, on the other hand, attempts to explain the incomes earned in society independently of any direct relation to individual or class productivity, but rather to macroeconomic forces such as the rate of accumulation and saving and consumption behaviour (Kregel, 1978). These principles are the fundamental blocks for later Post-Keynesian and Kaleckian interpretations of financialisation, which will be discussed in the next section.

2.2   How Do the Cambridge Theories of Distribution Relate to Financialisation?

In line with the emphasis put on the importance of aggregate effective demand, endogenous money appears as a conceptual necessity in this framework, because if the effective demand is determining for the economy, determined at the aggregate level, there should be a mechanism for the systematic transmission of that effect to the micro firm level. Endogenous money serves that purpose, by responding to facilitate supply meeting whatever the level of effective demand generated.

Many scholars have described a Post-Keynesian economy as a *monetary production economy*, an expression that is used by Keynes himself (Carvalho, 1984; Chick and Dow, 2001; Kregel, 1976; Lavoie, 1984). For Lavoie (1984), a monetary economy underpins the fundamental uncertainty in economy, because of the inability to determine monetary aggregates (especially with respect to monetary wages), and as a result the economy being not a self-correcting but a cumulatively unfolding process that is non-ergodic (Arestis, 1996). The monetary wages play an important role, because payments to workers are made with money; neither the workers nor the capitalists know their final share of output meaning that the rewards to the factors of production are not set a priori in real terms. Lavoie (1984) claims that this contrasts with the orthodox theorisation where the integration of money into the economic system is done when the output is already specified, therefore the specificity of money comes from its stock scarcity (as with the other commodities). In the Post-Keynesian theorisation, however, the money is introduced in the beginning of the production process with the flow of new commodities. In that sense, *all* money is generated as credit money upon the demand of producers and therefore any stock of money should be accepted as a residue which cannot play any causal role (Davidson and Weintraub, 1973). The residue of bank loans that has not yet been paid is reflected as the money stock (depending on liquidity preferences), therefore can neither explain prices nor employment as monetarists would suggest (Lavoie, 1984).

The Post-Keynesian theorisation of money differs from the conceptualisation of money accepted in this book, for various reasons outlined by Saad-Filho (2002). First, for the Post-Keynesian theory of the business cycle, any expansion starts with the expansion of credits conceptualising all money as credit money, ignoring the theoretical relevance of fiat money created by the state. It also ignores the fact that, even when all money is credit money, there can be some discrepancies between the demand and supply of credit (Saad-Filho, 2002). That is because, even the supply of credit money necessarily corresponds to individual demand, the total supply of credit may not reflect the needs of the economy as a whole, for example visible in the case of speculative price increases in the asset markets when there is excess supply from the side of lenders facilitated by speculative borrowers. Money has an essence, and a distinct use value, which is the monopolisation of exchangeability, fulfilling various roles in the economy as a means of payments, as a store of value, as a unit of account, as world money, which sometimes conflict with each other (Saad-Filho, 2002). The conflict is visible, for example, when there is a breakdown in the payments in moments of crisis, and money acts primarily as a means of payments to settle down the existing transactions. In that moment, who gets paid and who does not is independent of the nature of the original individual demand generated, that might lead to an overall breakdown of revenues.

These considerations are not raised to question whether credit money supply is endogenous or not, instead, to suggest that money cannot be defined on the basis of limited endogeneity. This book suggests that money's role for the economy does not come from what it does (facilitating transmission from demand to supply is one of its functions, for example), but rather from what it is, in other words, its use value to monopolise exchangeability.

A second difference is that, in the Post-Keynesian analysis, money is introduced when revenues are being distributed in the form of wages (at the beginning of a production process), rather than when they are spent from the stock (at the end of a production process). This implies a simultaneous determination of profits and wages. According to the conceptualisation of the capitalist economy adopted in this book, wages and profits are not determined simultaneously and wages are determined before profits. The production process starts when the labourer sells his/her labour power for a wage (wages are determined at that moment irrespective of the time of payment) and that is a distinct moment from the distribution between wages and profit and the end of previous production process. In that sense, the wages are not determined by the share of labourers, but rather the share of labourers from the final surplus value (which is unknown at the beginning of the production process) is determined by the wages (Saad-Filho, 2002). By introducing money when revenues are being *distributed* in the form of wages, the Post-Keynesian approach does not assign a specific use value to the labour power, distinct from the labour's collective share at the end of the production process, when the output is already specified.

Nevertheless, the Keynesian approaches are systemic in character, with money stock having some distributional (hence real) impacts by building upon the theories of distribution summarised in the previous section. In short, the money stock's impacts are (Fine and Dimakou, 2016):

1)   It can lead to differential rewards for those owning financial assets: This has a corresponding implication for effective demand (lower) from redistributing towards those with lower propensities to consume.

2)   In the real sector, it can redistribute towards speculative investment again at the expense of effective demand.

The existence of these channels implies that the financial sector is not theorised separately from the real economy with a primary function of channelling savings into investment, but has impacts on production, growth and accumulation. On the basis of these channels, there is an extensive literature on financialisation with respect to the endogenous impacts of finance on the rest of the economy coming from Post-Keynesian, new Keynesian and Kaleckian perspectives; explaining the impacts of a shift from bank-based to market-based financial systems on investment (Schaberg, 1999), the impacts of changing consumption expenditures and asset price inflation (Toporowski, 2000, 2009), shareholder value orientation or 'rise of the rentier' due to changing firm behaviour (Lazonick and O'Sullivan, 2000), the negative impacts of shareholder corporate governance on real investment and accumulation (Orhangazi, 2008; Stockhammer, 2005, 2004), increasing inequality as a response to shareholder value orientation and its negative effects on aggregate demand through decreasing wage share (Onaran et al., 2011; Stockhammer and Onaran, 2013), as well as increasing household indebtedness as a result of increasing inequality in line with the rest of the developments mentioned above (Barba and Pivetti, 2009).

Van Treeck (2009) divides the literature into two as the supply-side and demand-side analyses of financialisation. While the supply-side analyses concern phenomena like the productivity impacts of rent-seeking activities or the impacts of the growth of unproductive sectors on technical change, this side is less developed, considering that Post-Keynesianism is primarily a demand-side, macro theory. On the demand-side, the focus is on the impacts of the changing firm behaviour on effective aggregate demand and accumulation with some other macro distributive constraints, such as firm indebtedness and the nature of saving and consumption behaviours. These will be examined in greater detail in the following sections.

2.3   Empirical Analyses on Firm-level: Decreasing Real Investment, Slowing Down of Accumulation

The empirical studies on firm level data reviewed in this section broadly draw upon the Post-Keynesian theory of the firm. This suggests, the individual firm will make investment decisions according to its individual 'expansion frontier' and 'finance frontier'. Expansion frontier is based upon the notion of the 'growth-profit trade-off' at the firm level, suggesting that the firms will favour growth over profitability in the long-run (Lavoie, 1992). The finance-frontier, on the other hand, refers to the maximum rate of accumulation with a given profit rate. While firms maximise profits, their investment decisions will be determined by the intersection of these two frontiers. However, as Crotty (1990) mentions, this dichotomous trade-off between growth and profits assumes that the managers and shareholders are primarily the same economic agents with more or less unified interests and strategies.

As it is well documented, shareholders gained power in corporate governance after the shareholder revolution in the mid-1980s, which led many to argue that the result has been their imposing of higher profit pay-outs (through higher dividends or share buybacks), favouring short-term profitability over long term growth. In their well-known work, revealing a historical analysis for the change in firm behaviour in the US from 'retain and reinvest' in 1960s-1970s to 'downsize and redistribute' in the mid-80s, Lazonick and O'Sullivan (2000) argue that the shareholder value orientation affected long-term investment decisions of firms. By the end of the 1970s, there were two problems faced by the firms. First, through internal growth and mergers and acquisitions, corporations grew too big with too many diverse activities, which resulted in the detachment of central offices from the investment processes of their companies. Second, innovative competition was allowing only lowest cost suppliers with flexible employment structures to survive. As a result, agency theory was developed to address the issue of over-centralisation and competition. The theory suggests that because the agents (managers) were not disciplined by the market, they would opportunistically use their control over the allocation of resources, leading to overinvestment. There was a need for an increase in the shareholders' power through the capital markets that would function as a market for corporate control on managers.

Agency theory favoured the capital markets as behaviour-correcting mechanisms for the managers, which could reduce the risk of overinvestment and channel savings into most profitable investments. An OECD study summarises such developments as:

> One of the most significant structural changes in the economies of OECD countries in the 1980s and 1990s has been the emergence of increasingly efficient markets in corporate control and an attendant rise in shareholders' capability to influence management of publicly held companies. In particular, owing to the expanded possibilities for investors to use the capital market to measure and compare corporate performance of corporations and to discipline corporate management, the commitment of management to producing shareholder value has become perceptibly stronger; this represents a significant change in the behaviour of large corporations.
>
> cited in STOCKHAMMER, 2005, p. 198

However, as Lazonick and O'Sullivan (2000) argue, the impacts of this shareholder takeover on the firm level have been negative at the macroeconomic level, especially on employment and investment levels. Lazonick and O'Sullivan (2000) find that between 1979 and 1983, the number of people employed increased by 0.4 per cent, while employment in durable goods manufacturing declined by 15.9 per cent. Between 1983 and 1987, 4.6 million workers lost their jobs, 40 per cent of whom were from the manufacturing sector. Overall, the job loss in the first half of 1990s stood at about 14 per cent. Even when the economy moved to recovery from 1991, the job-loss rate rose to ever higher levels until 1995.

For Stockhammer (2004, 2005), financialisation is observed as two macro consequences of this hostile takeover movement which changed the firm behaviour internally. The first is that the accumulation rates (that is the rate of retained profits) in OECD countries have reached their lowest points in the first half of 1990s, whereas profitability was increasing (Stockhammer, 2005).[2] Second, the profits to investment ratio in most OECD countries also

---

2 Stockhammer (2005) measures profitability by the profit share in the business sector and finds that in the United States, the profit shares have increased from 29.83 per cent between

declined. For example, while the investment rate amounted to 80 per cent of profits in Germany in 1970, the ratio has fallen to 60 per cent in 2000 (Stockhammer, 2005).

In a well-known study drawing upon the USA firm level data for the period between 1973 and 2003, Orhangazi (2008) also finds evidence for the negative impacts of changing firm behaviour on real investment and accumulation through two channels. First, the increased financial investment and increased financial profit opportunities crowd out real investment by changing the incentives of firm managers. Second, and more indirectly, increased payments to financial markets in the form of dividends and stock buybacks decrease the available internal funds for investment, shortening the planning horizons. Onaran, Stockhammer and Grafl (2011) also presented econometric evidence for the negative effect of dividend and interest payments on firm level investment, giving rise to increases in 'rentier' income along with the rise of the profit share at the expense of wage share, which has been reflected in the worsening income distribution since the beginning of the 1980s. In a recent study by using panel data based upon financial statements of UK publicly listed non-financial companies, Tori and Onaran (2015) find further supportive evidence for the negative impacts of financial activity orientation on physical investment, hence stagnant and fragile growth. The next section will discuss how these developments identified at the firm level are translated into the aggregate level, also taking the wealth effects of increased consumption into account.

2.4   *Empirical Analysis on Aggregate Level: The Impacts of Worsening Income Distribution, Determination of Different Accumulation Regimes*

Although not defined as financialisation as such, the increasing shareholder value orientation also coincided with the disturbance of profit-wage distribution at the expense of wages since the 1980s. In line with the firm level analyses described in the previous section, Onaran and Galanis (2012), Onaran, Stockhammer and Grafl (2011), and Stockhammer and Onaran (2013) provided

---

1960-74 to 33.25 between 1985 and 1999, using the OECD Employment Outlook Dataset. The accumulation rate is measured as the rate of reinvested profits (the growth of capital stock).

Stockhammer (2005) claims that there is ambiguity in Marxian analysis as the term accumulation can both refer to the growth of profits or the growth of capital stock. In fact, in Marxian analysis accumulation refers to neither, but the rate of investment from surplus value that is newly created at the end of each production process, which differs from the growth of capital stock.

empirical analyses that combine how the changing firm behaviour and declining wage share are translated into the aggregate economy. When theorising at this level, the final pace of the growth of accumulation is not determined by the investment decisions of the firms alone, but also through consumption functions. When consumption functions are taken into account, the impacts of financialisation on the aggregate economy are not straightforward, given there are positive wealth effects of holding financial assets on consumption. In other words, although their income share is declining, households can continue consuming from their increasing wealth through the increasing value of their financial assets (Lavoie and Godley, 2001).

Giving the example of the USA, Onaran et al. (2011) argue that the decreasing share of wages since the mid-1990s could support a consumption-boom, instead of leading to a decrease in consumption, only through increased borrowing and wealth effects of the stock market inflation, mostly associated with housing price increases during the same period.[3] This had certain implications for accumulation, as the increase in wealth relative to income also led to a decrease in the personal saving rate (consumption increased relative to income).

To measure the impacts, Stockhammer and Onaran (2013) aggregate income and wealth effects into a consumption function. They also introduce investment (negatively related to worsening income distribution) and net export function (positively related to worsening income distribution). As a result, the total effect of the decrease in the wage share on aggregate demand is found to be dependent on the relative size of the reactions of consumption, investment and net exports to changes in income distribution. If the total effect is negative, the demand regime is called wage-led; otherwise, the regime is profit-led. Onaran and Galanis (2012) find that the demand regime in the aggregate Euro area (12 countries) is wage-led, indicating that a wage share decrease has negative impacts on total output. This is not a surprising result, as for a demand regime to be profit-led, the only channel is the positive impacts of inequality on exports to be greater than the negative impacts on consumption and investment.

In other words, under a dynamically demand constrained global economy, two types of accumulation regimes emerge: while some countries maintain consumption-induced demand regimes through increased borrowing hence widening current account deficits, other countries maintain export surpluses

---

3   Consumption as a share of GDP has increased from 0.65 in 1988 to 0.7 in 2007 whereas gross operating surplus as a share of GDP (profit share) has also increased from above 0.3 to just above 0.35, during the same period (Onaran et al., 2011).

through wage suppression, complementing each other. This approach acknowledges that the worsening income distribution might not lead to direct decreases in accumulation if the demand is profit-led. However, as demand is generally wage-led empirically, it is possible to argue that inequality is destabilising for the macroeconomy in itself by leading to decreasing aggregate demand levels as well as higher levels of debt (Stockhammer, 2012).

Hein and Van Treeck (2008), Hein (2009) and Van Treeck (2009) also contributed to this stream of literature. By drawing upon the Post-Keynesian theory of the firm, Hein and Van Treeck (2008) suggest that firms are interested in maximising their accumulation rate. They are only interested in the profit rate insofar as a higher profit rate eases the finance constraint, allowing for faster expansion. With financialisation, because the accumulation is below the maximum rate, profits appear to be no longer a means to an end, but rather they become an end in itself. They suggest that higher profitability at the firm level could lead to higher growth in the long run, if demand was taken as given. However, because higher profitability constraints lead to decreasing shares of wages, this has an impact of decreasing aggregate demand and hence a lower rate of accumulation.

Like Stockhammer and Onaran (2013), they also find a link between financialisation and increasing consumption expenditure. An increase in firms' profit pay-out ratio might lead to more consumption from financial wealth, because distributed profits will partly be consumed by the profit receivers who have higher propensity to consume. The overall outlook of an accumulation regime is, again, dependent upon the aggregated interactions of the investment and consumption functions through saving functions.

In the absence of compensating macroeconomic forces (i.e., impacting on saving), a higher profitability scenario has contractionary impacts for accumulation. Clearly, this impact depends on the propensity to consume of the recipients of capital income. The deregulation of the credit market may lead to an increase in the overall propensity to consume out of both income and wealth as well as increasing indebtedness levels. Depending on whether the negative impact on investment or positive impact on consumption dominates, the economy can be characterised as either 'debt-led' (higher leverage stimulates the economy) or 'debt-burdened' (higher leverage is accompanied by weaker aggregate demand and/or financial distress.

Van Treeck (2009) summarises the possibility of mechanisms for determining the final impact of financialisation on accumulation as follows. Financialisation can be associated with two micro level developments, higher profit pay-out ratio for firms and easier access to credit for households. If higher profit pay-out ratio leads to higher personal income and wealth and therefore higher consumption, multiplier/accelerator effects might lead to higher investment, but a debt-led accumulation pattern. The same pattern also emerges if the other primary exogenous determinant, easier access to credit, distributes towards lower income groups and higher consumption through increased indebtedness. On the other hand, if higher profit pay-out ratio leads to lower preference for expansion, lower retained earnings and higher leverage, lower credit worthiness and higher debt servicing might lead to lower levels of investment and higher risk of financial distress in a debt-burdened accumulation pattern. Again, the debt-burdened accumulation pattern also occurs if easier access to credit distributes towards higher income groups, followed by lower consumption together with higher debt servicing.

In short, although there can be positive wealth effects and the availability of credit further affect the overall macroeconomic trajectory, these analyses emphasise that financial profit seeking leads to lower accumulation rates in general, which then leads to lower profit rates, giving rise to a vicious circle in the long run.

2.5   Emphasis upon Increasing Levels of Debt and Securitisation

There is a certain tradition within the financialisation literature that puts the emphasis upon the impacts of increasing levels of indebtedness on accumulation. Contributions to this particular area came from different schools of thought including Marxists, Post-Keynesians and circuitists, especially after the sub-prime mortgage crisis in 2009.

For Barba and Pivetti (2009), rising household debts is a consequence of rising inequality as the households had to borrow for rising consumption expenditures along with increasing inequality. Because consumption tends to be inelastic with respect to reductions in income, given that wages have been stagnating since the beginning of the 1980s, relative standards of consumption were sustained through increased borrowing from the side of the households.

Dymski (2010) also puts emphasis on the increasing bank lending to households, especially to lower income households, from a Minskyian framework of business cycles. Although Minsky himself focused the attention on the indebtedness levels of financial and non-financial firms, instead of households, Dymski (2010) claims that Minsky's theorisation of business cycles can be extended to incorporate the household sector as lending to households reached certain high levels to have an impact on asset-liability structures of financial and non-financial firms.

In a Minskyan business cycle, all economic agents behave like banks, acquiring assets by issuing liabilities. In the beginning of a cycle, leverage ratios throughout the economy are low. However, as profitability rises along with optimism, agents start issuing more liabilities that increase the overall indebtedness levels as well as individual leverage. This process also signals a transition from robust financial positions towards fragile, speculative Ponzi-financing in which the increasing levels of indebtedness are only sustained through the payment of interest without the ability of full repayment. As the increased demand for credit also puts liquidity constraints on banks, the cycle comes to an abrupt end when decreasing liquidity from the side of financial institutions triggers a crisis in payments. In the case of the subprime mortgage crisis in 2008, securitisation in mortgage bonds enabled banks to liquidate their financial positions and extend their lending to lower-income households at a period of speculative lending and borrowing that was reflected in housing asset price boom. Hence, the increases in the household indebtedness were 'exploitative' in nature, as it was a strategy of banks to transfer the risks of inevitable bursts of speculative bubbles to lower-income households.

This view is also adopted by Lapavitsas and dos Santos (2008) in a Marxian framework, where financial profit is theorised as a form of profit which appropriates surplus from future flows of value in the form of interest. In the case of household lending for consumption purposes, because no production process in involved in the repayment of debts, the extra interest payment is deducted directly from the wage share of labour, giving rise to 'financial expropriation'. This approach will be discussed further as 'the financial expropriation approach' in the second half of the chapter.

Along similar lines, Sawyer (2013) adopts a circuitist framework and claims that increasing indebtedness levels of economic agents is significant in terms of leading to a macroeconomic instability, as the monetary circuit starts with the lending by banks, then is expanded or closed according to the portfolio choices of agents. For example, if the household saving level is low and the predominant source of savings is profits (in the form of retained earnings), credit money is generated through the loan demand and these are paid off after the profits are received. However, in the opposite case, when savings are primarily coming from households, loans are generated with demand, firms have paid off loans for investment, but now are indebted to households. When credit is extended for consumption purposes, the circuit still operates whereas in the other case, it is closed after the debt is paid off. Initially, increased borrowing contributes to aggregate demand in both cases. However, when the demand is coming from debt financed consumption instead of productive investment, the repayment of debt not directly related to an output increasing productive activity. Moreover, the payment of additional interest requires a compensating loss in consumption spending or extra borrowing (Sawyer, 2013). Therefore, the final impact of increased borrowing for consumption purposes on aggregate demand is more ambiguous as it has to be sustained through an increase in wages or extra borrowing.

2.6   *Asset Price Inflation Approach and 'Forced' Indebtedness*

The final stream of literature that will be discussed in this section is the asset price approach developed by (Toporowski, 2010, 2009, 2000). Toporowski is careful in using the term 'financialisation', in fact, in his later works, he favours an abandonment of the concept altogether (Michell and Toporowski, 2014). Nevertheless, using the term or not, from a Kaleckian perspective, he emphasises the destabilising impacts of inflation in capital asset markets along with a change in the saving and consumption behaviour of households. This approach differs from others summarised above, by introducing cyclicality to the picture. Moreover, it differentiates voluntary and 'enforced indebtedness', a concept adopted from Steindl, in order to distinguish endogenous aspects of rising household indebtedness as a response to rising asset prices in capital markets due to changing saving behaviour of middle classes.

In classical approaches to finance, Toporowski (2016) identifies two problems: which are first, a reduction of finance to credit in general, and second, the reduction of credit to saving or savings. While the latter is most prevalent within the neoclassical approaches, visible for example in attempts to reduce international debt problems to trade imbalances, the former is prevalent in both neo-classical and heterodox approaches that adopt a tradition to reduce financial crises to general banking crises arising from standard banking activities, such as speculation. By focusing on the psychological characteristics of economic agents as 'decision makers', these approaches do not differentiate capitalist firm and its financing decisions from other financing activities in the economy. His criticism to financialisation studies, such as the ones offered by Lapavitsas (2013) or Duménil and Lévy (2011), both of which will also be discussed in following sections, is that these studies incorporate basic debt into theories of production and distribution in an under-consumptionist framework, without an in depth understanding of the capital markets.

Instead, his framework of capital market inflation is as follows. From a Kaleckian perspective, investment determines savings. In Steindl's framework, household savings is a financial barrier to retained profits. If household saving exceeds the level of investment, then saving becomes a net financial deficit for firms (Toporowski, 2009). In other words, if investment falls below the level of household saving, firms find themselves paying to holders of their financial obligations and will borrow more to finance the deficit which will increase their indebtedness and further decrease their investment. This is a form of 'enforced indebtedness', in which an initial decrease in investment (or increase in household savings) creates a cycle of decreasing investment as savings are accepted to be more inelastic with respect to investment. This describes a typical business cycle in a pre-financialised economy.

With financial innovation and factors that affected the turnover in financial markets such as securitisation, active monetary policy that enhances liquidity, hedging operations and so on, the number of financial transactions and credit operations increases substantially. The ease of credit paves the way for a new saving opportunity for households in the form of borrowing and holding financial assets (Michell and Toporowski, 2014). Here, Michell and Toporowski (2014) argue that it is this aspect of changing middle-class behaviour for saving that is determining for a change in the accumulation patterns, and not the expansion of debt itself, as most of the expansion in consumer debt seem to be endogenous to the activities of the household sector. The change in the middle-class saving behaviour, on the other hand, refers to an increasing dependence on consumption from wealth gains: while past savings are kept for future consumption, current consumption is financed through borrowing and from capital gains.

When this change in the behaviour of saving is adopted widely among the middle classes of a society, asset markets grow with a large base of agents where the capital gains are not paid by the firms (like in the form of dividends), but rather by the other agents in the market through price increases. In this schema, deposits of late-comers (younger generation) provide the basis for repaying early savers and this creates a Ponzi-like capital market structure that leads to speculative price inflation (Toporowski, 2010).

What is observed empirically is first, capital market prices increase, and second, saving and consumption from capital gains increase. Because the vast bulk of household savings come from middle and upper classes as they have higher propensities to save, drawing upon the Kaleckian relationship between investment and savings, investment is negatively affected. Therefore, in a financialised business cycle, it is the high and stable form of middle class saving from capital gains that forces firms into enforced indebtedness, decreasing the investment levels. In Toporowski's (2009, p. 145) words, this is "how financial inflation makes companies overcapitalised, resulting in a decline in the trend of long-term investment and how forced company indebtedness is modified as the middle classes extend their consumption financed through inflating asset markets." As a result, an enhanced option to consume from wealth changes the character of capitalism and brings structural financial instability (Toporowski, 2010).

By looking at the subprime mortgage crisis, Toporowski (2009) argues that the housing market in the USA functioned as a 'welfare state of middle classes', giving rise to overcapitalisation and increasing indebtedness. In the case of housing, there is a limit to the amount of additional debt that households are willing to incur. As that limit is approached, more households extract capital gains from the market either to sustain consumption in the face of rising debt repayments or to repay debts. In either case, when the rate of credit withdrawal from the housing market (equity withdrawal) exceeds the amount of new credit coming into the market, the rise in housing prices reverses itself, resulting in a new era of debt deflation and household saving (Toporowski, 2009). This is different from the previous periods of financial inflation and the mechanism offered by the shareholder value approach, as the overvaluation of the financial assets is not obtained through draining the value of industry but rather by a general capital market inflation that is financed by the credit money that is put into the market by other participants (Michell and Toporowski, 2014).

The approach also differs from the consumer debt approach as it introduces the constraint of changing financing structures throughout a business cycle (towards Ponzi- financing) that limit the choices available to both firms and households. For this approach, the modern finance had changed the workings of the economy in general and an approach to financialisation should adequately address such a transformation instead of linking it to associated processes. In later works, such as in Michell and Toporowski (2014) mentioned before, the authors suggest that the term financialisation should be dropped altogether as what is needed is not a new definition for financialisation but rather a new theory for modern capitalist accumulation which identifies the endogenous factors and key determinants of the new economy following the unprecedented rise of finance.

2.7   Conclusion

This section briefly summarised some Post-Keynesian, Marxian and circuitist approaches to financialisation, which investigated the impacts of changing household and firm behaviour and changing distributional patterns on the aggregate economy, following the easier access to credit since the 1980s. First, it briefly outlined the Cambridge theories of distribution in order to introduce some of the underlying theoretical principles of these works, prioritising aggregate demand and its distributional components.

It is important to note that not all the approaches discussed in this section follow closely what has been offered as the fundamentals of this school of thought. However, there are some common assumptions especially regarding the role of money and credit within that framework. According to this, the primary role of money and credit is to fulfil a transmission role; first, at the aggregate level, through distributing to those with lower propensities to consume (capitalists) and second, within the real sector, distributing to those with speculative profit motives. Both of these happen at the expense of aggregate demand and imply an endogenously created instability within the capitalist system, which is why financialisation is accepted to be destabilising in general (whether endogenously or not). In the asset price inflation framework, destabilisation stems from the increasing prices in capital markets due to the increasing importance of the use of financial assets as a source of wealth. For Stockhammer (2013), inequality itself is destabilising for macroeconomy through the channels of decreasing levels of aggregate demand and higher levels of debt. In short, all the studies outlined in this section underline that financialisation is an endogenously destabilising process for the economy.

This book adopts an approach different than these studies, as financialisation is not necessarily theorised as a destabilising mechanism, but rather the material base of a phase in capitalist accumulation with or without destabilising impacts. Referring to the previous chapter, the book draws upon an analysis of capitalist accumulation has a two-fold nature, which involves the reproduction of both material (heterogeneous, context-specific) and value conditions. For that purpose, the circuit of capital is used for the analytical model to represent how labour and means of production is re-created as commodities at the end of each successive circuit while value also expands itself through money (Weeks, 1983). The Keynesian categories do not appropriately represent this dual nature as they do not assign a separate use value for labour power and treat the product of living labour as the revenue share of workers. Second, from the perspective of value expansion, these approaches assume that value created by living labour must be equal to the value of the consumption items plus the value of fixed means of consumption that can hold only under simple reproduction conditions (Weeks, 1983; Saad-Filho, 2002). Third, classes are identified according to revenues they share (with a unified motive in competition), but not according to the factors they supply during production process (with different motives) (Fine, 1982a).

The next section will introduce another method for conceptualising financialisation, as a reference point for periodisation.

3   Financialisation as a Reference Point for Periodisation

The first section discussed how financialisation can be conceptualised as an accumulation pattern in which profits accrue primarily through financial rather than commodity production channels. As such, conceptualised within a framework of supply-demand, this process is not limited to a specific time or space theoretically, irrespective of the special empirical emphasis given to its actual emergence in history. Another method for conceptualising financialisation is more historical, which is to define it in association with the current period of capitalism, which is named as neoliberalism, emerged around the late 1970s and early 1980s.

As pointed out by Jessop (2001, p. 285) periodisation is distinct from chronology in three particular ways:

> First, a chronology orders actions, events, or periods on a unilinear time scale that serves as a neutral parameter. Conversely, a periodisation uses several time scales that include the temporalities of the phenomena being periodised [...] Second, a chronology recounts temporal coincidence or succession [...] A periodisation focuses on conjunctures. It classifies actions, events, and periods into stages according to their conjunctural implications (as specific combinations of constraints and opportunities) for different social forces over different time horizons and/or for different sites of social action. Third, a chronology typically provides a simple narrative explanation, i.e., it refers to the temporal coincidence or succession of a single series of actions and events. Conversely, a periodisation presupposes an explanatory framework oriented to the contingent necessities generated by more than one series of events that unfold over different time horizons; it can therefore provide the basis for a complex narrative.

This distinction in fact refers to an important methodological principle about periodisation in terms of how to theorise on the basis of real flow of time/history. Simultaneity of different temporalities requires that the observant abstracts from excessively concrete elements of the real succession of events to identify sequential periods of relative continuity or discontinuity (Jessop, 2001). As discussed in Fine and Saad-Filho (2016), in terms of periodising capitalism, despite differences in criteria that can be adopted, there seems to be a broad consensus on its stages from a laissez-faire period in the nineteenth century later to give way to a more monopolistic stage in the first half of the twentieth century, which is later replaced by a stage involving significant state intervention, named as the Keynesian or Fordist period, and finally by the current stage, neoliberalism. This sequential structure is identified on a global level, by no means suggesting a convergence of different national economies, but rather identifying the common elements at a global level. The next sections will discuss how the concept of financialisation is used as a tool for periodisation, starting with a historical account by the Annales School.

3.1   *Annales School and Recurrent Financialisation*

In line with Fernand Braudel's notion of capitalism evolving in long-term historical cycles, *longue durée,* in which time is accepted non-homogenous, bounded by non-physical (conjunctural) and physical (geographical) space, Arrighi (1994) developed a notion of recurrent financialisation in his famous *The Long Twentieth Century.* In this well-established historical study of long cycles of capitalism, Arrighi's emphasis is upon the internal relations between the states, underpinned by the economic cycles of production, trade and finance. Each cycle is characterised by a hegemon, namely the dominant economic and political actor, emerging from an increase in its productive activities at the beginning of each cycle. However, when the intensifying inter-state competition starts to threaten the profitability levels and new production cannot lead to higher profitability, capital naturally shifts from production to trade and finance. This marks the falling of a hegemon and end of an era, implying that the current financialisation is not a novel phenomenon, but is rather a recurrent event signalling the 'autumn' in the *longue durée* of capitalism. This was for example observed in the falling of Dutch Empire in the late 17th century, and the falling of the British Empire from 1870 onwards, both of which were characterised by the substantial increases in volumes of trade and inter-state competition as well as decreases in production (Arrighi, 1994).

Arrighi's study later inspired Krippner's (2005) well-known longitudinal work on financialisation of the American economy. She found evidence for a similar financialised process in the modern economy, as the ratio of financial to non-financial profits in the USA increased from 0.1-0.2 band in 1960s to just above 0.7 in 2001. Similarly, the ratio of financial cash flows to non-financial cash flows increased three times from the 1960s until the end of the 1990s. For Krippner (2005), the rise of finance is the defining feature of contemporary capitalism, which signals the end of the current *longue durée* with the decline of the USA as a hegemon.

3.2   *Financialisation as Coupon Pool: Social Accountancy and Cultural Economy Approach*

This section will briefly discuss how financialisation is approached in a more encompassing sense in the everyday practices of contemporary capitalism. In these interdisciplinary studies from social accountancy and cultural political economy perspectives, the common emphasis is to show how the entrance of finance into everyday life alters the agents' behaviour and the capital markets emerge as a powerful social construct.

The advantage of this approach, as posed by Froud et al. (2002) is that instead of prioritising equity-based capital markets, which has been the emphasis of the literature under the influence of Anglo-Saxon economies, it conceptualises a generic 'coupon pool' system. In a coupon pool system, not only shares issued by private corporations, but all types of financial assets, such as debt obligations issued by the state are given importance as these securities equally contribute to the deepening of capital markets, which has acquired a dominant character to regulate firm and household behaviour.

From a cultural economy perspective, Langley (2004) discusses the emergence of a new welfare system on the basis of individualised middle-class savings through the asset markets in Anglo-American economies. In a coupon-pool system, the entrance of finance into everyday life transforms the society in way that credit borrowing becomes essential for sustaining living standards, reflected in the secular boom in the consumer debt levels. While savings are channelled into capital markets, in the form of pension funds or other financial assets, these savings are in turn used by the capital markets to create a volume of securities. In this way, the deepening of capital markets itself becomes a distributional issue, considering that the majority of lower-income households are too poor to meet the requirements of such a welfare system (Langley, 2008).

Erturk et al. (2007) discuss how the complicated nature of the financial products with considerable degree of opacity adds to the negative distributional impacts, given that financial literacy is not high among the lower-income households. In addressing the issue of distribution, Erturk et al. (2004) emphasise how the existing rhetoric on corporate governance remains inadequate, as it ignores the interactions between the agencies and structures and reduces all structures to a collection of decisions of individual actors. Instead, they suggest that the financial system is in need of an overall democratisation, taking these structural factors into account.

In later works, Engelen et al. (2010a) further contribute to the critique on the rhetoric of corporate governance by emphasising the unruly nature of the financial markets depending heavily on financial innovation as *bricolage*. This refers to the fact that financial innovation does not progress in a predictable or rule-bound fashion, rather it takes the form of bricolage, in which the structures are created out of a collection of improvised events, without a central, scientific rationality (Engelen et al., 2010a). Drawing upon such internal nature of financial systems, they argue that the regulation becomes not only a technical, but also a political issue, further complicating the picture.

They argue that three fundamental internal challenges must be addressed by the regulators, which are high volume, complexity and opacity within the financial markets themselves. High volume mostly arises from the fact that many innovations are designed to manufacture risk and leverage, instead of hedging risk, while complexity exists not only at the level of product, but also at the level of market relations. Related to these two, there is considerable degree of opacity about the nature of the financial products and the interactions, considering that many interactions are carried out through off-balance sheet, over-the-counter methods. In addition to these, the fundamental challenge for regulation does not come from the technical aspects of the financial markets themselves, but rather from the relative autonomy of political and technocratic elites to carry out improvised financial innovation techniques without sufficient rational foundations. As a result, the nature of financial regulation in the current period of capitalism also differs from earlier periods as it requires also a political solution. In this context, the fundamental principles of regulation revolve around reducing the detachment of technocratic elites and downsizing and simplifying finance as much as possible, in a transformative, rather than restorative attitude (Engelen et al., 2012).

The cultural economy approach prioritises the role of discourse and performativity in analyses of financialisation. It underlines how a new type of economy emerges through a discursive transformation. Erturk et al. locate the approach along a social constructivist line and emphasise how the economy itself becomes a performance "which combines stories and enactment through saying and doing so that the world can become more like our theories" (p. 34). Similarly, Haiven (2014) claims that this results in a cultural climate where all aspects of social life, including the creative processes, are shaped by the codes and logic of financial markets. In Bryan and Rafferty's (2006) conceptualisation, the performative aspect of the economy has much to do with the increasing importance of derivatives, as in a world without a single monetary unit backed up by gold or any other material resource, derivatives came to be used as global tools to anchor prices and construct the value of capital invested. But given that secondary financial asset prices do not move to stable equilibria, they cannot truly constitute an alternative to establishing the so-called fundamentals (Bryan and Rafferty, 2006, p. 35-36).

For Leyshon and Thrift (1997), not only the process of determining the monetary value of financial assets, the role of money in the economy itself is a social process. The authors emphasise how the contemporary conceptualisations of money are mostly based on a structural separation of the economic sphere from other spheres, and how in reality monetary relations are maintained through and out of geographical configurations and the corresponding social power balances. They especially point out to modern money's exceptional ability to co-ordinate different economic activity across geographies, rejecting a universal truth inherent in money existing in all times and spaces. Cutler (1978) also underlines the issue of the impossibility of a general theory for capitalist calculation, especially given the co-existence of various agents within the economy with different motives other than profit-maximisation.

Although the cultural economy approach offers exceptional insight, this book adopts a narrower and more specific definition for financialisation. In that sense, although the intensification of financial profit seeking and dominance of the logic of financial markets are instrumental in providing a base for the financialisation of the overall economy, the book examines the transformation of these social relations not in and of themselves, but within a more structured understanding of the economy as explained in the previous chapter.

The next section will introduce the French Regulation School and discuss how financialisation is conceptualised within a regulationist framework.

3.3 Finance-led Accumulation Regime as an Alternative to Fordist Regime: French Regulation School

Although the Regulation School does not use the word 'financialisation' per se, its early conceptualisation of a finance-led growth regime in the late 1970s contributed substantially to the financialisation literature. The framework of the Regulation theory was first developed by Michel Aglietta (1976) within a Marxist political economy analysis. Preoccupied with the identifying distinguishable systems of accumulation, through the interaction of different macroeconomic trajectories with already existing institutions and policy making practices, the contributors to this school such as Robert Boyer, Alain Lipietz, Antoine Reberioux, Francois Chesnais were among the first to claim the emergence of a new global accumulation regime in the 1980s, replacing the previous Fordist regime.

In 1990, Boyer (1990, p. 17) describes regulation theory as "[t]he study of the transformation of social relations, which creates new forms -both economic and non-economic- organised in structures and reproducing a determinate structure, the mode of reproduction." In that sense, the Regulation Theory offers a periodisation framework for capitalism based on, but not limited to, the changing macroeconomic structures at the level of national economies. In differentiating different macroeconomic configurations, the primary importance is given to changing demand or productivity regimes. In the case of a 'timeless' economy, these changes would alone be sufficient to determine how certain macroeconomic structures reproduce themselves through the interplays between a variety of possible demand or productivity outcomes, given a passively responding social sphere as an aggregated mass of individuals. However, the Regulation approach claims that the interacting macroeconomic outcomes of demand and productivity are embedded within the existing structure of institutions and political traditions, which gives the capitalist economy a path-dependent nature with a notion of irreversible (real) time (Jessop, 1997). It is in fact, this temporal nature in the development of capitalism that is captured by the periodisation attempts. For example, for Lipietz and Vale (1988), forms of regulation must at the very least concern the regulation of the wage relation, which is highly historical and political, concerning a variety of parameters such as the establishment of norms for working time, work pace, value of labour power, consumption standards, hierarchy of skills, segmentation of labour markets, regulation of the reallocation of monetary capital, management of money and its circulation as well as the forms of state intervention from legal to economic.

Although the Regulation theory evolves through time with some changes in its methods and arguments, its primary emphasis stays on the classification of capitalisms through time and space on the basis of dominant modes of regulation. In that configuration, a new accumulation regime only emerges, if a new set of institutions is being established or transformed in a way to allow for new regulation mechanisms, in line with the internal demands of a new macroeconomy, underpinned by its micro level determinants (Aglietta and Breton, 2001).

Drawing upon the experience of the US, Aglietta (1976) claims that the Fordist regime was an intensive, as opposed to extensive, regime of accumulation in the Post-World War II period. Its intensive nature was due to its dependence on the intensification of production techniques as well as working hours that gave rise to a significant rise in productivity and increasing returns to scale. This was only a part of the picture, as the productivity gains and mass production were combined with mass consumption due to corresponding wage increases. Fordist strategy came to an end from mid-1970s onwards with substantial stagnation in productivity levels as well as the loss of labour's organised power to sustain the wage share.

Following the demise of the Fordist regime, a finance-led growth regime emerges as a substantially distinct one from the previous period. According to Aglietta and Breton (2001), its distinction is first, due the change in the inner logic of the supply of new financial services, expanding the base of financial activities enormously, covering all economic agents instead of solely supplying credit to productive investors. Prior to the rise of the finance-led growth regime, finance was primarily in the form of bank finance, which is no longer the case. Second, this change in the supply of financial services in turn impacted upon corporate strategies, changing the interrelation between the capital accumulation and financial variables.

The microeconomic underpinning of such an approach is then, the changing relationship between finance and the rest of the economy which in turn changes the nature of the business cycle by abolishing the traditional trade-off between profitability and growth -that is because the debt decision of the firms is no longer determined by the trade-off between growth and market valuation, but rather by the dividend share. Aglietta and Breton (2001, p. 455) describe such process of change as:

> The pursuit of higher share prices through dividend distribution raises the financial cost of capital, which leads firms to limit their indebtedness. Corporate debt is then determined by the return on equity requirement of the majority shareholders. It is possible to conclude, therefore, that the influence of majority shareholders and the momentum of the market for control go hand-in-hand: they can be viewed as the twin offspring of the new economy.

The change in the financing structures means that asset price inflation becomes a determinant in the emergence of business cycles, as the companies' future dividend distributions are dependent on the assumptions made about asset price expectations. As a result, the interactions between speculative bubbles in asset markets, credit growth and financial imbalances become important for the patterns of business cycles in a finance-led growth regime (Aglietta and Breton, 2001). In addition to the changes in the firm level dynamics, the integration of wage earning strata in such an asset-based financial system introduces the household orientation towards wealth gains created by asset price increases, further re-imposing the importance of asset markets for the economy, leading to a virtuous cycle (Boyer, 2000).

In these earlier studies discussed above, the theorisation of the Regulation School is based upon the experience of the US. Later, in order to incorporate other national economies and to address the persisting diversity among different macroeconomic trajectories, Boyer (2005) defines four types of capitalisms (market-led, meso-corporatist, social democrat and state-led) existing simultaneously in the current phase, suggesting that the global emergence of a new accumulation regime does not lead to homogenisation, given the importance of institutional and social settings. Overall, the type of the accumulation regime will be determined by the speed of technical change captured by technical productivity increases (intensive as opposed to extensive), the nature of the demand (the distinction between wage-led and profit-led regimes), different finance regimes (bank-based as opposed to finance-based) and internationalisation of capital.

According to Boyer (2005), it was in fact the lack of this broader understanding that led to a premature generalisation of Keynesian policy suggestions on the basis of the context-specific success of Fordist regimes based on the productivity gains. The success of the Keynesian period was context-specific because, first of all, there were loose profitability constraints imposed by shareholders and the productivity gains were reflected in the wage increases with the help of collective bargaining (Aglietta and Rebérioux, 2005). Second, the circuit of accumulation was operating within the national boundaries, increasing the scope for policy success. Even during the Fordist era, not all the gains were stemming from productivity gains and there were differences between national economies. For example, Germany and Japan were export-led economies and their competitiveness was mainly stemming from a price effect instead of a mechanised Fordist model in less-open national economy conditions compared to today (Boyer, 2005).

By revealing the context-specific nature of the Fordist regime successes, the Regulation School provides a critique of the Post-Keynesian school, which draws its policy suggestions upon the previous period's bounded dynamics which no longer exist. Technically, Fordism was an intensive (increasing returns to scale), wage-led accumulation regime for which success was a combined product of its own conditions and therefore cannot now be simply replicated through following its policy schemata.

The next section will introduce the Varieties of Capitalism approach that also underlines the role played by the context-specific institutional settings in determining the macroeconomic trajectories.

3.4   *Varieties of Capitalism (VoC) Approach*

The Varieties of Capitalism approach developed by Hall and Soskice (2001) and later adopted by others such as Peck and Theodore (2007) and Streeck (2011) offered another method for understanding contemporary capitalism on the basis of the rising importance of finance. Rejecting the homogenising impacts of finance over the economy, they explained why different economies adopted different corporate strategies and have not been converging given their operation under the imperatives of an apparently homogenous global financial system.

Similar to the Post-Keynesian or Regulationist approaches, the starting point of analysis for VoC approach is the microeconomic changes in the firm behaviour towards shareholder-value orientation with respect to the rise of finance. When these changes are transmitted to the macroeconomic level, the shareholder-value oriented firms interact with the institutional forms such as the educational and training systems, intra-firm employee relations and inter-firm relations. Ultimately, the classification of the national economies depends on whether these relations are organised through 'markets' or 'hierarchies'.

While Liberal Market Economies (LMEs) are characterised by market-based relations, Coordinated Market Economies (CMEs) are characteristically dominated by hierarchical organisational structures (Hall and Soskice, 2001). However, Hall and Soskice (2001) also acknowledge that there is a range of relationships that are neither market-based nor hierarchical. In CMEs in particular, many firms develop close relationships with other firms as well as with their employees in a non-market and non-hierarchical 'third way'. In a restricted sense, however, the dominant form of the market and hierarchical relations determines the overarching institutional formation which in turn is impacted by the entrance of finance into the picture.

What are the differentiated impacts of finance in LMEs and CMEs? To understand, a comparison of corporate strategies in LMEs and CMEs is useful, as offered by Knetter (1989). Based on an empirical study conducted for British and German firms, Kneetter (1989) discusses how the exchange rate fluctuations would result in diverging outcomes in these economies due to their different institutional settings. When faced with an exchange rate appreciation which would make the country's goods more expensive in the international markets, British firms could sustain their profitability within an LME. As the structure of financial markets would limit the firms' access to capital and the fluid labour markets would allow them to change employment structures, they would favour sustaining profitability over sustaining their international market share. In contrast, the firms in a CME such as Germany, could afford a decline in returns because the firms have access to capital, independent of current profitability, given the bank-based financial structure. They would, however, attempt to retain the market share because the labour markets in CMEs favour long term employment, making downscaling more difficult.

Similarly, Hall and Soskice (2001) claim that the rise of finance has differentiated impacts on these different economies. It might disrupt the non-market relations in CMEs and have negative impacts on employment structures in LMEs. These impacts can be detrimental for both types of economies, and especially for CMEs easier access to capital can actually lead to unravelling of the national institutional structure by decreasing the reliance upon the long-term funds provided by banks.

The VoC approach is criticised by Ashman and Fine (2013), who show in the context of South Africa that the interventions of the financial system is not purely dependent upon the terms of its structural separation from industry and how they interact with one another, but rather is integrated into the specific systems of accumulation. Neither a coordinated nor a liberal market economy, South Africa has a well-developed and sophisticated financial sector with the dominance of London-based banks as a consequence of the particular pattern of its imperial past. These banks, however, neither primarily provide funds for accumulation nor expand their activities towards larger populations in a country where 37 per cent of the population do not even have a bank account.

Ashman and Fine (2013) report that this is because the dominant industry, mining, is not dependent on the funds provided by these banks but rather their own capital provided by the establishment of a strong oligopolistic structure given the large amounts of capital necessary for the mining industry. The six mining houses which controlled the industry had also shares in the two imperial banks, indicating that the banking sector was intertwined with the mining industry. But as Ashman and Fine (2013) notes, it was the productive industry which dominated the financial sector, and not vice versa.

Following the financial deregulation in 1985, although a consumer boom was developed due to high commodity and asset prices and household borrowing reached up to 65 of the GDP, the oligopolistic structure in South African industry has prevailed. The oligopolistic structure also remained, even deepened, with the top five banks owning 90 per cent of all banking capital in 2010 (Ashman and Fine, 2013). In short, the entrance of global finance did not result in the dissolution or transformation of existing relations, but rather exacerbated the oligopolistic, which is both non-market and non-bank based at the same time. This does not mean South Africa is historically unique, but rather shows that the role of finance in comparative economic performance could not be reduced to the changing relations between banks and industry, with predetermined patterns for funding investment.

The VoC approach shows similarity to the Regulation School in terms of emphasising the impacts of different institutional configurations on accumulation patterns. However, it differs from it by placing the emphasis more on the intra-class relations (between financial and other industry actors) rather than the inter-class relations. The next section will discuss the tri-partite regime approach developed by Duménil and Lévy (2004, 2011), which brings the investigation of the inter- and intra-class relations together.

3.5   Tri-partite Class Regime and the Crisis of Neoliberalism: Duménil and Lévy

Within a Marxists political economy framework, Duménil and Lévy (2004) describes the latest stage in capitalism as a tri-partite class regime, in which managerial classes acquire some degree of autonomy and form alliance with the capitalist class, at the expense of the popular class. In that sense, the current financial expansion is seen an attempt to restore the financial hegemony which was first established during the period between 1900-1929, with the help of three revolutions in the 1890s. These are first, the corporate revolution triggered by the growth in firm incorporations, financial corporation through a rapidly expanding banking system and a managerial revolution through the separation of ownership and control. This latter aspect had been fundamental in terms of giving way to a new capitalist class structure, where capitalists, managers and popular classes (production and clerical workers) constitute a tri-partite class configuration, which is fundamentally different from the previous periods.

In their analysis, the Great Depression is given specific importance in terms of defining the changes in the following periods As the first financial hegemony (1900-1929) was characterised by the bourgeois class getting less connected to individual firms and more connected to financial institutions, and there was dramatic progress in the organisational structure within the firms, they claim that the 1929 crisis occurred as a result of the exercise of hegemony that pushed the economic mechanisms beyond the frontier of sustainability (Duménil and Lévy, 2011). In that respect, Keynesianism came as a post-war compromise, which included the containment of finance, as well as the alliance of managerial and popular classes under managerial autonomy. During that period, the economic climate in general was favourable for investment and technical change for example through low interest rate policies.

Later, however, the authors claim that this period came to an end due to a declining rate of profits, by drawing upon the empirical developments in both the USA and Europe. While in the USA, the trend can be traced back to the end of the 1960s, when the slowdown of growth was accompanied by the rising inflation, stagflation; in Europe, it is dated to the 1974-1975 crisis, coinciding with the rise of oil prices.[4]

---

4   The rate of profit is accepted as the indicator of capital profitability, which relates "the mass of profits realised during a given period, one year, to the total sum of funds invested in a firm, sector or entire economy" (Duménil and Lévy, 2004, p. 22). Profits are calculated after all expenses (raw materials, depreciation, the cost of services and wages) are subtracted from the sales, but they might differ according to whether taxes and interest are paid. It is important to emphasise that the profitability is not measured by the share of profits (as opposed to that of wages) in the total revenue generated. That is because in Duménil and Lévy's words, "what interests capitalists is not to know how much they are to pay for wages to obtain one million dollar profits, but rather how much total amount of capital to invest in order to turn a profit of that magnitude" (2004, p. 22). The rate of accumulation is calculated as the rate of growth of the net stock of fixed capital.

The decline in the profit rate was coupled with the decline in investment (hence accumulation and employment), marking the end of the 'Keynesian compromise'. In the USA, the profit rates are found to decrease from 20.6 per cent on average during the period 1965-1974 to 15.4 per cent during 1975-1984. Similarly, it decreased from 18.1 to 13.8 per cent in Europe during the same time span. Unemployment rates on the other hand, increased from an average of 4.6 per cent between 1965 and 1974 to 7.7 per cent between 1975 and 1984 in the USA and from 1.8 per cent to 6.1 per cent in Europe (Duménil and Lévy, 2004).

The continuing fall of profitability resulted in the alliance of managerial and capitalist classes to sustain profitability, which gave rise to a hegemony of finance again, in the name of neoliberalism. As the accumulation system has changed towards over-consumption and under-accumulation, the Keynesian responses to crises of under-consumption or over-accumulation also became ineffective. In that sense, they claim that we witnessed a crisis *of* neoliberalism in 2008, which signalled the structural unsustainability of the current configuration.

The next section will introduce another Marxist interpretation by Lapavitsas (2009, 2013), named the financial expropriation approach.

3.6   *Financial Expropriation Approach: Lapavitsas and Dos Santos*

Another well-established Marxist approach to financialisation has been Lapavitsas' (2013) financial expropriation approach, which concerns first, the changing relationship between the banking system and the accumulation process, especially the shift to open market financing and the increasing reliance on the use of retained profits for investment. Second and more importantly, it theorises the rise of a new form of 'financial profit' through the extension of interest-bearing capital for consumption purposes since the 1980s, which resulted in the financial expropriation of workers. According to Lapavitsas (2013), credit extension for consumption purposes results in a direct deduction from workers' wages, as without a productive activity that follows credit extension, interest payments deduce their share from future flows of value, which are wages in the workers' case. Adopting the same theoretical framework, Dos Santos (2011) emphasises that as the ordinary households do not operate with profit maximising motives, excessive borrowing leaves them structurally disadvantageous compared to lenders.

Earlier, drawing upon Hilferding's (1981) *Finance Capital* and the Japanese Uno school,[5] Lapavitsas had established a business cycle framework in which

---

5   See Itoh and Lapavitsas (1999) for more details. Also see Weeks (1979) for a critique of Itoh's business cycle framework.

an upswing is characterised by a substantial reserve army of labour and high profit rates above the interest rates. As the accumulation proceeds, the volume of idle money that is necessary for the establishment of a financial system also increases. The increasing stock of capital available for credit, however, limits the incentives for technological innovation, resulting in unemployment to fall and wages to increase. This leads to an increasing demand from the consumers together with the decreasing stock of idle money available for credit; resulting in a subsequent crisis (Itō and Lapavitsas, 1999). This can be accepted as an over-accumulation explanation to crises in general, as Argitis et al. (2014) argue, which later led Lapavitsas (2009) to develop a new theoretical framework for the current stage of capitalism, as the latest crisis in 2008 clearly did not follow a similar pattern. Lapavitsas (2009, p. 124) argues that "the crisis did not emerge because of over-accumulation of capital, though it is already forcing capital restructuring on a large scale. Rather, this is an unusual crisis related to workers' income, borrowing and consumption as well as to the transformation of finance in recent decades."

He argues that three historical aspects have been particularly relevant for financialisation. First, productivity growth has been problematic from the middle of the 1970s to the middle of the 1990s, most significantly in the USA. Second, labour practices have changed, characterised by the intensification of casual work and the entry of female-labour into the labour-force. Third, global production and trade have come to be dominated by giant multinational enterprises through a wave of mergers and acquisitions throughout the 1980s and 1990s (Lapavitsas, 2009). Against the background of these historical developments, what was however, uniquely peculiar about the recent crisis was *financial expropriation*. It refers to the banks' increasing reliance on household credit extension, where capital is primarily extended for consumption rather than productive purposes, interfering with the ability of the credit system's contribution to the generation of new surplus value and resulting in a generalised form of usury through profit appropriation in the form of interest on a global level. This approach was criticised by Fine (2013) due to its understanding of the category of interest-bearing capital, which will be discussed in the next section.

3.7   *The Increasing Presence of Interest-bearing Capital*

Conceptualised by Fine (2013, 2010), financialisation can also be defined as the increasing presence of interest bearing capital (IBC) at the level of capital in general, drawing upon Marx's theories of money and finance. This is also the approach adopted in this book, in line with the methodological principles elaborated in Chapter 1. As explained, this methodological approach conceptualises accumulation within a structured and layered formation; consisting of the tendencies, countertendencies and contingencies, with categories of each layer coexisting and interacting with one another at all times. This means that although each category is specific to a level of abstraction and gets more complex as the analysis proceeds to more concrete levels, the simple concepts are not replaced with more complex 'versions'. Along these lines, this approach treats interest bearing capital as a simple analytic category that is purely abstract which is never observed directly but interacts with the categories of circulation.

As Lapavitsas (1997) argues, the possibility of IBC arises as a purely logical category, from the structural separation of the specialisation of 'monied' capitalists from 'functioning' capitalists, which is a distinction not posed by Marx himself, but existed in classical political economy, for example in works of Smith and Ricardo. The distinction between monied and functioning capitalists is purely abstract and simple: while the former simply owns money and advances loans to the latter without being involved in productive processes, the latter borrows money for possessing an investments project, directly engaging in productive activity. After the production process takes place and surplus value is generated, total social surplus is distributed between monied and functioning capitalists with profits earned in the form of interest and the profit of enterprise, respectively.

Without yet referring to the qualitative distinction between different uses of money lent and borrowed (for productive or other purposes including commercial activity), the division of total social surplus between interest and the profit of the enterprise refers to a quantitative one: the more one appropriates, the less remains for the other (Lapavitsas, 1997). In other words, in order for IBC (or more appropriately, loanable money capital at this undifferentiated level) to be able to appropriate surplus without being involved in productive activity, it takes its share from the total social surplus produced *elsewhere* in the economy, in the form of interest, which also include financial transaction fees and so on (Fine, 2013).

As mentioned before however, this separation is treated in purely abstract terms, without referring to empirical separation of different types of capitalists in the actual operation of economies. This is for various reasons. First of all, in the actual operation of economies, there is no clear distinction between 'monied' and 'functioning' capitalists, especially the latter operating purely through borrowing and engaging in productive activity without owning any capital of their own (Lapavitsas, 1997). Second, although they might have different motives in the abstract, as theorised by the literature on separation of ownership of control, in practice, revenue in the form of interest accrue both to industrial and rentier capitalists, blurring the distinction at an empirical level.

At this point, it is necessary to emphasise, however, there is a further distinction for IBC to appear as a separate category. The category of IBC does not simply arise from the existence of interest, but from the qualitative distinction of money lent specifically for productive purposes, which is when it requires a specific use value to function as capital (IBC) and expands itself through generation of new surplus value through productive activity. By possessing this use value, it also acquires the characteristics of a commodity, with an intrinsic ability to be bought and sold in the market with a price, which is interest. Lindo (2013) explains that the qualitative distinction arises from the dual aspect of capital as a both property and process, explained in Marx's (1981, p. 497) own words as:

> Interest is the fruit of capital in itself, a property of capital, without reference to the production process, while profit of the enterprise is the fruit of capital actually in process, operating in production process.
>
> cited in LINDO, 2013, p. 120

In other words, the qualitative division between IBC and other types of capital refers to a split in capital as a property and a process, the distinction of the former being its disengagement from the process of capital without forming a direct relationship with labour. This refers to the distinction between money-dealing capital (MDC) as money lent as money and interest-bearing capital as money lent as capital, both of which earns interest for different reasons. As Fine (1985) notes, however, the function of ownership of money is embodied in IBC on behalf of the society, and does not correspond to individual ownership of deposits. Fine (1985, pp. 398-399) summarises that IBC arises out of two factors: first, formation of hordes of temporarily idle money separates money from the mass of commodities and represents value in its purest form. Second, money as such represents potential capital, with an ability to renew and expand the production of surplus value.

Its separation form the sphere of production does not mean it is in no relationship to production, as the formation of a credit system is a precondition for the mobility of capital between sectors to form prices of production as opposed to values, which is an indispensable aspect for the rate of profit to be equalised across different sectors in an economy (Fine, 1985). Nevertheless, the important point is, because its formation does not depend upon systematic availability of money capital, but rather is contingent upon the actual hordes of money generated across the economy, the category of IBC (unlike money dealing capital), is formed *outside* the circuit of capital after money hoards leave the unity of production and circulation.

Lapavitsas (1997) explains this procedure as follows. Industrial and commercial capital are integral to the circuits of capital, while the former engages directly in productive activity, the latter minimises the costs of exchange process (although it might not be the case empirically), which is integral to the unity of production and circulation represented by the circuit. This means, industrial and commercial capitals take part in the process of redistribution of total surplus value at the level of capitals in competition, which is the process that determines the average rate of profit. Because IBC is formed only after money hoards leave the circuit of capital, on the other hand, it is not involved in the formation of average profit rate, despite appropriating a share from the total surplus value in the form of interest. This distinction explains why interest rate is qualitatively distinct from the profit of enterprise, without a material basis that connects it directly to the tendencies and countertendencies of accumulation, governed by the organic composition of competing capitals, length of the turnover of capital, as well as length and division of the working day (Lapavitsas, 1997). In other words, interest becomes a pure price category, determined by supply and demand, without a direct relation to the value system (Lindo, 2013).

Again, it is crucial to note that the division is a purely abstract one and the distinction between money lent as money and money lent as capital arises not from empirical validity, but from a logical possibility. That is because, the qualitative distinction of IBC expanding itself at the expense of other capitals is not observed at the more concrete level of capitals in competition, where IBC exists in combination with money dealing capital under the category of loanable money capital (LMC), acting both as money as money as well as money as capital. In other words, while the former merely involves a redistribution of existing monetary wealth and the other depends upon the expansion of monetary wealth, the distinction cannot be made from the perspective of the lender as long as each of these forms require interest to be paid by the borrower (Fine, 2013). At this empirically observable level, borrowing and lending activities that accrue interest are made for both productive and simply purchasing purposes. This has certain implications for the restructuring of capital in general, and interest-bearing capital in particular.

The important implication of this on accumulation is that once IBC requires its qualitative characteristic to expand itself to generate more money, there is an obligation to repay, irrespective of the success of the initial issuance of the money loan. In that case, the debt can take on a market life on its own through being bought and sold separately from the original debt. This explains why independent (secondary) circulation of IBC is called fictitious accumulation, not because it does not exist, but because it is not directly underpinned by productive value relations (Fine, 2010, 2013). In other words, it refers to the well-known fact that the value of mortgage-backed securities, for example, is determined irrespective of the value of the original debt it represents. Once accumulation acquires a fictitious character, it is subject to volatile boom and bust cycles as documented extensively and discussed throughout this chapter. Nevertheless, because interest-bearing activities are made for both productive and purely money lending reasons, the expansion of IBC might as well contribute to real accumulation through facilitating capital mobility between individual circuits of industrial capital at an inter-sectoral level.

For example, as discussed, the financialisation literature underlines how the deregulation of labour and financial markets benefits the expansion of a rentier layer at the expense of industrial capital (Stockhammer, 2005). From the Marxist political economy interpretation adopted in this book, these developments taking place at the level of capitals in competition may equally benefit financial and industrial interests (Fine, 2010). In the case of financial deregulation, while leading to an increase in the formation of secondary circuits of capital, it might as well lead to an expansion of credit in general, including consumption credits for simple purchase purposes. Many scholars who contributed to the literature on financialisation acknowledge that the expansion of pure credit does not necessarily refer to financialisation (Gabor, 2010; Toporowski, 2000; Van Treeck, 2009). Nevertheless, it might contribute indirectly through expanding the base for future capitalisation through financial deepening; or, it might equally lead an expansion of credit extended for productive purposes with positive impacts on real accumulation, which might in return contribute to the restructuring of IBC elsewhere, as long as newly created secondary circuits are realised with successful productive activity pursued through initial credit expansion. Hence, at this more concrete empirical level, where sectors are differentiated and competition is taking place with the help of money going in and out of sectors, it is not possible to pursue a purely theoretical discussion on financialisation.

It is, however, possible to talk about how a seemingly undifferentiated credit expansion has differential impacts on both production of individual wage goods, and their consumption across different income groups. In that sense, for example, the role of credit in electricity provision is differentiated from its role in housing, which will be discussed in the context of Turkey in Chapters 5 and 6, respectively. In the former case, it will be shown that the intervention of finance has facilitated productive investment. In the latter case, where the intervention of credit relations is usually linked to capital gains through asset price inflation in mortgage markets, Chapter 6 will show that the destabilising impacts of a strategy of boosting of overall revenues through price appreciations were limited, given the relatively limited intervention of landed property.

In short, the emergence of secondary circuits of IBC in the form of equity or debt-based securities taking a separate market life detached from the original values of loans (or shares) has been a common characteristic of the neoliberal period. Nevertheless, whether this emergence happens at the expense of production is an empirical question, depending on the success of the realisation of the circuits with surplus generated through productive activities elsewhere in the economy. In that sense, fictitious and real accumulation can and does take place simultaneously, as in the case of Turkey which will be discussed in the following chapters.

4   Conclusion

This chapter provided a selective literature survey on financialisation, on the basis of a methodological distinction between approaching financialisation as an object of study and using it as a reference for periodisation of capitalism. The first half of the chapter discussed the primary financialisation argument suggesting a slowing down of accumulation and crowding-out of investment, mostly associated with Post-Keynesian school of thought, based upon the principles of the primacy of aggregate demand and the impacts of distribution, laid out by the school's early pioneers. Some studies that find evidence for the negative impacts of increasing shareholder value orientation and short-termism on firm-level investment decisions are discussed, together with the investigation of the impacts of the shifts in firm behaviour on the national accumulation patterns (Orhangazi, 2008, Stockhammer, 2004, 2005; Onaran et al., 2011, Stockhammer and Onaran, 2013). The asset price inflation approach (Toporowski, 2000, 2009, 2010) is also discussed, which prioritises changing household saving behaviour for financial instability.

The second half of the chapter is devoted to financialisation as a tool for periodisation. Specifically, contributions from cultural economy and social accountancy approach (Froud et al., 2002; Langley, 2004, 2008; Erturk et al., 2007; Engelen et al., 2010a, 2012), Annales School (Arrighi, 1994; Krippner, 2005), Regulation School (Aglietta and Breton, 2001; Aglietta and Rebérioux, 2005; Boyer, 2000, 2005), Varieties of Capitalism approach (Hall and Soskice, 2001; Peck and Theodore, 2007), tri-partite class regime approach (Duménil and Lévy, 2004, 2011) and financial expropriation approach (Lapavitsas, 2009, 2013; Dos Santos, 2009, 2013) are discussed. Lastly, the approach adopted in this book, which is to explain financialisation as the increasing presence of interest-bearing capital at the level of capital in general is introduced (Fine, 2010, 2013).

It is argued that in line with Marx's theory of money and finance, although IBC expands itself at the expense of other capitals in the abstract, what is observed empirically is not the slowing down of accumulation, but rather an undifferentiated expansion of credit, appropriating interest both as capital and simple purchasing credit. Here, what this book suggests is a context-specific exploration of these differentiated impacts, which are never predetermined theoretically. Specifically, the book investigates the impacts of the financial expansion on the provisioning of wage goods in order to identify the impacts of this process on the value of labour power, the significance of which is explained in the previous chapter. The next chapter will move on to the discussion of financialisation within a context of developing and emerging economies.

Financialisation in Developing and Emerging Economies

1   Introduction

This chapter provides a selective review of literature on financialisation in developing and emerging economies in order to compare different developing country[1] patterns in light of financialisation. As introduced and discussed in the previous chapter, the financialisation literature has expanded considerably especially during and after the 2008 crisis, primarily focusing on the processes that led to the crash of financial markets triggered by the dysfunctional mortgage markets, starting in the USA. This particular focus had been biased towards developed country experiences where financial markets are well-integrated and deep enough with a wide pool of actors and institutions to sustain a growing volume of secondary markets, a considerable portion being mortgage-backed securities. As a result, the literature on financialisation in developing countries emerged both to extend the scope of the existing literature and to introduce some of the aspects that are specific to them mostly due to the dependent nature of these economies on the core. This chapter aims at introducing the existing literature, which will provide a theoretical framework to discuss how the case of Turkey compares to other developing country experiences that will be outlined in the following chapter.

During the late 1980s and 1990s, as the financialisation process accelerated, the world economy experienced more than seventy crises, about two-thirds of which hit the developing countries (Adelman, 2000). Historically, the process of financial integration of developing countries into global capital markets included experiencing systemic financial crises (Kaltenbrunner and Karacimen, 2016). For Dos Santos (2013), these crises are structural because of the very nature of the growth sustained through financial accumulation due to the source of profitability, which comes from future claims from net credit extension in the first place. As a result, the critical literature on the financialisation of developing countries has primarily focused on first, the destabilising

---

1   Although the term "developing country" is broadly used here, throughout the chapter it mostly refers to the transition economies or emerging markets such as BRIC countries, Mexico, Indonesia and South Africa, among which Turkey also stands.

impacts of increased financial integration such as the crowding-out of investment and the subsequent slowing-down of accumulation that have been discussed in the previous chapter, and also, the increasing need for costly financial reserves in response to the enhanced vulnerability to financial crises (Ergunes, 2009; Painceira, 2012; Powell, 2013; Rodrik, 2006), as well as the narrowing down of the scope of domestic policy manoeuvre due to debt management and exchange rate requirements (Gabor, 2012a, 2012b; Kaltenbrunner, 2011).

Many suggested that similar to the path in developed country cases, the increasing importance of finance in developing economies imposes a minimum rate of return on production, which is ultimately determined by the return on securities. In other words, production decisions become dependent on shareholder value (Crotty, 1990; Boyer, 2000). As a general trend, earlier studies on financialisation had observed that non-financial institutions increasingly became more involved in stock accumulation which had crowding out effects on fixed investment with shortening time horizons within the firm (Stockhammer, 2004; Orhangazi, 2008). In the context of developing countries, the question was whether the same processes were to be observed given the shallow nature of primary financial markets and individual or firm-level access problems especially for lower- and middle-income groups as well as SMEs, although it is clear that the role of finance in developing countries has increased along their deeper integration into the world economy (Demir, 2009b; Karacimen, 2013; Painceira, 2009).

At the micro level, it was emphasised that firms in both developed and developing countries were not able to make decisions independently of balance-sheet considerations. Drawing upon a firm- level empirical study on Mexico and Turkey, Demir (2009b) supported the argument that firms chose short-term financial over fixed investment especially during the 1990s where rate of return on financial investments had been higher than the productive investments given overall macroeconomic uncertainty. Karwowski (2015) supported the same argument by finding how South African firms increasingly engaged in speculative stock market activities, turning away from productive investment.

There were some significant macroeconomic distinctions, however, between the developing and developed country financialisation experiences, mostly due to the former's dependent integration into the world economy. For Bonizzi (2013), for example, the most important distinction in developing country experiences in that respect has been the underdevelopment of the second circuits of securities to give rise to financial asset price inflation as in the case of mortgage markets prior to the 2008 crisis. Instead, the main channel of financialisation has been the primary interest income which facilitated dependency on capital inflows through the sustained adoption of high interest rates. Similarly, Erturk (2003) emphasises that many developing countries are bank-based, contrary to equity-based financial systems of the Anglo-Saxon economies that dominate the literature on finance. Therefore, instead of carrying out speculative activities through buying and selling private corporation shares, many developing countries are now characterised by state-dominated bond markets through intensified issuance of government securities which regulate firm and household behaviour.

As a general theme, the literature on financialisation in developing and emerging economies emphasised the structural dependency on capital inflows, which were mostly assumed to be destabilising in and of themselves due to their very short-term characteristics (Grabel, 2011, 1995; Vasudevan, 2009a, 2009b). Global capital inflows are believed to reinforce the structural dependency and unevenness, as while the maintenance of flows had huge impact on domestic economy choices, the direction of flows was influenced very little by the individual domestic policies. In that respect, the primary emphasis on developing country experiences has been on their disproportionate turn to foreign capital in an attempt to shield themselves against fluctuations in exchange rates together with the attempt to maintain a consumption- driven demand structure. While profit opportunities such as carry trade, or debt characteristics of domestic economies played a great role in the determination of exchange rates, they diverted from their corresponding levels in line with the macroeconomic fundamentals which, as a result, limited the domestic policy scope (Gabor, 2012a; Gabor and Ban, 2013; Kaltenbrunner and Painceira, 2015).

As Toporowski (2007) points out, while in advanced countries, the depth and range of financial institutions meant that debt management was not a constraint on government policies, developing economies which cannot easily take on debt in their domestic currencies become practically tied to international portfolio considerations. From a Minskyian perspective, Palma (2012) emphasises how a country's outstanding stock of external liabilities can be the main determinant of structural vulnerability, as opposed to macroeconomic fundamentals, by investigating the commodity price-boom driven cycles in Latin America since the debt-crisis in the late 1970s and early 1980s. Levy-Orlik (2012) argued that how the structurally high trade deficits in developing economies have contributed to the import of developed country experiences through macro mechanisms of intensified capital flows, and found evidence accordingly in the case of Mexico. Following the debt crisis in 1982, increased financial integration has resulted in Mexican firms' participation in new global supply chains to provide high technology manufactured goods with lower prices which, as a result, lowered the gross capital formation necessary for investment.

As argued in the previous chapter, this book accepts financialisation not as strictly destabilising an economy that is otherwise stable, but rather as an inherent feature of a certain stage of development of contemporary capitalism, on a global yet differentiated scale. As such, although it draws upon the literature covered here, it has a slightly different focus in terms of shifting it away from the destabilising impacts of financialisation on sectoral or national economy levels. Differentiated from the increase of credit as such, the investigation of increasing prominence of interest-bearing capital is concerned with the ways of attachment of credit to the rest of the economy which is itself attached to a particular understanding of the capitalist economy evolving systematically that is both productivity-enhancing and labour-reducing, as summarised in Chapter 1. The aim is, then, to understand financialisation as part and parcel of the workings of the economy as a whole, not a variable that simply has its own causes and consequences contingent on presence of other variables. The next chapter on the political economy of Turkey will discuss how the Turkish experience compares to the examples summarised in this chapter, with the emphasis being upon how the increases in productive investment went hand-in-hand with the policy and structural limitations imposed by capital account liberalisation since 1989.

Section 2 provides a historical narrative for the development of financialisation in developing countries, starting from the implementation of the Brady Plan in Latin America, in light of the literature mentioned above. Section 2.1 discusses reserve accumulation strategy and the narrowing down of the domestic policy scope in developing countries. Section 2.2 covers the majority of empirical findings with respect to the crowding-out of production. Section 3 concludes by providing a brief summary of the literature.

2   Historical Development of Financialisation in Developing Countries

When the term financialisation gained prominence in the aftermath of the 2008 financial crisis, the literature on the developing country experiences stayed limited compared to those of the developed countries, especially with respect to the developments related to the secondary financial market formations. Because the extent and depth of such formations in the developing economies were limited, the literature did not go beyond discussing the possibility of a 'contagion' of financial instability through the increasing financial dependence.

Financial dependence was mostly arising from increasing financial indebtedness, coinciding with the global movement of capital flows out of developed economies, the first major wave of which occurred in the mid-1970s due to the USA's efforts to sterilise OPEC surpluses through syndicated loan channels after the oil shock in 1973 (Vasudevan, 2009a).

During the 1970s, oil surpluses were absorbed by the international banking system and then were recycled in the form of sovereign debt to emerging economies, particularly to Latin America. As a result, syndicated loan lending to emerging economies has increased substantially, reaching from insignificant amounts to $46 billion in 1982, replacing bilateral lending (Gadanecz, 2004). As it is well known, this movement came to a halt with the USA's attempts to stabilise the dollar during the last couple of years of the 1970s through increased interest rates, creating a sudden debt crisis in many developing economies that manifested itself first in Mexico's suspension of interest payments on its sovereign debt in 1982. After the Volcker shock, the capital flows to emerging markets in the form of loans suddenly decreased to $9 billion in 1985 (Gadanecz, 2004). Following the crisis in Mexico, many Latin American countries were affected by the sudden stop of capital flows including Brazil, Argentina and Venezuela.

As a response to alarming levels of sovereign debt after the oil shock, the implementation of the Brady Plan in 1989 is considered to be the beginning of a 'financialised' process in developing economies, which resulted in the creation of sophisticated financial markets for sovereign debt and the facilitation of financial reforms (Painceira, 2009).

The Brady Plan was implemented to provide sovereign debt relief to these countries through the diversification of risks. As mentioned above, Latin American debt was mostly in the form of syndicated loans, of which risks were very concentrated, as 80% of sovereign debt was concentrated among nine big banks (Vasudevan, 2009a). The trading of such concentrated debt had started in a small secondary market among smaller commercial banks right after the beginning of the debt crisis in Latin America in 1982. Trading activity was intensified in 1986 with the introduction of debt-for-equity exchange programs as part of debt restructuring programmes. The implementation of the Plan in 1989 was a formalisation of these trading activities within the framework of a two-step programme to allow debtor countries to experience debt relief from these interactions, instead of direct debt restructuring of the original loans which were highly illiquid.

The logic behind the Plan was to offer creditors capital gains from the purchase of sovereign debt bonds from emerging economies, hence transferring the risk from domestic to international capital markets (Vasudevan, 2009b). Debt reduction came in two forms: as direct loans from international financial institutions and as trading of Brady bonds with different menus. The menus included a wide range of risks from creating new money/debt conversion to direct buyback options, and the overall observed impact for debtor countries has been a combination of partial debt buyback at market prices and a restructuring of the remainder (Clark, 1993). Mexico being the first country to adopt, the plan involved a two-step process. First, creditor banks and debtor countries negotiated the amount of discount to be applied to existing debt and the availability of new lending opportunities. Second, the individual creditor banks chose between the options to exchange their outstanding sovereign debt with bonds at a discount or lend new money or both. If they chose not to give new money, a portion of sovereign debt was 'forgiven', for which in return, creditor banks received US Treasury bonds which are less risky than debt bonds.[2] Through this mechanism, the IMF and World Bank continued to provide loans to debtor countries, further contributing to the deepening of financial systems. In that sense, the Brady Plan was in accordance with the more or less unified global policy rhetoric of the time, which is famously known as the Washington Consensus that offers reformative steps to developing economies such as opening domestic markets to international capital markets, full financial and capital account liberalisation and the abandonment of control over financial markets as well as the promotion of the establishment of national stock markets (Fine, 2001).

Nevertheless, despite positive prospects and efforts, the Plan had heterogeneous impact on banks across the board with respect to their exposure levels to developing country debts. Moreover, its overall aim of reducing the sovereign debt to sustainable levels was unsuccessful (Unal et al., 1993). In some countries, such as Argentina, Brazil and Mexico, debt service payments even increased after the implementation of the Plan.

In Clark's words (1993, p. 47):

Net cash flow impacts have varied, however, for different countries. Countries that were paying full interest before their Brady deals, that is countries not benefiting from new money loans nor incurring arrears, achieved the largest expected savings in cash outflows. In contrast, for

---

2   For a more detailed explanation of how the Plan was implemented and how it worked, see (Unal et al., 1993) and Clark (1993).

Argentina and Brazil, restoring normal relations with creditors through Brady restructurings required significant increases in debt service payments [...] For Mexico, which had benefited from large new money packages in 1983, 1984, and 1987, projected debt service payments after the Brady operation were slightly higher than the average net payments made in 1986-88.

Regardless of its mixed consequences, the nature of capital flows to developing countries has changed after the implementation of the Brady Plan. In line with the Washington Consensus, the Plan allowed banks to transfer debt from their balance sheets, while it also facilitated the deepening of the financial sector in many developing countries by creating an established market for debt securities, which was previously absent (Kaltenbrunner and Karacimen, 2016). During the 1990s, substantial capital flows from abroad primarily took the forms of private portfolio flows and direct investment instead of sovereign loans (Kaltenbrunner and Karacimen, 2016). Private equity flows to developing economies increased from $5 billion in 1989 to $25 billion in 1992 (Vasudevan, 2009a). While the share of the bond market was insignificant during the 1980s, outstanding bonds reached 24% of total GDP of emerging market economies in 1994 (BIS, 2002). There was a substantial growth of domestic bond issuance as well. The outstanding stock of domestic bonds exceeded one trillion USD in the mid-1990s (Peiris, 2010). In the development of domestic bond markets, the participation of foreign investors has been crucial, which increased sevenfold between 2002 and 2006 based on national data and information from the Emerging Markets Trade Association (EMTA) (Peiris, 2010).

As a result, the financial sector continued to deepen in many developing countries during the 1990s, facilitated by the increased volume of capital flows. Nevertheless, throughout the period between 1987 and 1998, emerging economies experienced 44 episodes of capital inflows with more than a third of these episodes ending abruptly in a currency crisis or a sudden stop (Vasudevan, 2009a). Mainstream theories assume that probability of a sudden stop of capital inflows initially increases in the early stages of financial integration but then gradually decreases (Calvo et al., 2008). In general, it was argued that capital flows to emerging economies during the 1990s may have resulted in more vulnerability and financial instability due to three explained by a BIS report (2009, p. 11) as follows:

1) Local banks financed a major expansion of bank lending by short-term borrowing in foreign currency from international banks creating both maturity and currency mismatches.

2) The lack of long-term local currency debt markets resulted in the excessive accumulation of short-term foreign currency denominated debt securities (hence contributing to their 'original sin').[3]

3) Equity and other financial markets were thin which led to disruptive boom and bust cycles. In many cases, foreign capital was diverted into non-tradable instruments that were easily collateralised (such as real estate instruments).

Eichengreen and Hausmann (1999) emphasise the different theoretical nature of the changing views on the relationship between the exchange rate and financial fragility, arising either from moral hazard, original sin, or institutional weakness, all of which has different exchange-rate policy implications for emerging economies. For example, Demirguc-Kunt and Detragiache (1998) emphasised that although the mechanism behind such crises seemed to be triggered by the abandonment of control over capital accounts, the sole reason for the crises was a weak macroeconomic environment such as low growth, excessively high interest rates and high inflation. Although capital account liberalisation might have contributed to the adverse terms of trade and an increased risk of sudden capital flows, trade and fiscal deficits did not seem to play an independent role in the making of these crises, according to Demirguc-Kunt and Detragiache (1998).

In general, Demirguc-Kunt and Detragiache's (1998) approach can be generalised as the 'macroeconomic fundamentals first' approach supported by the global policy institutions, especially by the IMF throughout the 1990s and 2000s (Gabor, 2012a, 2010; Grabel, 2011; Kaltenbrunner and Painceira, 2015). Gabor (2012a, p. 714), for example, emphasised how the IMF's policy response to capital flows has followed a sequenced structure: "first, allow the exchange rate to appreciate to equilibrium levels, then lower domestic policy interest rates if no threats of overheating or use sterilised currency market interventions to bring foreign exchange reserves to adequate precautionary levels, and tighten fiscal policy".

Nevertheless, capital control measures taken by some countries, such as Malaysia after the Asian crisis, resulted in considerable policy debate whether there was room for other macroeconomic measures, other than correcting the macroeconomic fundamentals (Kaplan and Rodrik, 2001).

---

3 'Original sin' hypothesis refers to an incompleteness in financial markets, which prevents the domestic currency from being used to borrow abroad or to borrow long-term domestically. For a more detailed theoretical and policy implication investigation of this aspect, see (Eichengreen and Hausmann, 1999).

Heterodox views on the issue, therefore, emphasised that a rising deficit in the balance of trade, non-residents' involvement in domestic financial markets as well as residents' acquisition of foreign currency denominated assets put speculative pressures on exchange rates and, as a result, exchange rate speculation becomes structural (Akyuz, 1993; Kaltenbrunner, 2011). A structural implication of this process in developing countries is that, once a current account deficit occurs in a developing country, it is hard to maintain a stable foreign exchange regime given their limited foreign exchange reserves (Lapavitsas, 2013). In the absence of control over free capital flows, governments could not prevent speculative attacks and the foreign exchange outflows were followed by sharp devaluations of domestic currencies. As a result, especially countries with large current account deficits and a huge amount of foreign currency liabilities experienced frequent financial crises.

It was argued that in accordance with the expansionary phase of a Minskyan cycle, such foreign exchange crises were easily translated into financial crises given high asset prices and financial crises were further translated to the real economy through the channel of a weak banking system (Palma, 2012). When faced with sudden stops of capital flows, banks with solvency problems started looking for immediate rescue loans which resulted in increased interest rates with seriously negative impacts for productive investment. Aybar and Lapavitsas (2001a) argued that it was through this channel the increased financial integration through foreign capital movements led to more frequent financial crises in developing economies. As a result, especially after the surge of capital flows came to another halt with the eruption of Asian Crisis in 1997-1998, many developing countries especially in Latin America adopted a reserve accumulation strategy mostly in the form of dollar to avoid sudden foreign exchange crises which were now structural (Painceira, 2009). The next section will discuss how the increasing indebtedness resulted in unproductive strategies such as reserve accumulation, and the narrowing down of the policy scope in developing countries in general.

2.1   *Reserve Accumulation Strategy and the Narrowing Down of the Policy Scope*

A new wave of capital inflows to emerging economies started in 2002, increasing the total volume of net private capital flows from $90 billion to $600 billion in 2007 (BIS, 2009). During 2006-2007, the rapid rise of gross capital inflows peaked at over $1 trillion compared to the previous peak of $300 billion in 1996 (BIS, 2009). Between 2002 and 2007, developing countries accumulated short-term capital worth more than $2 trillion cumulatively (BIS, 2009). The inflow of capital mostly took the form of direct investment and portfolio flows.

Nevertheless, it is assumed that the sharp rise in capital flows took place in quite different macroeconomic and financial circumstances than the 1990s, with different global implications. First of all, such flows were not needed to supplement inadequate saving levels. From 1999, increases in saving rates outpaced investment while the current account balance of emerging economies as a whole was in surplus (BIS, 2009). This phenomenon can be explained by the reserve accumulation strategy in the emerging economies. It was argued that in order to keep liquidity at sufficient amounts, these flows were used to purchase financial assets from the USA mostly in the form of short-term Treasury securities instead of being transferred to productive investment (Painceira, 2009; Powell, 2013; Lapavitsas, 2013). As a result, the emerging economies have become net positive lenders, when the crisis in Asia came to an end in the early 2000s.

By 2006, reserves have climbed to almost to 30% of developing countries' GDP from a range of 6-8% of GDP while the share in developed countries steadily remained below 5% since the 1950s (Rodrik, 2006). These flows were held mostly in dollars. The dollar share of emerging economies' external debt has risen from 49% in 1974 to 63.4% in 1984, decreased to 43.4 in 1991 after the international flows dried up and then reached a peak in 1997 with 77% (Vasudevan, 2009a). Globally, while the USA absorbed 34% of capital imports in 1995, in 2009 it absorbed 65% of total capital imports indicating the dominance of its currency in circulation globally (Vasudevan, 2009a).

As pointed out by Feldstein (1999) and Rodrik (2006), in accordance with the Guidotti-Greenspan rule, that was because countries with higher net levels of liquid assets were better able to cope with sudden capital flow reversals, which has been a costly strategy for many developing countries including Brazil, Argentina, South Korea and other Asian countries.

From the perspective of international development, the primary argument of the advocates of the establishment of a global financial economy in which there are no controls over financial flows is that such a system would contribute to the equalisation of rates of return and capital-labour ratios throughout the world, hence helping developing countries benefit from the excess supply of capital in developed countries (McKinnon, 1973; Shaw, 1973). This argument has been criticised by the financialisation literature on empirical grounds bu documenting reverse trends of capital transfers from periphery to core. Lapavitsas (2013), Painceira (2012) and Powell (2013) find that contrary to expectations, developing countries have started to systematically finance the increasing financial debts of core economies since the 1980s, by accumulating high cost financial liabilities but earning much less on their low-return short-term financial assets which mostly consist of short-term USA Treasury securities.

For Lapavitsas (2013), a dependent reserve accumulation strategy is one of the most important reasons why the developing economies faced structural instability during the 2000s, due to the role of the dollar as world money. Lapavitsas (2013) argues that since the collapse of the Breton Woods system, the world economy has been functioning without a 'true' world money, yet the dollar has been acting as the only monetary anchor. The USA took the role of the banker by borrowing short-term and lending long-term and as long as its economy was able to keep its external deficit under control and attract financial investments in dollar assets, the dollar could function as the monetary unit of the global world economy. Such a development, however, had an important implication for emerging economies, namely the structural requirement to accumulate dollar assets, intensified with financial deepening.

The hoarding of dollar increased the level of indebtedness in developing countries, which had already been systemically high, and ensured continual purchase of the USA public debts and a transfer of surplus from developing to developed countries. As a result, Powell (2013) argues that the uneven global development structure was further reinforced by the financialisation process, leading to a 'subordinate' form of financialised accumulation in developing economies. As Rodrik (2006) also argues, holding excess foreign currency reserves had significant social costs for developing countries. Representing the social cost by the spread between the yield on liquid reserve assets and external cost of funds, and assuming reasonable spreads between the yield on reserve assets and the cost of foreign borrowing, Rodrik (2006) calculated the income loss amounted to close to 1% of GDP.[4]

It was argued that the mechanism of transferring financial risks to the periphery worked relatively well until the beginning of the 2000s. Nevertheless, when a currency functions as the world money, the hegemonic state faces a contradictory trend. While the continuation of the credit system lies in the hegemonic state's ability to generate international liquidity in the form of debt, the growing debt burden threatens the hegemon to face speculative

---

4   Rodrik (2006) explains that liquidity is achieved through three strategies which are reducing short-term debt, creating a collateralised credit facility and increasing foreign exchange reserves of Central Banks. The socially optimal way of sustaining liquidity would be not just building up foreign assets, but also reducing short-term liabilities, therefore the question of why many developing countries chose solely to depend on increased foreign assets has stayed rather as a mystery, according to Rodrik (2006).

outflows of capital (Vasudevan, 2009b). The USA has been able to preserve its hegemonic position until the 2000s through the mechanism of countercyclical capital flows despite its external debt being over 25% of its GDP (Vasudevan, 2009b). After 2002, however, both flows to the USA and periphery have started to increase, breaking the countercyclical trend and therefore introducing the question whether the dollar's ability to settle the debt globally as the world money was coming to an end (Vasudevan, 2009b). For Lapavitsas (2013), this was due to the USA's inability to control the flows given its huge external deficits and the existence of huge surplus countries such as China.

The growth of financial assets held by peripheral countries was accompanied by the growth of public debt, a shift from foreign currency denominated debt to domestic currency denominated debt with shorter maturity and a further growth of the financial sector (BIS, 2007). In accordance with the inflation-targeting strategies of the Central Banks of the periphery, large foreign exchange surpluses were sterilised through issuance of domestic government securities in order to avoid inflationary pressures. While the total financial assets in emerging economies rose from $3.9 trillion in 1995 to $23.6 trillion in 2006, domestic public sector debt rose from 8.8% of developed countries to 35.4% during the same period (Painceira, 2009). As documented extensively by the Bank for International Settlements (BIS) (2007), this refers to a carry-trade position, a cross-currency investment strategy which involves leveraged borrowing in low-interest rate currencies to fund placements in high-yielding currencies without hedging the attending currency risk (Gabor, 2012a). As Gabor (2012a) argues, the carry-trade contradicts with the dominant theoretical explanation for currency movements, as the uncovered interest parity (UIP) condition traditionally predicts that under flexible exchange rate regimes, high interest rate countries normally experience depreciating exchange rates, offsetting speculative gains from interest rate differentials.

Intensified carry-trade activity suggests that there is also a link between reserve accumulation strategy and increasing domestic debt levels, as the sterilisation of capital flows mostly took place through Central Banks' issuance of public securities, held mostly by domestic financial institutions, which further contributed to the expansion of the financial system (Gungen, 2012). In the context of Eastern European countries, Gabor (2010) highlights how the Central Banks' sterilisation attempts in creating the pool of liquidity resulted in financial institutions increased engagement with speculative activities such as carry-trade and currency arbitrage, as well as increased foreign currency denominated lending to households. As Rethel (2010) documents, a shift towards households to sustain consumption was evident in Malaysia. From

1999 to 2006, total Malaysian household debt grew at an annual rate of 15%. In 2005, total household debt to GDP amounted to 72.6%. This is also discussed by Karacimen (2013) in the context of Turkey, as will be discussed in the following chapter.

Nevertheless, not all capital flows took the form of financial assets and liabilities, as FDI flows also increased both from and to developing countries showing both an increased capacity for internationally competitive investment from the side of developing countries as well as an increased placement of such capacity in non-domestic territories which might raise concerns for domestic regional growth and development. In 2014, outward FDI from middle income transition economies jumped by 84% reaching a peak at $99 billion, while FDI from developing countries also reached a peak at $454 billion (UNCTAD, 2014). Together, developing and transition economies were accountable for 39% of total FDI outflows compared to 12% at the beginning of the 2000s (UNCTAD, 2014). Meanwhile, FDI inflows to developing countries also reached a new high of $778 billion, constituting 54% of the total. In total, the net balance of $108 billion went to transition economies, increasing by 28%.

As pointed out by Powell (2013), capital flows do not account for systemic instability by themselves and the quantity or direction of capital flows cannot be taken as an indicator of financialisation at any one time. That is because under flexible exchange rates, Central Banks take costly measures to manipulate the flows which can result in positive or negative cash flows at a given time period depending on the external availability of funds. Moreover, global production chains are so intertwined that most developing economies are structurally import-dependent which contributes to the foreign exchange inflows (Powell, 2013).

Nevertheless, reserve accumulation has been an important empirical observation to underline the volatile nature of capital flows and their corresponding impact on foreign exchange policies. The literature on reverse capital flows emphasises three major implications for developing countries. First, it finds that the flows resulted in net capital transfers from developing to developed countries despite expectations for the contrary (Painceira, 2009; Lapavitsas, 2013). Second, it created huge social costs by hampering investment and employment (Rodrik, 2006). Third, maintaining a stable foreign exchange regime became more difficult for countries with huge current account deficits and the efforts to prevent inflationary pressures increased the domestic public debt, leading to intensified carry-trade (Gabor, 2012a, 2012b).

The next section will discuss whether the crowding-out of investment hypothesis of financialisation is prevalent in the context of emerging economies.

2.2   Crowding-out of Investment and Changes in Firm and Institutional Behaviour

As argued in the previous chapter, one of the primary arguments of the financialisation literature is that it has negative impacts on both aggregate and firm-level investment given the turn of individual firms to financial profits. In the context of emerging and developing economies, this picture is further complicated by the governments' efforts to maintain both financial profitability and liquidity, which ultimately restrict their domestic policy choices.

As argued in the previous chapter, this book does not support the crowding-out argument of financialisation. Kaltenbrunner and Karacimen (2016) also emphasise that productive investment might fall (or indeed continue to grow) at the aggregate level, dependent on the dynamics fundamentally differing according to the dominant firm size, sector and openness in an economy. This section will examine the studies of developing country cases of financialisation empirically, which report crowding-out of investment and changes in firm behaviour across the board.

Demir (2009b) uses micro-level data for Mexican, and Turkish firms and finds that the increased availability of finance had a negative impact on productive investment, as the firms favoured financial investments with higher returns. Karwowski (2015) conducts a similar study on South African firms and claims that there has been a tendency for South African firms to overcapitalise themselves and hold excessive financial assets which made them the largest holders of bank deposits. This trend was also visible in Mexican firms, which underwent transformation toward downsizing and distributing (Levy-Orlik, 2012). As firms were required to invest in financial services, they moved away from high-technology manufacturing and reduced their employment levels. Moreover, more profits generated in the previous period were distributed as dividends, decreasing fixed-capital consumption. On the asset side, firms turned towards more liquid, short-term financial assets and there was a decrease in fixed investment items such as net equipment. On the liability side, they tended to borrow more from open markets in the form of bonds and more complicated financial instruments, especially OTC derivatives, instead of long-term bank loans (Levy-Orlik, 2012; Powell, 2013).

In Malaysia, Rethel (2010) finds that the country has shifted from a bank-based to a market-based financial system in the post Asian crisis period (1997-1998). This affected both individual and corporate financial cultures, leading to the emergence of a new politics of debt which was embedded in the domestic system and reproduced itself. Because a market-based system privileges firms over certain size, this transformation exacerbated unevenness of access to credit. Levy-Orlik (2012) also emphasises Rethel's (2010) point that financial integration brings unevenness in access to credit and foreign exchange reserves as a constraint and creates differentiation among firms according to size and international openness. High domestic interest rates in order to sustain attraction of foreign capital resulted in the decreased competitiveness of domestic small/medium enterprises with no international partnership since they lacked funds to borrow from expensive domestic credit markets. Because the SMEs traditionally rely more on bank lending, the increasing reliance on equity-based financing methods is found to affect their access to credit in a negative way (Levy-Orlik, 2012; Rethel, 2010). This resulted in large international corporations' increased domination in domestic markets where they could access cheap international funds.

Correa, Vidal and Marshall (2012) and Correa and Vidal (2012) also document that the financialisation process in Latin American countries resulted in the transformation and evolution of certain key institutions, such as the Central Banks and the commercial banking sectors which affected the ways in which the economy functioned. They claim, "[t]he ample accumulation of reserves in the region during the past years correlates to the ample issuance of non-resident actors in financial markets, as well as the balance sheet administration of foreign bank entities whose headquarters confront a process of deterioration of their capital, a growing need for reserves, and diverse programs of government bailouts." (Correa and Vidal, 2012, p. 545).

In line with the growing need for reserves, many Latin American countries witnessed huge capital inflows in the form of direct investment especially in energy and minerals, as well as the privatisations of select sectors of basic public services and telecommunications, especially during the second half of the 1990s. Meanwhile, the financial policies shifted towards those that respond to the needs of creditor banks such as a diversification of portfolios, widening the capacity of payments for debtor governments and sustaining stability through providing liquidity and depth in domestic currencies and widening the capacity of transfer earnings, dividends and interest payments. As a result, these requirements put considerable restraint on the autonomy of central banks to finance structural public deficits (Correa et al., 2012; Correa and Vidal, 2012).

The limitation of the policy choices was especially visible, for example, in the inflation-targeting strategy's class dimension, manifested as the decreasing share of wages, especially as opposed to that of the 'rentier' layer with strong financial interests. Many argue that considering that inflation was already showing a downward trend in both inflation-targeting and non-inflation targeting countries in late 1990s and early 2000s, inflation-targeting strategy was not solely a price stability mechanism, but also another way to provide financial profitability through the deterioration of labour gains (Ergunes, 2009; Papadatos, 2009).

In many countries, it is argued that the cost of low inflation and high interest rates has been socialised through decreased labour costs by keeping wages low. Onaran (2009) finds in Korea, Mexico and Turkey that frequent crises of the 1990s and 2000s resulted in downward pressure on wages. This was especially through exchange rate depreciation and recession. In Turkey and Mexico, increased export intensity has led to a decline in the manufacturing wage share, although this had no significant impact in Korea. In all three countries, however, both recessions and nominal exchange rate depreciations had a negative impact on wages. The depreciation rates had reached up to 90.2% in Mexico in 1994, and 169.5% and 96.0% in Turkey in 1994 and 2001 respectively, 47.3% in Korea in 1998 (Onaran, 2009). Correspondingly, wage share in manufacturing industry decreased from approximately 50% in all countries during the late 1970s to 30% in Mexico, 20-25% in Turkey and 40-45% in the early 2000s. While labour costs were kept low, Marois (2011) argues that the financial interests were protected as seen in the bank rescues in the post-2001 crisis in Turkey.

3   Conclusion

This chapter provided a selective literature survey on financialisation in developing countries that first, primarily focused on their increasing dependency due to the role of the dollar, changing exchange rate and debt management strategies and increasing profit opportunities from speculative activities such as intensified carry-trade. Second, empirical evidence for decreasing investment levels in line with the developments in the core is discussed. The first half of the chapter focused on how capital flows played a determining role as while they reached unprecedented levels, helping the core countries sustain financial earnings, it also caused developing countries to import monetary policies directly from the core. This resulted in many developing countries to adopt systematically tight monetary policies in the 2000s, in order to prevent the inflationary effects that would arise from the excess liquidity of capital flows.

As a result, exchange rate speculation has become structural and the excess accumulation of short-term debt securities mostly in the form of domestic bonds led to a growth of domestic public debt, and capital transfers from periphery to the core (Gabor, 2010, 2012a, 2012b; Kaltenbrunner and Painceira, 2015; Painceira, 2012). It was argued that the import of the USA monetary policies, specifically, through reserve accumulation led to the emergence of a dependent form of financialisation that is highly historical, political and institution-specific in nature (Powell, 2013). In the second half of the chapter, empirical evidence for declining productive and fixed investment is provided (Demir, 2009a; Levy-Orlik, 2012; Karwowski, 2015).

The next chapter is on the political economy of Turkey, in order to discuss how the Turkish case compares to the experiences summarised in this chapter. Until 2017, the Turkish economy has followed a rather optimistic path in which aggregate expenditure was not adversely affected significantly by financialisation. Instead, it led to a simultaneous development of construction and energy sectors which will be discussed in Chapters 5 and 6.

CHAPTER 4

The Political Economy of Turkey since 1980

Towards Differentiated Global Integration

1   Introduction

This chapter provides a political economy of Turkey since 1980, which marks the beginning of the financialised period. As argued in Chapter 2, periodisation of capitalism on the basis of methodological principles adopted in this book economy requires an understanding of the global economy in the abstract of which constituent parts are national economies which are neither mere manifestations of the global abstract nor separate subsets. In that sense, the analysis of the particular trajectory in Turkey is aimed neither to prove the existence of financialisation as a specific causal mechanism at the level of national economy nor to reject it as a rule. Instead, this chapter has two interrelated objectives. First, it has an aim in itself which is to give a detailed historical account of Turkish political economy that contributes to the understanding of how labour power is reproduced contextually through electricity and housing provision to be investigated in following chapters. Second, by drawing upon the historical formation of industry with respect to its actors, and investigating the impacts of 2001 crisis on this particular formation, it underlines the complex nature of the connections between finance and industry and examines the developments in light of the previous discussion of financialisation.

At the time of writing this book in 2020, the world economy is experiencing an almost unprecedented uncertainty due to Covid-19. Obviously, the Turkish economy is not exempt from such volatility and the impacts of the crisis will be immense. However, this book will not discuss the impacts of this particular event for two reasons. First, the crisis is still ongoing at the time of writing this book and most of its impacts are not observed yet. Although the Turkish economy has grown by 4.5% in the first quarter of 2020 according to TURKSTAT, it is expected to shrink by 8-9% in the second quarter due to the pandemic. Second, the impacts of Covid-19 in Turkey are to be shaped by the new, volatile macroeconomic phase since 2018, which is also not discussed at great length in that book. As the book is primarily interested in the deeper, long-term trends of the economy, it instead analyses the previous period from 1980 to 2017, which paved the way for such volatility and instability today.

The chapter goes back to the 1980s, as the period in which the global integration of the economy has started especially since the full capital account liberalisation in 1989. As discussed in the previous chapter, there are conflicting theoretical views on the impacts of capital account openness on growth and development, reinforced by the inconclusive empirical results (Eichengreen, 2001; Rodrik and Velasco, 1999). As Rodrik (2009) suggests, the results primarily depend on whether countries are constrained by finance or low returns on investment. Basically, while countries that are constrained by low savings and weak financial markets without structural return constraints on investment benefit from the increasing capital flows through directing them into productive investment; other countries where the costs of overvaluation outweigh the profitability of investment do not benefit much from capital flows through overcoming credit insufficiency. With the examples of Brazil and Argentina as constrained by finance and low returns, respectively, Rodrik (2009) shows that while capital inflows contributed to the investment levels in Brazil, exchange rate management of the overvalued peso has been more effective to maintain investment in Argentina, due its impacts on the profitability of tradables.

For Rodrik (2009), Turkey can be considered to have a finance-constrained macroeconomy, given its better macroeconomic performance especially during the 2000s. The annual rate of growth for both GDP per capita and GDP per worker have been higher during the 2000-2008 period compared to the previous two decades, with GDP per worker annual growth rate increasing from 0.02 during 1980-1990 to just below 0.025 during 1990-2000 and well above 0.035 during 2000-2008. During and after the global financial crisis in 2008, the Turkish economy continued to perform relatively well with an average growth rate of 5.4% between 2010 and 2014. After 2012, the growth started decelerating although it grew above expectations by 2.9% in 2016 during a period of global subdued demand. This optimistic trend has continued until the mid-2018, as mentioned earlier.

This chapter aims at portraying how this was made possible in a period that is associated with slowdown of growth and accumulation. Similar to other developing country cases, Turkey's integration process has also been accompanied with greater instability and deep financial crises in 1994 and 2001 both of which started as foreign exchange crises which later were translated into real economy busts. It also experienced, however, an increase in fixed capital formation especially during the 1990s which later constituted the base for a more stable growth after the financial crisis 2001,[1] as opposed to the decreasing

---

1   See Figure 3.

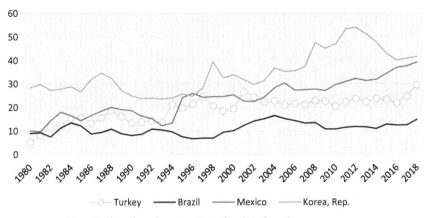

FIGURE 3   Exports of goods and services in Turkey (% of GDP)
            SOURCE: WORLD BANK

trend in the developed world. The next two sections will discuss these developments; first, during the 1980s and the 1990s, when accumulation stemmed from increased exports due to wage suppression and currency devaluation as well as government expenditures together with intensified speculative activities mostly through dependence on government bond markets. Second, the chapter will cover the period from early 2000s to the late 2010s, when the economy performed relatively well, despite the concerns with respect to decreases in gross savings, high unemployment, widening current account deficit and a consumption-induced demand structure (Rodrik, 2009; Yeldan, 2007).

From the 1980s onwards, the share of exports in GDP (94% of which is manufactured goods, in 2017) has increased steadily after the boom in the first half of the 1980s.[2] Figure 3 demonstrates that Turkey had a better export performance from Brazil since 1980 and followed a similar path with Mexico until the early 2000s, although Mexico's export share continued to grow after 2002, while Turkey's share remained stagnant at around 20% of the GDP.

It is argued by many that the real success of the export performance was due to wage suppression and currency devaluation accompanied by a consumption boom, instead of long-term structural change (Demir, 2009a; Onaran, 2009; Yeldan, 2011). However, in line with what Rodrik (2009) suggests, there is also evidence for a shift from labour-intensive industries towards capital-intensive industries within the manufacturing sector (Atiyas and Bakis, 2013; Sengul,

_____

2 See Figure 4.

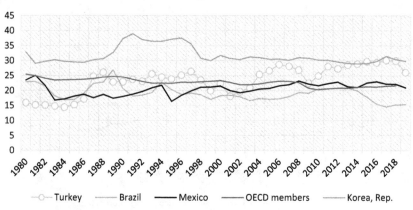

FIGURE 4   Gross fixed capital formation in Turkey (% of GDP)
             SOURCE: WORLD BANK

2015; Taymaz and Voyvoda, 2009), which might contribute to the export performance in the international markets, especially after the 2001 crisis.

Figure 4 demonstrates that although the gross fixed capital formation as
a share of GDP did not substantially increase, it remained above some other
emerging economies such as Brazil, Mexico, as well as the OECD members'
average throughout the 2000s.

On the other hand, this success came at the expense of a widening current
account deficit and increasing unemployment which increased to a 9-12%
plateau from an average of 7% during the 1990s (Onaran, 2006; Rodrik, 2009;
Yeldan, 2006). Gross savings as a share of GDP decreased from 25% of GDP
in 1998 to 21% of GDP in 2010 by the end of 2015, then increased back to 25%
in 2019.[3]

Figure 5 demonstrates that the external debt stock has been rising steadily as
a share of GNI since the early 2000s, which makes the economy vulnerable to
exchange rate fluctuations. Although the corporate sector's external liabilities
to GDP stayed relatively stable suggesting that the growing indebtedness was
not disproportionate to the expanding economy in the 2000s, indebtedness
continued to increase in the 2010s, when the growth path was not as promising
before. This has made the economy vulnerable to exchange rate fluctuations,
as seen in 2018.

The next section will give a brief historical account of the Turkish economy
during the 1980s and 1990s to discuss how an export-oriented accumulation

---

3   World Bank.

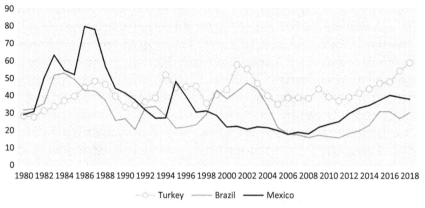

FIGURE 5   External debt stock (% of GNI)
            SOURCE: WORLD BANK

regime was maintained through wage suppression and labour shedding practices. This is believed to be the counterpart of the expanding financial arbitrage
opportunities, especially through the deepening of short-term government
securities market, in line with other developing country experiences covered in the previous chapter. Nevertheless, this chapter argues that there was
also evidence for early capital restructuring from labour-intensive to capital-
intensive industries within the manufacturing sector in that period signalling
an economy-wide structural change in the following period. Section 3 will discuss how the 2001 crisis contributed to this, and constituted a turning point,
by preventing the emergence of a fragmented financial structure through its
differentiated impacts on different actors of the economy. By favouring the
internationally competitive larger conglomerates with tight connections to
the financial sector over smaller and financially constrained enterprises in
Anatolia, it reinforced an oligopolistic structure with positive impacts on productive profitability, through maintenance of mark-up rates. In conditions of
shrinking domestic demand, it also pushed less-flexible capital-intensive firms
towards export-orientation, further contributing to the restructuring process.
Section 4 will discuss the deepening of the financial sector and increasing
indebtedness following the 2001 crisis, while Section 5 will specifically be dedicated to the implications of the corresponding expansion of consumption
credits.

While acknowledging the increasing scope of speculative activities such
as intensified carry-trade and simple arbitrage trading, Section 6 will discuss
the capital restructuring process within the manufacturing sector, to which
financial deepening during the 1980s and 1990s has been conducive. In that

sense, capital account liberalisation and enhanced access to credit facilitated not only speculative, but also industrial structuring, as the manufacturing firms could channel appreciated currency into capital deepening, following the capital account liberalisation. Meanwhile, fiscal expansion contributed to aggregate demand during a period when private demand was not so strong. Section 7 will conclude by emphasising the methodological argument of the book, which is to shift attention away from identifying national patterns and towards identification of a more abstract pattern (with implications for the value of labour power) with differentiated impacts on individual wage goods.

2   1980s and 1990s: Capital Account Liberalisation, Export Boom and Public Indebtedness

Turkey followed an import substitution industrialisation strategy in the 1960s-1970s after it completed its transformation into a nation state from the remnants of an empire. By the end of 1970s, this strategy was no longer feasible in the face of increasing pressures for financial liberalisation which started as recycling of accumulated surplus in developed countries in the form of lending and borrowing. As a highly vulnerable economy, it was impossible to continue financing the industry for import substitution, since the firms were already mature, but not competitive enough internationally (Yeldan, 1995). During the second half of the 1970s, there was a severe foreign exchange shortage after the oil crisis and the economy had high production costs due to protective tariffs and high labour costs due to the structure of the manufacturing industry consisting of low technology-intensive sectors with highly organised labour. The military coup in 1980 substantially suppressed wages through the dissolution of labour organisations and gave way to the replacement of the import-substitution strategy by an export-orientation programme in open economy conditions (Boratav et al., 2000).

   The new development strategy resulted in substantially increased exports, which had taken place mostly through rising private manufacturing capacity utilisation observed as an increase of the manufacturing sector's share in total exports from 55.3 per cent in 1980 to 73.5 per cent in 1987 (Sengul, 2015). Total exports also increased from below 5 per cent of total GDP in 1979 to almost 20 per cent of GDP in 1988. It has been well documented that the export orientation strategy was made possible not primarily through structural change, but through existing capacity utilisation as industry was extremely dependent on wage suppression and real devaluation of TRY for exports, as well as import and export subsidies (Onaran, 2006; Senses, 1989; Voyvoda and Yeldan, 2001; Yenturk, 1999).

Through making use of a Hodrick-Prescott filter to disintegrate the cyclical variations in productivity growth and wage rates from their historical trends, Voyvoda and Yeldan (2001) find the increases in labour productivity throughout the 1980s were only maintained with the help of the dissolution of powerful labour organisations after the military coup in 1980. They find that the average real value added per worker employed increased by 160 per cent from 1980 until 1996, with real wage earnings barely reaching the 1980 levels by 1996. Formal labour employment has increased by 31.8 per cent over the same period. On the other hand, the share of wage labour in manufacturing value added decreased from an average of 35.6% in 1977-1980 to 20.6% in 1988 (Voyvoda and Yeldan, 2001). Voyvoda and Yeldan (2001) argue that although it was theoretically expected from the process of outward orientation to contribute to both productivity and wage increases by exposing the sector to more competition and technological know-how of the global markets, this was not the case in the export-boom period during the 1980s in Turkey.

Meanwhile, during the first half of the 1980s, Turkey received a substantial amount of foreign private credit as one of the first developing countries to implement structural adjustment policies. As a result, the primary sources of demand shifted from heavy public sector borrowing and spending, especially in the form of infrastructure investment, to private sector manufacturing. Throughout the decade, net domestic borrowings hovered around 50 per cent as a ratio of the stock of the existing debt (Boratav et al., 2000). Still, indebtedness stayed rather manageable with the ratio of domestic borrowing to GNP increasing from 1.1 per cent in 1980 to 2.9 per cent in 1987 (Celasun and Rodrik, 1989).

The size and importance of the financial sector was not so significant, and the ratio of total financial assets to GDP hovered around 25% of GDP in the late 1980s. Most of the securities comprised public securities, amounting in 1989 to 66% of all securities despite the rapid increase of private securities (Gungen, 2012). 1989 was an important year to mark the transition to full capital account liberalisation, although liberalisation took place step by step throughout the 1980s through liberalisation of the foreign trade regime, removal of exchange rate controls, adoption of special policies to attract FDI, liberalisation of market interest rates and shifting to income transfer through public spending instead of price mechanisms (Demir, 2004). The classical strategy of surplus extraction through 'labour shedding' came to its natural limits in 1988, resulting in large current account deficits, high inflation and no significant real improvement in the overall competitive power of the economy in terms of global trade (Senses, 1989; Yeldan, 2006).

Throughout the 1990s, the manufacturing exports continued to grow, reaching a peak in 1997, rising from 18.6% of GDP in 1988 to 24.5%. Throughout the 1990s, exports grew at an annual rate of 6% while GDP growth was 5%. The growth of fixed investment remained considerably lower at an average of 1.5%. In general, distinct from the 1980s, the 1990s has been characterised by high levels of domestic, especially public borrowing to sustain the economy. The ratio of net domestic borrowings to the stock of the existing debt increased from 50% level in 1980 to 105% in 1993 and 163.5% in 1996 (Boratav et al., 2000). The share of the total public sector borrowing requirement (PSBR) increased from 4.7% of GNP in 1975 to 16.4% of GNP by the year of 2001, while the share of interest payments in the consolidated budget increased from 0.5% to 23% during the same time period (Demir, 2004).

Erturk (2003) pointed towards the speculative nature of this activity, facilitating a transition towards a 'coupon-pool' system, where the capital markets are no longer simply vehicles of financial intermediation but instead regulate firm and household behaviour in a destabilising manner. As mentioned in the previous chapter, many developing countries including Turkey are bank-based, therefore the establishment of a domestic debt market through the issuance of government securities increased the volume of speculative carry-trade activities in the overall economy.

From 1989 onwards, domestic borrowing continued to increase significantly, the stock of domestic debt in GNP increased from 5.7% in 1988 to 14% in 1994, and to 28.7% in 2000 (Yeldan, 2006). The indebtedness mostly took the form of short-term domestic public debt liabilities, mostly consisting of treasury bills with maturities less than a year. Between 1990 and 1999, the share of government bonds in the total assets of banks increased from 10% to 23%, while the share of loans to the private sector declined from 36% to 24% (Erturk, 2003). According to Akyuz and Boratav (2003), during the 1990s, the economy suffered from short-sided populist strategies such as Ponzi-financing debts and lack of fiscal discipline that resulted in unsustainable public indebtedness. For the Ponzi-financing strategy to work, domestic financial markets required the continued inflow of short-term capital to overcome the credit and monetary constraints. While the incoming flows were not sterilised by the Central Bank, they were used as a source for public expenditures by issuing short-term domestic debt (Yenturk, 1999).

Gungen (2012) supports the same argument and claims that the 1990s were characterised by a speculative accumulation strategy where the private sector avoided productive investment and profited from the gradual financial deepening via public securities since government debt securities offered higher yields than the expected profits to be gained from investment. As a result, the primary channel for indebtedness has not been external debt although it increased nominally from 41,751 billion USD in 1989 to 113,592 billion USD in 2001. Instead, the economy depended heavily on domestic borrowing, facilitated by the increase of total financial assets to GDP from 31.5% in 1990 to 99.2% in 2001 (Gungen, 2012). Most of the domestic debt instruments consisted of government bonds and treasury bills, the share of which increased from 4% in 1990 to 50.9% in 2001. Meanwhile the private sector securities also increased, albeit much less significantly, from 3% of GDP in 1990 to 4.4% in 2001.

In the face of such developments, Turkey experienced two big crises in the 1990s. The first severe financial crisis was faced in 1994, which was a traditional foreign exchange shortage crisis experienced by many developing countries during the period. The triggering of foreign exchange shortage was transmitted to the banking system through weak banks, which were becoming increasingly insolvent. Between 1992 and 1999, while the annual growth rate averaged less than 4%, the real interest rate paid on all domestic debts averaged 32%. By the end of 1999, the net open position of the Turkish banking system stood at 13.2 billion USD, showing the dependence of the banking sector on arbitrage income (Alper, 2001).

The Ponzi-financing of debts through foreign funding continued until 1999, which was the year when unsustainability concerns about the path of indebtedness and increasing fragility led to the implementation of a three-year stand-by agreement with the IMF in 2000, amounting to 4 billion USD to combat the chronically high inflation. The programme was a standard currency-peg exchange rate package for inflationary developing countries that included tightening of fiscal policy, implementation of structural reforms and exchange rate stabilisation as its main pillars. Although it has been partially helpful for achieving some of these goals, it could not overcome the complications created by price stickiness and the downward pressure on interest rates in an economy dependent on capital inflows. As a result, the stabilisation Programme resulted in further deterioration of the economy that was signalled by the increase of the ratio of current account deficit to Central Bank's international reserves from 5.9% by the end of 1999 to 29% in June 2000 and 49.7% by the end of the year (Yeldan, 2002). Just before the crisis erupted in 2001, the amount of net capital outflow reached a record level at 11.1 billion USD (Alper, 2001). It was classified as both a currency and banking sector crisis which was, again, similar to the crisis in 1994, and other developing country crisis experiences following capital account liberalisation, such as in Argentina in 2001 and in Mexico in 1994.

For Onis (2006), the 2001 crisis was due to a policy design failure of the IMF stabilisation programme, based on strict fiscal and monetary control, which could not be maintained in an open capital environment. For Cizre and Yeldan (2005) and Yeldan (2006), it was not the policy design, but the premature liberalisation attempt itself that led to the crisis by leading to an overvaluation of TRY and a loss of trade competitiveness in the international arena, as fiscal targets of the stabilisation programme could be reached despite ongoing difficulties. According to Alper and Onis (2003), especially in transitional financial systems in Turkey, Brazil or Argentina, the fundamental asymmetry between the liquidity structure of banks' assets and liabilities as well as between real sector and financial sector brings a systemic risk of financial crises to turn into long-lasting real economy crises. Demirguc-Kunt et al. (2000) argue, on the other hand, liquidity and banking crises that took place during the 1990s in developing countries did not have long lasting negative impacts on real economy and instead, had good prognosis in terms of rapid recovery by showing that although initially output levels declined sharply, they returned to pre-crisis levels in the second year after the crisis.

The 2001 crisis followed a similar trajectory described by Demirguc et al. (2000), with the economy contracting by 5.7% in 2001 but recovering growth by 6.9% in 2002. Between 2002 and 2009, the structurally high inflation rate was finally reduced to stable levels and a relatively high growth rate was achieved at an annual level of 6.6% on average until 2009.

The 2001 crisis has been analysed extensively (Akyuz and Boratav, 2003; Alper and Onis, 2003; Celasun, 2002; Marois, 2011; Yeldan, 2002). This chapter will not go into further details with respect to how the chain of events unfolded. Nevertheless, as this book argues, it is important to investigate how the crisis had an impact on the specific development trajectory of Turkey, how it had differentiated impacts on different actors in the economy, especially with respect to the access to credit. The next section will discuss this issue from a political economy perspective.

3   Political Economy of Transition: The Differentiated Impacts of the 2001 Crisis

In this section, I will briefly introduce the actors that played an active role in the establishment of the state apparatus and the design of social and economic policies as well as the productive relations in Turkey. This is to set a relational framework to understand how a global change has been incorporated into the specific set of productive relations in a particular domestic economy, and also to understand the differentiated impacts of the 2001 crisis on different actors.

Turkey can be classified as a late industrialising developing country in the sense that it heavily relied on a nationalist development agenda driven by the state in more or less closed economy conditions with very limited accumulation and productive capacities after the dissolution of the Ottoman Empire and the end of World War I. From the 1930s onwards, Turkey adopted an interventionist and protectionist development strategy for which the partnership between the members of the state apparatus and capitalist class was of great importance. At the early stages of primary capitalist accumulation, state intervention to the economy was direct in the form of étatist policies, which shaped the direction of the state's position in the following stages. In that regard, the Turkish state shared many characteristics with East Asian late comers who successfully implemented such techniques towards a successfully growing economy. Yet, there was a marked difference that, while the role of state in East Asia has always been market-augmenting, the state has been a major source of uncertainty for business with considerable variation in policy stances in Turkey (Bugra, 1994).

When the Republic was founded in 1923, the political aim of creating a 'classless society' through giving the state the absolute power of social and economic organisation seemed in conformity with both the global nationalist movements of the time as well as the traditional productive relations in the Ottoman Empire, where the infrastructural mechanisms were deliberately designed to prevent and suppress any form of non-political hierarchy. By the time the Empire came to its end, there was no significant capitalist accumulation and industrial production was confined to the limited number of small-scale establishments with an artisanal character.

The Ottoman Census of Industry in 1915 states that the Empire had 14,060 employees and workers in 182 operating industries 70 per cent of which specialised in the production of wool, cotton, cloth, yarn, raw silk, flour and tobacco (Boratav, 1981). These industries were mostly based in Western Anatolia where transportation links were more developed, while the commodity flows between the cereal growing regions of inner Anatolia and big cities were almost non-existent due to poor transportation links. To indicate the severity of the infrastructure problem, Boratav (1981) compares that while transporting one tonne of wheat from central Anatolia to Istanbul cost $8.8 in 1924, it cost only $5 from New York to Istanbul. The late Ottoman economy was operating in open economy conditions with no protective tariff rates for the industry due to the capitulations given to the European economies. Large-scale population transfers during and after wars and war losses had a serious negative impact on the existing labour force.

The Lausanne Treaty in 1923 maintained that the Republic took the heritage of the Empire and continued operating in open economy conditions until the 1930s. Due to the increasing discontent among social classes and the state's failure to establish productive capacity, the 1930s marked a distinctive difference for the Turkish economy in terms of the methods for capitalist accumulation. After the state has taken control of its tariff rates, the economy swiftly went into an étatist phase with the aim of the state taking absolute control of the internal markets by giving it the rent of production as the only price setter for strategic commodities (wheat, cotton, tobacco). The Central Bank of Turkey was established in 1930 and two official economic policy programmes were prepared: The Report on the Economic Situation (Sakir Kesebir Plani) and The Economic Programme. The full transition to the étatist period was complete with the preparation of First Five Year Development Plan in 1932. The ultimate aim of such programmes was explicitly declared to achieve external and internal equilibrium via an import-substitution strategy.

Despite the unfavourable conditions for the national economy, the programme was executed during the stagnant period of the Great Depression and became successful in establishing infant industries and eliminating trade deficits in a protective environment. Between 1933 and 1939, the GNP growth rate was 9.1%, the industrial growth rate was 10.2%, the share of industry in GNP rose to 16.9% from 11% in 1929 and share of imports decreased to 6.6% from 14.5% in 1929. Protective tariffs were successful in that imports decreased from a level of 256 million TRY in 1929 to 101 million TRY in 1932, creating a positive trade balance for the first time (Boratav, 2012). To move the country from an agriculture-based economy towards industrialism, 21 enterprises were decided to be opened under the First Five Year Development Plan, including a paper-mill in Izmit (Marmara Region), a cement plant in Sivas (inner Anatolia), an iron and steel plant in Karabuk (Northwest Anatolia), a brimstone factory in Keciborlu (Isparta, Western Anatolia) and a copper factory in Ergani (Diyarbakir, Southeast Anatolia).

In his well-known comparative historical study of industrialisation, Gerschenkron (1962) stated that étatist policies of the time were not entirely pragmatic measures taken at times of global uncertainty, but also had socio-political aspects which can be seen in the selection of sites in Turkey. Practically, étatism seemed to address primary capital accumulation for a state which only had a small entrepreneurial class. Nevertheless, according to the Thornburg report in 1949 on the Turkish planning experience, when the state started implementing investment projects in the form of State Owned Enterprises, social and political considerations played a greater role than economic considerations in selecting sites for the enterprises (Arnold, 2012). According to the Report, the cities for the establishment of SOE s were chosen to help create an urban culture in Anatolia (the urbanisation rate was below 25%) while not disrupting the agricultural production through large-scale migration to big cities.[4]

Establishing big industrial plants in scarcely populated cities required the state to create and regulate its own industrial workforce as well. For that purpose, Sumerbank and Etibank were founded in 1933 and 1935, respectively. While Sumerbank was in charge of the textile industry, Etibank was in charge of the mines; together they employed over 8% of the industrial workforce during the 1940s. They also acted as commercial banks with opportunities to make loans, despite their primary duty staying to support the textile and mine industries. From 1940 onwards, Sumerbank and Etibank also started to provide social benefits such as housing, food, clothing, education and health services (Arnold, 2012).

It was these conditions through which the capitalist accumulation was started with a small amount of internationally competitive big businesses in Istanbul, which had established powerful connections with the banks as well as the state elite, while the Anatolian economy was characterised by the monopolistic presence of the state (Aybar and Lapavitsas, 2001a). To a great extent, the actors in the financial and the real sector were the same. Large Turkish conglomerates competitive enough to survive in the world market had a variety of interests in banking and trading as well as industrial production, the most important examples being the Sabanci and Koc families, owning the majority of productive capital in refineries, automotive and metal industry as well as the fourth (Akbank) and fifth (Yapi Kredi) largest banks respectively.

This structure had important implications for the development of the productive industry, as bank ownership provided great access to credit, sometimes even beyond legal limits (Ergunes, 2009). While the accumulation proceeded from the étatism of the 1930s-1940s to the import-substitution strategy of the 1970s, the structure of the financial and the real sector with respect to their actors stayed more or less the same. It was only during the export orientation phase of the 1980s, some small and medium enterprises in Anatolia had emerged by taking advantage of low wages and state support especially in

---

4   The urbanisation project through the establishment of SOE s will be discussed in more detail
     in Chapter 6 on the political economy of housing provision.

textiles. These enterprises had limited access to credit, with a financial system in which the large banks were owned by the large conglomerates.

During the stabilisation period after the crisis in 1994, extra-budgetary funds were kept under strict control and state-owned enterprises started to be privatised in an accelerating phase. The two public banks Ziraat Bank (State Agricultural Bank) and Halk Bank (People's Bank) became channels for rent distribution with limited capacity for facilitating private entrepreneurship. While Ziraat Bank was the main channel to help agricultural producers, Halk Bank specialised in subsidising and lending to small and medium enterprises in cities. New bank entry was limited due to political limitations. Foreign bank presence, on the other hand, was almost absent.[5] In this environment, the access to credit for Anatolian entrepreneurs was through two channels which were, first, to buy shares from privatised Etibank and Sumerbank and, second, to establish their own banks such as Egebank and Yurtbank, almost all of which were inadequately capitalised and engaged in highly risky operations which contributed to the making of the 2001 crisis (Aybar and Lapavitsas, 2001b).

Throughout the 1990s, financing public deficit through attracting foreign capital with high interest rates along with the low-risk lending to state was sufficiently profitable for large firms and banks, as discussed in the previous section (Boratav, Yeldan and Kose, 2000). This created an opportunity for increased rentier income through the financial system throughout the 1990s which was exploited aggressively (Yeldan, 2006). In a disadvantageous environment dominated by huge public banks owning one third of all banking assets and big private banks with close links to large conglomerates, small private banks tried to maintain profitability through arbitrage opportunities and taking open positions by borrowing foreign currencies at high interest rate to capitalise TRY denominated government securities in an open capital environment. These small banks were eliminated during the financial restructuring in the post-2001 crisis period.

As covered in the previous section, the decade of 1990s is mostly discussed in the literature with respect to the establishment of a coupon pool system maintained through issuance of short-term government debt instruments. According to Sengul (2015), however, there were two important constituents of capital accumulation during the 1990s that formed a basis towards structural change in the following decade. On the one hand, recently consolidated import-substitution oriented manufacturing sector enjoyed the benefits of

---

5 Foreign bank entry stayed negligible in Turkey, with no entry during the 1990s and foreign bank assets in total bank assets ratio not exceeding 14% in 2012 (World Bank, Global Financial Development).

capital account liberalisation by turning the appreciated currency into capital deepening. The manufacturing sector grew by an average of 6.8% between 1990 and 1993, and by 5.7% between 1995 and 2000, with the exception of the 7.6% contraction during the 1994 crisis. The growth of the manufacturing sector was higher than the overall GDP growth, itself at an average of 5% during the decade. As mentioned above, the growth of exports also continued albeit through the help of wage suppression and currency depreciation after the 1994 crisis by 24%.

On the other hand, fiscal expansion also continued contributing to aggregate demand when the manufacturing sector demand was not as strong. As Boratav and Yeldan (2006) report, from 1980 to 2000, the contribution of government expenditures to GDP outpaced the contribution of investment and exports. During the 1990-1999 period, public sector borrowing requirement (PSBR)/GNP ratio had an average of 9.4%, rising from an average of 4.5% from 1981 to 1988. Although this meant a costly demand management, as by 2000, interest costs on domestic debt reached 80% of the overall tax income of the public sector (Boratav and Yeldan, 2006), it was helpful in providing a capital basis for private sector manufacturing growth.

Meanwhile, the financial sector restructuring following the 2001 crisis further contributed to this, through elimination of smaller 'risky' banks hence restricting the access of credit for smaller enterprises. As mentioned above, large Istanbul actors had no problem in terms of access to credit; therefore such conglomerates were the advocates of financial liberalisation during the 1980s and onwards, which rescued them from the burden of public investment concerns of the nationalist governments (Aybar and Lapavitsas, 2001b). Therefore, an improved banking regulation and supervision that favoured big banks (Marois, 2011), also contributed to the maintenance of the existing oligopolistic structure, despite the emergence of new actors after the election of the AKP government in 2002. This turned out to be a facilitating environment for productive investment, as it prevented the emergence of a fragmented financial sector with heavy reliance on foreign financing and open market liabilities, for example similar to the case of Mexico where the relationship between banks and large conglomerates were not tight prior to capital account liberalisation (Powell, 2013).

In contrast, the banking sector in Turkey displayed traditional characteristics, with the primary function remaining to allocate financial resources for industry, especially in favour of larger industries given they could more easily maintain mark-up rates through the restriction of entry of smaller competitors. The 2001 crisis constituted a turning point for Turkey in many respects. First, it led to a substantial restructuring of the banking system and second, its differential impacts on different actors (along with the impacts of financial restructuring), reinforced the oligopolistic structure through elimination of small banks and tightened connections between big businesses and banks – which in the following period facilitated channelling of available funds into productive investment, to a certain extent.

The next section will give an outline for the characteristics of the financial sector following the financial sector restructuring after the 2001 crisis.

4   After 2001: Restructuring of the Banking Sector

In the aftermath of crisis that erupted in February 2001 and resulted in the contraction of the economy by 5.7%, the IMF-led *Transition to the Strong Economy Program* was prepared to address the difficulties in the banking sector. The Program's primary targets were disinflation, fiscal discipline and structural banking sector reforms. To address the chronic vulnerabilities in the banking sector, Banking Sector Restructuring Program (BSRP) was prepared carried out by the Banking Regulation and Supervision Agency (BRSA). The programme had four pillars which were reforming the state banks, resolution of the banks under management of Savings Deposit Insurance Fund (SDIF), strengthening the private banks and strengthening the relevant legal and institutional environment.

It should be noted that a reform process in the financial sector had already started in the late 1990s, including the stabilisation programme based on a crawling peg exchange rate package in 1999/2000, mentioned before. The *Transition to the Strong Economy Program* was not dramatically different than these packages, although it put more emphasis on the financial sector directly in terms of regulation, transparency and accountability. Without doubt, the programme was more successful than its predecessors in terms of contributing to deepening and widening of the financial sector with effective monetary and fiscal management as well as stronger banking regulation and supervision.

Although the banking sector had grown and banking system assets in aggregate increased from 63% of GDP in 2005 to over 90% of GDP in 2012 reaching 1.4 trillion TRY and 121% in 2016 reaching 2.5 trillion TRY[6], Turkey still can be considered as relatively unbanked with domestic credit to GDP ratio at 93%.[7]

---

6   BRSA (Banking Regulation and Supervision Agency in Turkey) statistics: www.bddk.org.tr.
7   Domestic credit to GDP ratio is 237% in the US, 162% in the UK and 154% in Euro area, as an indicator of financial depth. In Brazil, it is 107% and 53% in Mexico (https://data.worldbank.org).

The Turkish financial system is still considered to be a traditional bank-based system in which banks play the most dominant role and the primary channel of profitability for banks is lending for productive investment. Banks own 86% of total assets of the financial sector and stock market capitalisation does not exceed 50% of GDP while it has been above 100% of GDP in the US and the UK for the last 15 years, except the year 2008 when the financial crisis erupted.[8] Even in 2008, however, the ratio did not decrease below the 50% of GDP level in developed countries, reflecting the relatively un-securitised nature of the Turkish financial system although the scope for market based financing in terms of securitisation, repo transactions and inter-bank money lending is increasing.

By 2016, the largest share in Turkish banks' total liabilities consisted of deposits at 53% and the largest share in total assets was credits at 62%. The first five banks held more than 50% of all banking assets, the largest three of which being public banks holding 32% of all banking sector assets.[9] After the crisis, loans increased rapidly to 29% of all bank assets by the end of 2010 with a 25% annual rate of growth reaching 64% by the end of 2016. Among total banking sector assets, 38.9% were foreign assets. While deposits also grew, it was at a slightly slower pace, exposing the banks to greater liquidity risks, since this imbalance indicated a further reliance on foreign funding opportunities although the reliance on wholesale FX funding was low (13% of total liabilities) in 2012, compared to other countries in the region (IMF, 2012).

As Figure 6 shows, the primary borrowers of the bank credits were the financial and non-financial corporations, and the non-financial institutions' long-term borrowing did not seem to decrease contrary to the latest trends in the core countries. Domestic bank credits mostly took the form of long-term TRY loans and by March 2017 the share of TRY loans in total loans was 66.3% (see Figure 7)[10], while the share of long-term credits among total credits issued was almost 75%.

The share of the largest 25, 50 and 100 credits is decreasing, which could indicate a decrease in large-scale productive investment. The share of largest 25, 50 and 100 credits has declined from 14%, 19%, 25 % in 2011 to 13%, 17% and 25% in 2012, respectively (BRSA). Nevertheless, the share of investment funded by banks has been 7.4% in 2004, which increased to 38% in 2009 (although it

---

8   The World Bank data on financial sector: https://data.worldbank.org/topic/financial-sector.
9   CBRT (Central Bank of the Republic of Turkey) Statistics: www.tcmb.gov.tr.
10   All domestic credit data is from BRSA (Banking Regulation and Supervision Agency) website (www.bddk.org.tr), unless otherwise stated.

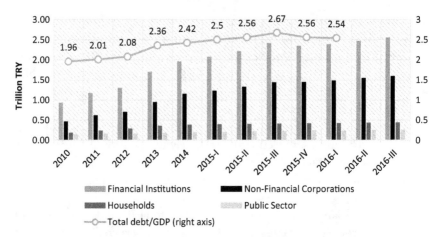

Disaggregation of total debts in Turkey according to sectors
           * Total indebtedness is calculated as the sum of currency and deposits, debt
           securities and loans under total liabilities.
           SOURCE: CBRT FINANCIAL ACCOUNTS STATISTICS

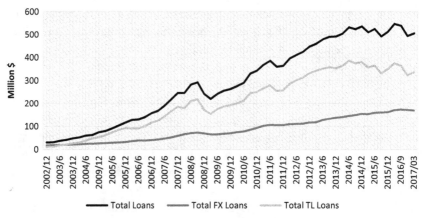

FIGURE 7   Total loans issued by domestic banks in Turkey (according to currency types)
           SOURCE: BRSA

decreased later to 31.4% in 2015).[11] Investments funded by equity and sales, on
the other hand, decreased from 33.4% in 2004 to 4% in 2009 and stayed at that

11   Investments funded by banks and investment funded by equity and sales ratios are from
      The World Bank Global Financial Development Database (https://data.worldbank.org/
      data-catalog/global-financial-development).

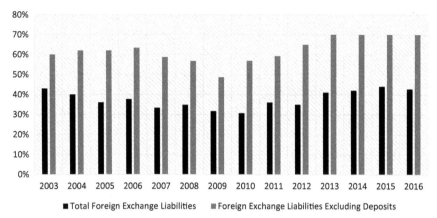

FIGURE 8   The share of foreign exchange liabilities in total liabilities of financial sector
             SOURCE: BRSA

level until 2015. In Latin American countries, on the other hand, an opposite trend was observed, and the share of investment funded by banks decreased from 23.8% in 2006 to 21% in 2010 on average.

In the period following the 2001 crisis, one concern about the financial sector was its heavy dependence on foreign exchange due to its high level of FX liabilities. As Figure 8 illustrates, although the share of total FX liabilities in total liabilities stayed stable at around 40% during the period between 2003 and 2017, this ratio increases to over 70% when deposits are excluded which are almost exclusively in domestic currency.

The largest share of foreign currency denominated liabilities among non-deposits came from the payables to banks item, which indicates foreign currency came into the domestic financial market mostly in the form of short-term interbank credits. Supply of foreign exchange credit mostly took the form of one-year maturity participation loans from international banks and off-balance sheet transactions. Among total bank liabilities, credits have a share of around 20%, 80% of which have been in FX from 2005 onwards. In 2014, 20% of such credits have been syndication credits with an average maturity of 1 year and 11% are securitisation credits with an average maturity of 6.5 years.[12] As a result, the net balance sheet open position of the financial sector reached a peak in 2015 at 92 billion TRY.[13]

---

12   BRSA (2014), Turk Bankacilik Sektoru Genel Gorunumu.
13   See Figure 9.

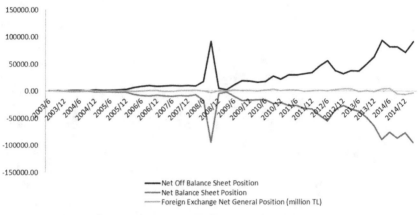

FIGURE 9   Financial sector FX position in Turkey
SOURCE: BRSA

As Figure 9 shows, the open FX balance sheet position of financial institutions was balanced with positive off-balance sheet position. By the end of
2016, the net balance sheet foreign exchange position of the financial sector
was around -64 billion TRY, balanced by off balance sheet flows reducing the
total net foreign exchange position to -1.6 billion TRY. The maturity structure of
such off-balance sheet structure is not officially known, but most of them are
assumed to have short-term maturity. In the long term, the financial sector has
a positive foreign exchange balance due to long-term investment loans.

Despite increasing off-balance sheet activities, the Turkish financial sector
stayed more or less a traditional one, especially when its asset side is observed.
As Figure 10 demonstrates, most bank loans are long-term which stayed persistently around 60% of total loans since 2010. Given 30% of all banking assets
are loans, banks mostly operate through issuance of long-term TRY loans to the
domestic private sector.

This indicates that although the capital flows enter the country in the form
of short-term foreign exchange credit, once it is absorbed by the domestic
banks, it is transferred to the private sector, in the form of long-term investment and commercial loans in TRY (see Figure 11 and 12) which had positive
impacts on real output growth while it also gives the advantage of profiting
from exchange rate differences to the financial sector until 2017. Figure 11
shows that most of the short-term external debt stock is absorbed by the private sector. Figure 12 shows that especially after the global financial crisis in
2009, the short-term external debt stock of the banking sector increased dramatically, outpacing the debt stock of the non-financial sector, which has been
indebted mostly domestically in long-term TRY credits. However, we can see in

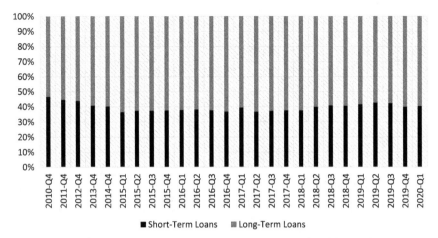

FIGURE 10   Turkish financial sector loans maturity structure (% of total financial
            sector loans)
            SOURCE: CBRT FINANCIAL ACCOUNTS

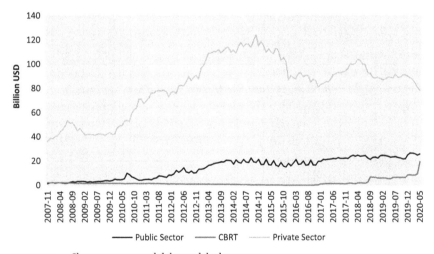

FIGURE 11   Short-term external debt stock by borrower
            SOURCE: CBRT

Figure 12 that the trend shifted again in mid-2017, as the non-financial institutions' short-term external debt stock increased its share as opposed to banks.
This was because while the banks substantially decreased external borrowing
in 2017, due to steady depreciation of Turkish Lira which culminated in a sudden devaluation in mid-2018, non-financial institutions could not immediately
respond to that development.

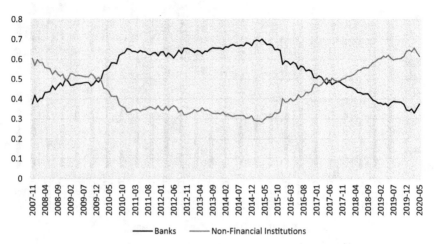

FIGURE 12   Short-term external debt stock by borrower (% of total short-term external
             private debt)
             SOURCE: CBRT

On the asset side of the financial sector, the most striking development has
been the increase of credits given to the non-financial sector, from 462 billion TRY in 2010 to 1.5 trillion TRY by the end of 2016. Figure 13 demonstrates
that the total credit liability flows in the non-financial corporations' segment
increased substantially since the 2009 crisis. During the period, public sector borrowing stayed insignificant as the high yield of government securities
declined gradually in domestic markets after the crisis in 2001, signalling a shift
in the primary accumulation channel.

Figure 14 further reflects the traditional nature of the Turkish financial sector, by showing that around 70% all credit liabilities of the non-financial sector
is long-term.

Despite the improvements in long-term lending capacity, it should be noted
that the largest proportion of total credits was issued for trading and commercial reasons, constituting almost 40% of all credits by January 2017. Figure 15
demonstrates that credits to small and medium enterprises also increased substantially, although their share in total credits declined from 27% in 2006 to
24% in March 2017. Still, considering that the SME credits are given in smaller
quantities, the nominal increase in the amount of SME credits from 60 billion
TRY (40 billion USD) in 2006 to over 448 billion TRY (120 billion USD) in 2017
reflects the improvement in the total number of SME credits from 1.7 million
in 2006 to just over 3 million in March 2017.

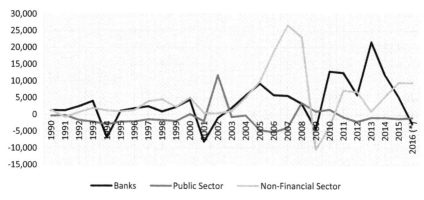

FIGURE 13   Total credit liabilities in Turkey (flow – million USD)
             SOURCE: CBRT BALANCE OF PAYMENTS STATISTICS

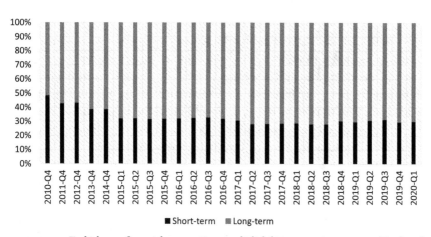

FIGURE 14   Turkish non-financial corporations credit liabilities maturity structure (% of total
             credits)
             SOURCE: CBRT FINANCIAL ACCOUNTS

The IMF Financial System Stability Assessment in 2012 states that the
CBRT's financial stability approach in the post-crisis period had been quite
unorthodox in the sense that it started differentiating and increasing TRY and
FX reserve requirements to lengthen maturities and increase the cost of funding. It widened the interest rate corridor and reduced the policy rate to lower
the front end of the yield curve in order to discourage very short-term capital
inflows. It increased reserve requirements, introduced tight rules for the FX

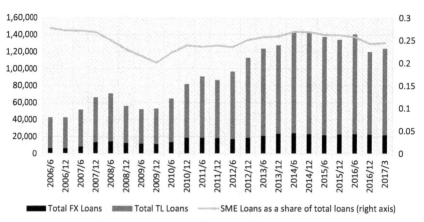

FIGURE 15   Credits given to SMEs by domestic banks in Turkey (million USD)
SOURCE: BRSA

open positions, liquidity and capital adequacy ratio (CAR requirement was increased from 8% to 12%, the absolute value of foreign exchange net open position standard ratio may not exceed 20%). As a result, reserves increased substantially, and CBRT increased its reserves from 18,741 million USD in 2001 to 87,128 million USD by March 2017. Nevertheless, the accumulation of short-term debt outpaced the growth of reserves, increasing the vulnerability of the financial sector to sudden stops of capital inflows which were otherwise relatively robust (IMF, 2017).

Figure 16 shows that there were also net positive FDI inflows to the country, even during the period of financial crisis in 2009. During the 2000s, FDI inflows were the most important item in financing the current account deficit, until 2009. According to the IMF Financial System Stability Assessment in 2012 such financial inflows were the primary reason behind strong post-crisis recovery, despite an externally financed boom presenting a very challenging macro financial environment given that domestic demand had been import-intensive and credit-dependent. Total FDI was only $10.6 billion in aggregate during the period in between 1984-2001, it increased to $52.2 billion between 2002 and 2007, foreign portfolio inflows also increased to $32.4 billion by 2007[14]. Between 2002 and 2009, the majority of capital flows took the form of foreign direct investment, after the global crisis, the primary source of flows has become portfolio investment instead of foreign direct investment. In 2012,

---

14   OECD website (https://data.oecd.org). Also see Figure 15.

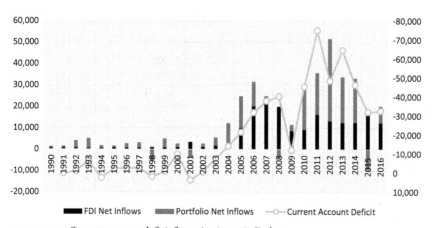

FIGURE 16   Current account deficit financing items in Turkey
             * Current account deficit on the right axis, in reverse order
             SOURCE: CBRT BALANCE OF PAYMENTS STATISTICS

when portfolio inflows reached a peak, 75% of capital flows became portfolio instruments, more than 80% of which were debt instruments.

These stylised facts raised concerns about the increasing risks that come with an increasing short-term debt stock in open market conditions. For example, in 2012 and 2017, the IMF's Financial System Stability Assessment for Turkey emphasise the fundamental macroeconomic vulnerabilities as the high proportion of savings and debt held in foreign currency at short maturities, the dependence on cross-border financing, and the risk of a large structural maturity mismatch, since the majority of deposits had maturities of less than three months and banks also relied on short-term CBRT funding. The average maturity of banking system deposits did exceed three months and banks held large amounts of government securities at longer maturities, although a BIS study in 2008 stressed that the risks are lower, as the share of securities decreased substantially from 41% in 2002 to 28% in 2007 (Yorukoglu and Cufadar, 2008). According to the same study, it was the participation of foreign investors that enabled Treasury to issue longer-term debt securities and rely less on the domestic banking system which as a result reduced the domestic debt rollover ratios below 100% and increased the loanable funds available for credit.

The Financial Stability report published by the CBRT in November 2014 stressed similar points but also indicated that the financial system had been under the threat of normalising monetary policies of the global economy triggered by the monetary measures taken by China, The European Central Bank as well as the Fed (CBRT, 2014). During 2012-2015, inflation levels had been below the targets for many advanced economies bringing the risk of a deflationary spiral. Rapidly depreciating interest rates and the weak outlook of economic activity in developed countries transferred the risk of financial instability from developed countries to emerging economies like Turkey which were extremely dependent on external borrowing.[15] It was also stated by the IMF in 2015 that volatility in major exchange rates had also increased by more than during any similar period since the global financial crisis, which was another disadvantage for Turkey. Reduced liquidity in both the foreign exchange and fixed-income markets, as well as the changing composition of the investor bases in these markets, added to the volatility level of portfolio flows. Oil prices declined sharply in 2014 by 45%, largely due to the insufficient levels of demand in advanced economies together with the large gap between exchange rates creating a reallocation of real income between different actors but favouring advanced economies while extracting resources from developing countries (IMF, 2015).

One interesting feature of the Turkish financial sector emphasised in these studies is the reliance of banks on private sector lending especially since 2010, which constitutes over 75% of all loan issuance by domestic banks, which is most probably due to a response in macro-prudential measures (IMF, 2017). After discussing the developments within the household sector in the next section, which has certain important implications for the financialised accumulation, the rising indebtedness will be explained in Section 6 with respect to a general restructuring process alongside rising vulnerabilities.

5   After 2001: Household Indebtedness

As Painceira (2009) argues, in most of the developing countries, the 2000s has been characterised by growing internal public debt to sustain the flows of capital from developing to developed countries, external debt being held mostly in the form of US Treasury bills. Another important feature has been the accumulation of household debt, which has also been emphasised in the Turkish context by Karacimen (2014). As discussed before, household indebtedness is given a specific focus within the financialisation literature, due to its distinctive implications for demand, profitability, growth and financial stability, as the dependence on household demand implies weaker contribution to capital outlays (Dos Santos, 2013).

---

15   IMF (2015), World Economic Outlook: Adjusting to Lower Commodity Prices.

Drawing upon the middle-income country examples of Brazil, Mexico, Turkey and Poland, Dos Santos (2013) claims that the expansion of consumer credit has some structural properties, because first, consumption credit makes a greater dynamic contribution to inflationary pressures than credit financing productive enterprise in closed economy conditions and second, consumption credit contributes to aggregate profitability by sustaining the systemic demand for credit through extracting profits from future income flows. As a result, this indicates that as long as sufficient levels of demand for household credit are present, competitive signals in the credit-market process will tend to push the economy to greater levels of consumption lending, increasing the susceptibility of the economy to financial crises due to increasing level of indebtedness as opposed to capital formation (Dos Santos, 2013).

After experiencing a decade of growing public indebtedness followed by a huge financial crisis in 2001, the Turkish economy has followed a similar path in terms of rising household indebtedness, to be later followed by a shift in the burden of indebtedness from public to the private sector. As Karacimen (2014) finds out, household credits as a share of all credits increased dramatically in 2004, after the legislation in 2003 that brought some regulatory arrangements for consumers to have greater access to credits such as outstanding debt relief, interest rate decreases and easier access to credit cards. Accordingly, in line with the general declining trend of interest rates due to deflationary pressures, monthly interest rates on housing loans declined from 2.57% in mid-2004 to 0.99% by the end of 2005 (Karacimen, 2014). As a result, the share of consumer credits as a share of GDP increased from 4.7% in 2002 to 18.7% in 2012.

However, as Figure 17 depicts, the rising trend reached a peak in 2012, when consumer credits reached 35% as a share of all credits. By early 2017, the share of consumer credits (including credit card expenditures) in all credits declined to 25%, although its share as a percentage of GDP increased steadily from just over 1% in 2004 to 15.9% almost 25% by 2017 (see Figure 18). After 2017, we can see that the amount of consumer credits as a share of GDP started to decrease simultaneously with commercial credits. As the Turkish economy entered a new volatile macroeconomic path since 2017, this development can be accepted as a reflection in the change of expectations of borrowers in an uncertain environment.

In terms of the content of household indebtedness, as Figure 19 illustrates, until 2009, the primary channel of increasing household indebtedness was through the increased use of credit cards. The total number of credit cards in use has been increased from 13,372,600 in 2000 to 44,392,600 in 2009. The credit card liabilities of the household sector as a whole increased from 33,990 billion TRY in 2008 to 83,806 billion TRY by the end of 2013, which is more than

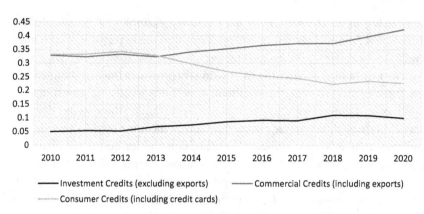

FIGURE 17   Credit types issued by domestic banks in Turkey as a ratio of total credits
            SOURCE: BRSA

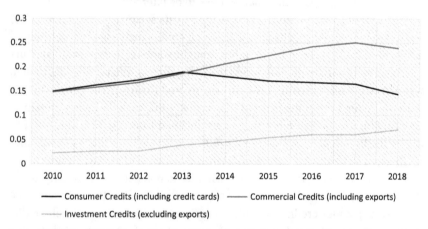

FIGURE 18   Credit types issued by domestic banks in Turkey as a ratio of GDP
            SOURCE: BRSA AND CBRT (GDP NOMINAL ACCORDING TO INCOME METHOD)

triple the amount in the early 2000s (see Figure 20).[16] In 2013, BRSA implemented a regulation regarding the credit card usage in order to prevent further
indebtedness and credit defaults which was represented by a decrease in total
credit card debts in 2014 (BRSA, 2014).

   After the mortgage regulation of 2004, housing credits increased substantially, reflecting the shift towards individualised housing provision that will

---

16   BRSA Statistics (www.bddk.org).

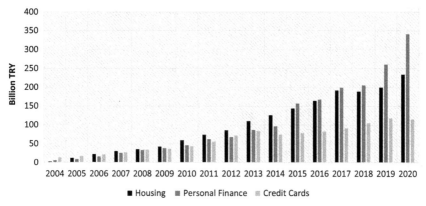

FIGURE 19   Disaggregated consumer credits in Turkey (nominal, billion TRY)
             SOURCE: BRSA

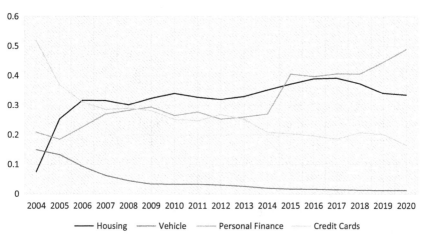

FIGURE 20   Disaggregated consumer credits (% of total consumer credits)
             SOURCE: BRSA

be discussed in Chapter 6. However, Figure 20 shows that although mortgage credits increased dramatically since 2004, their share in total consumer credits peaked in 2017 at 40%, and started to decline gradually afterwards, while the share of personal loans continued to increase. More importantly, the share of housing credits in GDP never exceeded 7% throughout the 2010s, which determines the ultimate 'depth' of the mortgage markets in an economy (see Figure 21). Considering that the mortgage debt to GDP ratio is around 80% in England, Netherlands and New Zealand, and around 70% in the US, even after

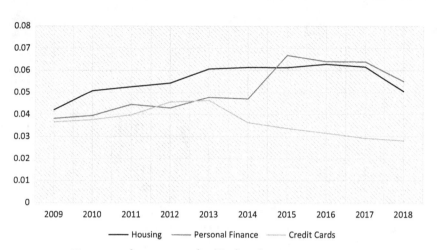

FIGURE 21   Disaggregated consumer credits (% of GDP)
            SOURCE: BRSA AND CBRT (GDP NOMINAL ACCORDING TO INCOME METHOD)

the 2008 crisis, it is crucial to emphasise that the rising household indebtedness in Turkey does not present a picture similar to the cases which are mostly referred to in the literature.

Moreover, households do not hold considerable debt instruments other than TRY denominated credits. Although household liabilities are outpacing the growth of assets and loan defaults jumped in 2009, reflecting the high unemployment level,[17] loan defaults stayed more or less stable throughout the period, never reaching 3%, due to safe lending practices. In short, we can conclude that the household balance sheets are still relatively strong, and the rapid credit growth during the period of 2004-2017 did not result in a highly indebted household segment although the increasing trend has been undeniable. Especially in comparison to the high levels of fragility of the private sector due to high FX denominated debts, the household segment had a stronger balance sheet position in the face of dramatic exchange rate volatility since 2017, although the depreciation of Turkish Lira and high levels of inflation resulted in rapid devaluation of their assets.

How to interpret these developments, does this trend prove that the household balance sheets are not financialising in Turkey? Although this is one way to go forward, either answer to that question is meaningless in terms of identifying the source and the direction of real change in the economy. This

17   IMF (2017), Financial System Stability Statement.

book instead shifts the analytical focus elsewhere and argues that housing consumption is in fact increasing alongside housing production in an almost unprecedented manner, which reflects a certain qualitative change in the way households and firms operate in the economy. This trend will be discussed within the context of housing market itself in Chapter 6. The next section is about the developments within the private sector on a macroeconomic level.

6   After 2001: Capital Restructuring?

As mentioned in the previous sections, especially after the global financial crisis in 2008, non-financial corporations' indebtedness increased substantially along with the increases in financial sector indebtedness. Corporate sector debt rose by about 19% to 40% of GDP during 2010 and to over 150% by the end of 2016.[18] It was argued that although non-financial corporations are profitable, increasing leverage also exposed them to FX risks. Although the majority of credits taken by the corporate sector are in the form of long-term TRY credits, FX credits also increased substantially, 68% of which are issued by the domestic banks. Over 60% of FX credits are denominated in dollars. Both in the long and short terms, the real sector took a short position in foreign exchange with a net position of -200 billion USD (Figure 22).

The fragility of the sector was clear by the end of 2017, as the IMF financial assessment report drew attention to the high levels of leverage (IMF, 2017). As the Turkish economy was considered to get riskier in the international arena, foreign capital flows slowed down in early 2018 and the Turkish Lira started depreciation. By the end of 2018, Lira has lost more than 40% of its value as opposed to dollar in a year, exposing the FX indebted private firms to even greater risks of default (Orhangazi, 2020).

However, although the fragility in this segment is clear, this chapter argues that the move towards higher capital-intensity in the late 1990s and early 2000s was one of the reasons which pushed the firms towards increased export orientation, which was certainly a factor in their increasing indebtedness level. Such restructuring process is reported in detail within the manufacturing sector in Atiyas and Bakis (2013), Taymaz and Voyvoda (2009), and also in PhD study by Sengul (2015) manifested as a shift from labour-intensive low-technology industries towards higher-technology, capital-intensive industries.[19]

---

18   See Figure 5 above.

19   According to CBRT classification, Manufacturing sector consists of Food Beverage and Tobacco Industry, Textile and Textile Products Industry, Leather and Leather Products

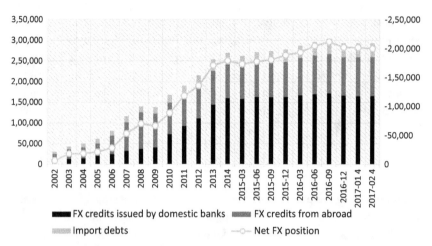

Turkish non-financial corporations' total FX liabilities
* Net FX position on the right axis, in reverse order
SOURCE: CBRT (ANNUAL FROM 2002 TO 2015-3, QUARTERLY STARTING FROM 2015-3)

The manufacturing sector has been a powerful segment in the Turkish economy especially in terms of export performance. In 2016, the manufactured exports to total exports ratio was 83%.[20] Before 2002, the manufactured exports were highly dominated by labour-intensive industries such as textiles and food industry. As mentioned above, after the crisis, the share of capital-intensive industries, such as motor vehicles or machinery production in total exports had remarkably increased.

The industrial investment oriented strategy aiming for this goal had been explicitly declared as a state strategy in the 8th Five Year Development Plan in 2000, hence between 2001 and 2005, the state has been actively involved in industrial policy design despite the lack of a complete industrial programme (Oguz, 2009). There were some institutional attempts to provide incentives for technical change, and for example, the enactment of Law No: 5084 regarding investment and employment brought tax deductions as well as generous

---

Industry, Wood and Wood Products Industry, Paper, Raw Materials and Paper Products Industry, Nuclear Fuel and Refined Petroleum and Coke Coal Industry, Chemical Products Industry, Rubber and Plastic Products Industry, Other Mines Excluding Metal Industry, Main Metal Industry, Machine and Equipment Industry, Electrical and Optical Devices Industry, Transportation Vehicles Industry, and Manufacturing Industry not classified in other places.

20   TURKSTAT, Foreign Exchange Statistics (www.tuik.gov.tr).

energy and land subsidies in the form of a 20% deduction in electricity bills and the free allocation of public land to enterprises employing more than ten employees for at least five years.[21] Initially, the Law concerned 36 provinces with an income per capita of 1500 USD or lower. Later in 2006, Law No: 5350 was enacted adding thirteen more provinces to the jurisdiction of Law No: 5084. In 2009 and 2012, a more comprehensive incentives package program was introduced, named the General Investment Encouragement Program (GIEP). While preserving the subsidies offered by Law 5084 and 5350, GIEP also introduced other incentives such as exemption from customs duties, value added tax exemption for machinery and equipment industry and direct credit allocation from the budget up to 50% of total fixed investment costs (Acar and Caglar, 2012).

Despite the state incentives listed above, however, the restructuring process should not be considered to be a result of a deliberate state initiative. It was rather a response to the crisis conditions. For, while lower-technology industries with flexible employment conditions continued to produce less for shrinking domestic demand through labour adjustments, medium-low and medium-high industries channelled capacities into export demand in order to preserve their pre-crisis production levels, which resulted in further increasing debt levels, together with the requirement to obtain foreign exchange to hedge against FX liabilities. An indispensable aspect of this has been low costs of labour, which has been well documented by Yeldan (2011) and Onaran (2006). There were, however, also signs of technical progress which will be discussed in this section.

The evidence for this improvement is documented by Taymaz and Voyvoda (2009) and Sengul (2015) as follows. Between 1998 and 2002, the share of textiles industry production in total output increased from 2.82% to 5.38%, while the share of the wearing apparel industry increased from 2.11% to 3.10%. Nevertheless, the remarkable change was in their decreasing exports share in production, as both almost halved from 74.3% to 38.3% and from 41.2% to 20.8%, respectively (Sengul, 2015). It should be noted that these two industries had been the locomotive of the Turkish manufacturing sector in terms of exports especially during the export boom of the 1980s.

Medium-low and medium-high technology industries such as basic metals, machinery equipment and transport equipment, on the other hand, increased their export shares substantially, although the increases in their total output

---

21   For a full list of investment incentives legislation including foreign direct investment and bilateral investment treaties, see Republic of Turkey Ministry of Economy website (www.ekonomi.gov.tr).

share were less significant. Between 1998 and 2002, the basic metals and metal products sector increased its export share from 16.1% to 24.7%, the machinery and equipment sector from 13.2% to 21.6%, while the transport equipment sector increased its share from 19.9% to 44.2%. Their shares in total production during the same time span only slightly decreased from 3.92% to 3.34%, from 1.97% to 1.79% and from 1.74% to 1.78%, respectively.[22]

From 2002 to 2007, the restructuring had been more visible, also due to the crisis conditions. The share of the textiles sector in total output declined from almost 7% to 5.2% while the decline in the share of the wearing apparel sector was from 4.6% in 2003 to 3.7% in 2007. During the same time period, the machinery and equipment sector increased its share in total production from 2.8% to 3.4%, the electrical and optical sector from 2.6% to 3.1%, and the transport equipment sector from 4.4% to 5.7%. A more striking change has been in gross fixed real investment as a ratio of total production, as while almost all sectors experienced a decrease in their gross real investment shares, the machinery and equipment sector increased its share from 1.6% to 2%, the basic metals sector from 3.5% to 4.1%, and the transport equipment sector from 2.9% to 4.9%. It should be noted that the sectors with the highest share in total production performed weakly in terms of fixed investment. For example, the textiles sector decreased its investment share in total production from 7.8% to 4.3%, between 2002 and 2007.

The indicators of restructuring were best observed in the transport equipment sector, driven by the motor vehicles (automotive) industry. The automotive sector's export share of production tripled from 14.6% to 43.6%. It has been the fastest growing medium-high capital-intensive sector, with its share in total exports rising from 2.5% in 1993 to 16% in 2006, and its average growth rate being 10% between 1993 and 2001 (Taymaz and Yilmaz, 2008). Between 2001 and 2006, its growth rate has been even higher at 20%.

For some, the success of the automotive sector is due to a considerable degree of import-dependency (Atiyas and Bakis, 2013; Gros and Selcuki, 2013; Taymaz et al., 2008). In terms of global competitiveness, Turkey is still involved in the global supply chains with limited domestic value-added capacity. By March 2017, low technology exports in total exports still have the highest share at 34.3% although medium-high exports follow closely at 32.1%.[23] Medium-low

---

22   All data for sectoral comparison is from Sengul (2015) unless otherwise stated. For a more detailed comparison including all sectors and other criteria such as real growth production, value added and import/production ratios, see Atiyas and Bakis (2013), Taymaz and Voyvoda (2009) and Sengul (2015).

23   All foreign trade data are from TURKSTAT website (www.tuik.gov.tr), unless otherwise stated.

technology sectors had a share of 30% while the high technology sectors are only responsible for the 3.7% of all exports.

For Taymaz and Yilmaz (2008) it was the successful trade links especially with the European Union and a high level of vertical integration as the primary driver of the growth of the automotive industry, which did not contribute significantly to increases in domestic value-added levels. Since automobile production is highly producer-driven (Ng and Kaminski, 2006), Turkey's trade links with the European Union enabled it to be involved in the international automobile supply chains as an assembly point. The vertical integration ratio (value added/output) of Turkish automotive industry is 0.330, which is significantly high compared to its counterparts in East European countries and Spain (0.154), India (0.177), UK (0.183) indicating that the Turkish automobile industry engages in more manufacturing operations through intra-firm trade and production (Taymaz and Yilmaz, 2008).

In 2012, the share of the automotive industry in total sales from production was 14%, and its share in total exports reached 24%, while the gross value-added share only remained at 5% relative to total industry, showing the dominance of low value-added assembly practices. Overall, the economy has been highly import-dependent as the imported component of the total manufacturing increased from 40% in 2010 to 43% in 2011. The growth of imports for manufacturing was even higher than the growth rate of manufacturing itself, showing the great level of import dependency (Gros and Selcuki, 2013). In a CBRT study, Saygili et al. (2010) also document that intermediate goods imports of Turkey have increased 2.5 times more than the increase in manufacturing output between 1994 and 2008. In 2011, total aggregate imports outpaced total exports – reaching $240 billion, compared to exports of $134 billion. Overall, imports of goods and services as a share of GDP has increased from 23% in 2000 to 31% in 2015, while gross savings decreased from 18% of GDP to 14% during the same time period.[24]

As a result, Taymaz and Voyvoda (2009, p. 167) argue that although the turn towards higher-technology sectors within the manufacturing was evident, it was unlikely to lead to economy-wide structural change, given that it was triggered by over-valued Turkish lira, rapid increases in intermediate imports to substitute domestic production and persistent dependence of the new production and export lines on imported components, which seriously restrained the economy's capacity to generate value-added and employment.

---

24   World Bank Data (https://data.worldbank.org).

Although it cannot be disputed that there is a considerable degree of import-dependency, it is important to address two issues that also reflect the focus of this chapter in line with how the workings of the economy are conceptualised in this book. First, it should be noted that the restructuring is in its early stages where total output levels were more or less preserved, therefore it was expected to see increasing import/production ratios. Despite this, the import ratio in total production decreased almost by a half in the transport equipment sector from 90.19% in 1998 to 52.17% in 2002 (Sengul, 2015).

Second, in addressing restructuring, this chapter is less concerned with its results with respect to improvements in international competitiveness or gross output increases, as such successes are dependent on many other considerations, but rather aims at understanding why such restructuring occurred in the first place, in a period of financialisation that is readily associated with low levels of accumulation and growth. Surely, one important constituent part of this strategy was the fact that the medium-low and medium-high technology sectors had to channel their production into exports given they required FX reserves to hedge against currency fluctuations. More importantly, however, given their capital structure with higher concentration of constant capital and less flexible productive techniques, their strategy to turn towards export demand was to maintain existing production levels in a competitive environment, which was conducive to the overall real accumulation. This, however, does not suggest a novel phenomenon, but explains how systematic productivity increases occur, in line with the conceptualisation of the capitalist economy outlined in the previous chapters.

As mentioned above, the change was more visible in the increasing export shares in production of different sectors rather than shares in total production, because it was easier for the lower-technology sectors to preserve their production levels in response to demand shocks given their flexible employment conditions. The increasing flexibility in low-technology industries was for example documented in considerable informalisation and subcontracting practices within labour-intensive sectors especially in textiles in the aftermath of the crisis (Demir and Erdem, 2010; Taymaz and Kilicaslan, 2005).

In a study with a broad dataset including Turkey as well as Latin American and African countries, McMillan, Rodrik and Inigo (2014) reported that labour productivity increased as a trend due to reallocation of labour from low productivity industries to higher productivity ones during the period 1990-2005. In countries such as Turkey however, there were huge productivity gaps, as productivity in construction was more than twice the productivity in agriculture, and productivity in manufacturing was almost three times as large (McMillan et al., 2014). This was accepted as a sigh of underdevelopment, as in such economies with large inter-sectoral productivity gaps, it was found that structural change did not always go towards the desirable direction of contributing to overall productivity growth, as displaced labour from high-technology industries would easily go to lower productivity activities, also given the expansion of services or informality. The contribution of the Marxist political economy analysis is to put the emphasis upon how these differences in productivity occur systematically, in line with such internal division of labour between different sectors, itself subject to change as accumulation proceeds. In that sense, it suggests a different focus than that is offered by McMillan et al. (2014), for whom the emphasis is not where systematic productivity increases come from, but rather how structural change follows from more or less arbitrary changes in productivity.

In short, the purpose of examining the restructuring within the manufacturing industry is not to draw a conclusion over whether the Turkish economy has been successful or not, especially considering that the aggregate investment level stayed stagnant, short-term external debts increased sharply, gross savings decreased from 18% of GDP in 2000 to 14% in 2015, and the unemployment rate increased from below 8% during the 1990s to well above 10% during the 2000s on average. Nor it is to examine if the restructuring has been successful in terms of cutting down import dependency or contributing to international competitiveness, as questioned by Taymaz and Voyvoda (2009) and Taymaz and Yilmaz (2008)

It does, however, instead underlines how restructuring took place simultaneously together with increasing informalisation in labour-intensive industries. Although the financialised accumulation path since the 2000s increased the overall vulnerability of the economy given the scope of speculative activities such as carry trade, it also contributed to industrial restructuring through increased availability of funds, especially for larger industries with higher levels of capital-intensity through reinforcing tight connections between banks and businesses after the financial sector restructuring in the post-2001 period. The next section will conclude this chapter in light of what has been discussed before.

7   Conclusion

This chapter provided a political economy of Turkey since the early 1980s. It outlined how the economy transitioned from an export-orientation strategy during the 1980s, maintained by wage suppression and domestic currency devaluation, towards structural change during the 2000s, especially following the developments within the manufacturing sector. However, as the increased availability of finance simultaneously contributed to the productive investment levels and provided increased scope for speculative activities, the economy was characterised by increasing macroeconomic volatility in the 2010s, which culminated in the Turkish Lira to lose 40% of its value against dollar in 2018.

As suggested by the financialisation in emerging economies literature, the 2000s were globally characterised by the increasing reserve accumulation against exchange rate fluctuations together with the increasing volume of speculative activities such as carry trade (Erturk, 2003; Gabor, 2010; Gungen, 2012; Kaltenbrunner and Painceira, 2015). Another important feature of the 2000s was the rapid increase in the consumption credits, with possible negative impacts on growth and production. Turkey was no exception and all three of these trends were observed especially in the 2000s. Nevertheless, the 2010s was characterised by the increasing indebtedness of the non-financial corporations, which almost tripled nominally from 463 billion TRY in 2010 to 1563 billion TRY in 2016, raising concerns over sustainability especially after the exchange rate crisis in 2018.

As a result, many have suggested that the previous growth path in Turkey during the 2000s was maintained through export-orientation based on wage suppression and a consumption-induced demand without overcoming previous fragilities (Demir, 2009a; Onaran, 2006; Taymaz and Voyvoda, 2009; Yeldan, 2011). This chapter suggests that despite the existence of fragilities emphasised by Demir (2009a) as sky-rocketing external debt, extremely high and worsening current account deficit, high country risk, low fixed capital formation rates, and falling industrial and manufacturing value added in GDP, there were also some developments within the manufacturing sector that signalled early stages of capital restructuring from low-technology labour-intensive sectors to higher-technology capital-intensive sectors visible especially in the growth of automotive sector (Sengul, 2015; Taymaz and Voyvoda, 2009; Taymaz and Yilmaz, 2008).

This was mostly due to the elimination of the small banks in the post-2001 crisis period, which restricted the credit access for smaller industrial producers in Anatolia, and contributed to the profitability of larger, internationally competitive industries incorporating capital-intensive activities in Istanbul, while labour-intensive sectors turned towards increased informality. As a result, the historically close connections between the big conglomerates and banks maintained a traditional financial sector in Turkey, which continued to provide 'patient' finance for the industry, while also profiting from primary interest and foreign exchange arbitrage opportunities. The share of investments funded by banks has been 7.4% in 2004, increasing to 38% in 2009 although it decreased later to 31.4% in 2015.[25] Investments funded by equity and sales, on the other hand, decreased from 33.4% in 2004 to 4% in 2009 and stayed on that level until 2015. This contrasts with what is suggested by the financialisation literature, predicting a move towards equity-based financing techniques for all actors in the economy (Boyer, 2000).

This indicated that loanable money capital entered the economy in the form of short-term portfolio flows and bank credits, which were later used for speculative purposes by domestic banks in the interbank money market, but also lent to the private sector in the form of long-term TRY loans. The following chapters will investigate how they are used by the energy and construction sectors specifically, which contributed to the restructuring of capital (including the industrial capital) in general and interest-bearing capital in particular, with negative impacts on the value of labour power in the abstract.

25   World Bank Global Financial Development Database (https://data.worldbank.org/data-catalog/global-financial-development).

CHAPTER 5

The Political Economy of Electricity Provision in Turkey

1 Introduction

This chapter provides a political economy of electricity provision in Turkey since the 1980s. Its aim is twofold. First, it explains how electricity is produced and consumed as a wage good, with an importance in and of itself in order to investigate how the relations of production and consumption have changed over time. Second, it examines recent developments in electricity provision to provide an empirical example for two interrelated aspects of financialisation that have been discussed in earlier chapters. The first concerns how the process initially involves the extension of commodity relations to a broader base of the population. At a later stage, regular payments from this base contribute to the emergence of a secondary circuit of capital through securitisation of stable revenue streams. Another aspect is to show how the expansion and intensification of commodity relations can go hand-in-hand with increases in productive capacity.

In Turkey, after a long period of a state-owned vertically integrated structure, both electricity distribution and generation segments were gradually privatised, starting from 1984 until 2014. Private sector investments were mostly made in electricity generation infrastructure. Given the high start-up costs in this segment, private sector participation was heavily subsidised by the state through take-or-pay agreements especially in the early period of privatisation. The costs were reflected in higher consumer prices as well as higher transfers from the public budget. Privatisation of distribution, on the other hand, has been completed through the introduction of cost-reflecting pricing system which was designed to reflect the increases of costs directly in consumer prices while allowing any improvement in performance to be appropriated by private firms, protecting and sustaining their profitability. Although securitisation has so far remained negligible, these developments signal a considerable movement towards market-based forms of electricity provision.

There is a wide literature on financialisation of natural resources especially in the context of water, although the literature on electricity per se is comparatively limited. Within the financialisation of natural resources literature itself, there are different streams with important differences in terms of the place of emphasis as well as method. The distinction is most visible in the different ways finance is addressed in economics as opposed to other social sciences. As discussed in detail previously, within economics, increased financial activity is most readily associated with short-termism, with implications for long-term productive activity. In the context of natural resources, the impacts of short-termism on production are more direct and easily captured due to the involvement of long-term infrastructural investments. As a result, critical economics literature on energy industries places the analytical focus on the impacts of different types of investors and ownership structures that might offset the short-termist production strategies following the developments within the financial sector itself.

Haldane (2015) finds that because the short-termism distorted the perception of long-term projects' net present value in investors' eyes, projects that take long time to mature, such as energy and infrastructure, are under-financed by the private banking system in the US and UK (Haldane, 2015). For the OECD in 2015, this observation contributed to the acknowledgment that alternative sources and strategies were needed to finance infrastructural investment which necessitates a long-term asset structure from the side of investors given the long-term liabilities undertaken to finance projects. Mazzucato and Semieniuk (2016) further emphasise that finance is not neutral and especially as the newer technologies in energy towards lower-carbon emission are adopted, traditional 'patient' finance might be necessary to support the high risks involved. Based on a global dataset on renewable energy asset finance from 2004 to 2014, they find that when there are high risks involved, the involvement of finance is more traditional, and the funding is more likely to be provided through state banks and utilities. In fact, 58% of all deployment investment is made by public investors globally in 2014, which underlines the role of traditional finance in such capital-intensive sectors with high initial costs.

In human geography literature, the discussion of the role finance in the natural resources sectors is made mostly within the context of privatisation with the emphasis being on the incompatibility of public good provision with profit seeking motives. Bakker (2007, 2005, 2004), for example, investigated how the full water privatisation in England and Wales has been unsuccessful which resulted in the retreat of government from full competition attempts in 2001. She claimed that the failure was due to water's public good characteristics, as market failures and common property rights make water an 'uncooperative' commodity that is resistant to short-termist market reforms (Bakker, 2004).

Castree (2008a, 2008b) and Swyngedouw (2005) emphasise similar aspects that are associated with the increasing marketisation of nature and natural resources. Swyngedouw (2005) points out how some hybrid forms of regulation in water emerged after the failure of privatisation attempts. In these forms, state has been actively involved in the infrastructure investment projects, in order to make sure that the private sector stayed within the sector by enabling them to profit from the natural monopolistic conditions of water supply. For Castree (2008a), the single case studies on the experiences of privatisation in these sectors signal how certain commonalities operate among these cases, although the outcome depends upon the local institutional context in the last instance. In a table of comparison, he contrasts the different outcomes of privatisation from price increases for water in Buenos Aires to erosion of peasant livelihoods in Bolivia due to water and gas privatisation (Castree, 2008b). He claims that despite such big differences in the outcomes, privatisation mostly resulted in the emergence of complicated market mechanisms in these sectors with possible destabilising impacts. Bayliss (2014a) detects a similar trend in UK water companies, where a byzantine structure of complicated corporate mechanisms emerged after the commodification of water.

With these findings in mind, this chapter provides a political economy of electricity provision in Turkey with a twofold aim. First, it examines how the commodity relations for electricity, distinct from financialisation as such, developed in Turkey following the gradual privatisation process that might give rise to the emergence of secondary circuit of capital through the securitisation of long-term bank loans. In the case of electricity and infrastructure in general, securitisation requires; first, the simultaneous creation of markets through privatisation on the production side and the promotion of these markets through commodification on the consumption side, mostly achieved through the help of the state. The completion of this scenario would result in a fully financialised sector the implications of which are discussed extensively in the previous chapters.

This is, however, only a partial picture as far as Turkey is concerned. As discussed in Chapters 3 and 4, financial markets in Turkey are still relatively shallow with a limited scope of asset securitisation. Therefore, the electricity markets in Turkey do not provide a sufficient base for examining the changing nature of financial relations directly through the extent of asset securitisation. There is, however, a striking increase in the degree and scope of commercial relations within the sector that is in line with the developments around the world, which is the primary focus of this chapter. In this light, the second aim of this chapter is to investigate how these commercial relations evolve through time in the context of electricity provision in Turkey, where there is also considerable growth in the long-term productive investment, *because of* the increased availability of finance.

For the reader who has followed the highly abstract discussions of finan-cialisation in the previous chapters, this chapter is highly empirical. In line with the methodology adopted in this book, as Castree (2008a) argues that these 'case studies' are areas of analysis in their own right, which are qual-itatively distinct from the more abstract analysis. In earlier chapters, it was claimed that financialisation is the increasing presence of interest-bearing capital (IBC) at the level of capital in general (Fine, 2013). At this level, interest bearing capital feeds upon other types of capital due to the requirement of an interest, for which the payment is dependent upon successful productive activity elsewhere. This is however, a purely abstract category and the profita-bility of IBC depends on how the economy functions and pursues productive activities as a whole (Fine, 2013). At the level of all capitals in competition, IBC exists as loanable money capital (LMC), acting both as 'money as money' as well as 'money as capital', the distinction of which cannot be made from the perspective of the lender. There, the borrowing and lending activities are made both for productive and simply purchasing purposes, as in the case of expan-sion of LMC as simple credit, which might act as a *facilitator* for competition with positive impacts on accumulation as long as the newly created secondary circuits are successfully realised with productive activity pursued elsewhere in the economy. In that sense, the analysis of the electricity provisioning in Turkey provided in this chapter is not the analysis of the financialisation pro-cess as such, but the investigation of the changing commodity relations along the chain of activities in the sector in order to contribute to the understanding of the abstract process discussed earlier (Bayliss et al., 2013).

Along these lines, Section 2 introduces the policy rhetoric for privatisa-tion and a brief historical summary of privatisation of electricity experiences around the world. The changing theoretical rationale behind privatisation that paved the way for these experiences is briefly explained, which shifted from emphasising ownership transfer as an end itself to emphasising the nature and extent of competition within the sector. While the state's presence within the utilities sectors including electricity has stayed rather constant throughout, the radically shifting rhetoric and scholarship of privatisation demonstrate a relative detachment of these from the actual practices in and around these sectors. The actual practice has been the increasing degree and scope of com-modity relations around these sectors alongside with the state's involvement, the degree of which changing according to the relative success of the produc-tion of these goods as use values as well as values.

Section 3 moves on to the Turkish case. After giving a general outlook of the energy sector, the political economy of electricity provision in Turkey is dis-cussed. It shows that how the industry has been transformed with the gradual privatisation of the sector starting from 1984 along the lines mentioned above. Section 4 investigates the extent and sources of finance within the sector with the help of balance sheet data obtained from The Central Bank Company Account Statistics in order to show that the increasing degree of commodification and subsequent emergence of secondary circuit of capital could occur alongside the increases in productive capacity. Section 5 concludes by underlining the theoretical premise that the global trend towards a market-based provisioning of wage goods such as electricity provides a base for future capitalisation of revenues with ambiguous impacts on sectoral levels of production due to the possibility of sustained profitability for both productive and financial interests.

2   Privatisation of Electricity Provision: Rhetoric and Experiences
       around the World

Historically, electricity provision has been dominated by the state-owned vertically integrated institutions, which were considered natural monopolies worldwide until the 1980s, because of huge sunk costs, inelastic demand and coordination problems with generation, transmission and distribution systems (Dagdeviren, 2009). During the late 1980s and early 1990s, the rationale for vertical integration and public ownership has weakened following the technological progress that eased the conditions of entry that were assumed to make the sector a naturally monopolistic one. Privatisation of the electricity sector usually follows a process in which first state-owned vertically integrated enterprises are unbundled according to type of activities, namely generation, wholesale, distribution and retail, and then each segment is privatised. Electricity generation is considered to create the largest potential gains from competition given the capital-intensive structure of its production methods. It is assumed that with the withdrawal of the state as the single producer, the output restricting monopolistic structure will erode with the help of stricter contracting of generators with profit motive. The only obstacle to such gains in efficiency is considered to be the entry conditions, big infrastructural investments, which is to be overcome with the help of state subsidies.

The pioneers being the UK and Argentina, the early 1990s was a period during which almost all countries attempted to privatise their electricity sectors with specific emphasis on the privatisation of the generation segment. During the early phase of privatisation, along with the Washington Consensus principles in policy making, the rhetoric on privatisation was one that perceived private ownership as an end in itself, with anticipation of increased efficiency following the transfer of ownership from the public to the private sector. A World Bank document in 1991 explicitly states that:

> Ownership matters. In theory, ownership may not affect efficiency, but in practice it almost always does –because governments tend to tilt the economic/financial playing field toward 'their' firms in ways that are difficult to perceive and harder to correct. Thus, the telling argument for privatisation is that it enhances competition.".
>
> cited in BAYLISS AND FINE, 2008, p. 60

In accordance with this policy rhetoric of the World Bank, the UK has privatised all of its state-owned electricity distribution and generation between 1990 and 1992. After the government sold its golden shares in 1995, a huge takeover wave, mostly from the US companies, has started. However, there were some negative outcomes of this experience especially due to the failures in implementation. Wholesale and retail markets were created, but until 2005 the share of total electricity traded in the markets stayed only at 1% (Thomas, 2004). In general, there were serious miscalculations in privatisation investments. In 2001 four US companies (AES, AEP, NRG and Mission Edison) purchased 20% of British generation capacity which were based on inaccurate forecast of wholesale prices and therefore within 18 months the investments had failed (Thomas, 2004). UK investments also played a role in Enron's bankruptcy in 2002 by financially over-stretching and therefore contributing to the collapse of the parent company (Pond, 2006). Nevertheless, between 1990 and 2005, significant price cuts were made to customers, reaching to 30% in transmission and 50% in distribution (Pollitt, 2007). For Pond (2006), this was due to major switch to lower cost long-term gas contracts instead of increased competition. Moreover, price reductions were made possible also because the industry was sold for only a fraction of its accounting value which effectively wrote off much of the costs. Still, despite the failures in implementation, the UK has been one of the few countries that were able to decrease end-user prices after power reforms.

In general, privatisation process has been followed by increased prices, especially in developing countries (Bayliss and Fine, 2008; Erdogdu, 2013; Hall et al., 2013; Nagayama, 2007; Steiner, 2000). An OECD study following the period of rapid privatisation based on 19 OECD countries over a 10 year time period also showed that, although there were differences in the relative efficacy of different reform strategies across countries and time, retail prices for electricity especially for industry increased after privatisation (Steiner, 2000). Considering the high start-up costs of these systems, an initial increase in the prices was expected only to decrease later through increased competitiveness. Contrary to expectations, in many of the developing countries, the result has been increasing prices despite years of reform (Bayliss and Fine, 2008).

In Latin America, retail competition raised prices for industry, while in ex-members of Soviet Union and Eastern Europe, higher energy tariffs were needed to secure the return on investment (Nagayama, 2007). Some developing countries, such as Australia, also experienced 40% higher prices since the privatisation of the sector in 1994 (Cahill and Beder, 2005). Especially in low-income countries, high prices led to decreased services level provided by the private sector, because where the majority of consumers are unable to afford a full transition, privatisation actually resulted in increased state subsidies to keep the sector alive for private investors. In order to attract private investors, governments had to make power purchase agreements such as fixed prices, foreign currency agreements and take-or-pay agreements. For example in Tanzania, privatisation of the vertically integrated electricity company TANE-SCO resulted in transmission and generation expenses tripling between 2001 and 2003, primarily due to huge state payments to two thermal IPPs (Bayliss, 2008). In general, during the first wave of privatisation, the shift to private ownership did not result in a retreat of the state, but rather directed the state to take on new responsibilities. By the mid-2000s, approximately 70 per cent of infrastructure investment in developing countries was still financed by governments or public utilities either from their own resources or from non-concessional borrowing (Bayliss and Fine, 2008).

These examples emphasise how the policy rhetoric was not in line with the practices and how the issues that are associated with privatisation required a much wider debate than the ownership debate itself. Following the shift from Washington Consensus to Post-Washington Consensus in the beginning of 2000s, there was also a shift in the global policy rhetoric with respect to privatisation, favouring public private partnerships (PPP) instead of full privatisation (Fine, 2008). The increasing dissatisfaction and failure stories related to fully liberalised energy markets were shown as the reason behind such shift, although the state's involvement has been more continuity than a break in reality. Despite substantial efforts for privatisation, the state had continued to stay in the sector as generator, regulator and/or financier. By 2004, the private sector's participation in electricity generation was not more than 41% in low-income countries and 58% in upper middle-income countries (Bayliss and Fine, 2008).

As Fine (2008) notes, a World Bank document in 2004 (p. 6) claims:

As with all economic elixirs, privatisation has been oversimplified, over-sold, and ultimately disappointing--delivering less than promised.[1]

The same document also reports (p. 43):

The limits of state ownership are numerous and widely accepted. But that does not imply that private enterprise is a superior organisational form for all infrastructure activities and in every country. Before state ownership is replaced, the properties and requirements of the proposed alternative must be carefully assessed--not just generally but also specifically for the activity and country in question.

In 2013, however, another World Bank document concluded that (pp. xiii-xv):

It is difficult to find conclusive evidence of the consistently beneficial effects of the reforms actually implemented in many countries.[2]

Therefore, in line with the shift in the theoretical emphasis from ownership structures to the degree and extent of competition within the sectors, the policy recommendation for privatisation has become the promotion of public private ownership schemes instead of full liberalisation, beginning from the second half of the 2000s. Investment commitments to PPP electricity projects in developing countries reached $46.5 billion in 2007, about double that of the previous year which represents an increase over 150 per cent from the level in 2004, and brings investment just 17 per cent below the peak level reached in 1997.[3]

In the 2000s, the involvement of the state was actively encouraged in the utilities sector as these industries with considerable degree of capital-intensive, non-incremental technological innovation were believed to go through two distinctive phases: the first is the deployment of new innovational technologies with higher risks and the second is the diffusion of mature technologies in incremental and less-risky ways (Mazzucato and Semieniuk, 2016). In a study with a global dataset, it was found that during the initial high-risk period,

---

1 See Kessides (2004) "Reforming Infrastructure: Privatization, Regulation and Competition" (http://elibrary.worldbank.org/doi/abs/10.1596/0-8213-5070-6).

2 See Vagliasindi (2013) "Revisiting Public-Private Partnerships in the Power Sector" http://elibrary.worldbank.org/doi/abs/10.1596/978-0-8213-9762-6.

3 Vagliasindi (2013) "Revisiting Public-Private Partnerships in the Power Sector" http://elibrary.worldbank.org/doi/abs/10.1596/978-0-8213-9762-6.

especially in countries such as Germany, China and Brazil, state investment banks have been providing patient finance for the energy sector and participated actively within the sector (Mazzucato and Semieniuk, 2016).

Due to privatisation related problems such as increased social opposition, increased prices, oligopoly, increased state subsidies, in some countries there was even a tendency for full re-nationalisation especially in electricity services since the mid-2000s (Hall et al., 2013). Several studies conducted by PSIRU (Public Services International Research Unit) in 2009, 2012 and 2013 reveal that nationalisation was very common especially in Latin American countries, because while the prices increased, investments did not increase to decrease prices and meet the demand (Hall, 2012; Hall et al., 2013, 2009; Thomas, 2009).[4]

Between 2007 and 2012, Germany has set up over 60 local public utilities for electricity distribution while cancelling 190 concessions for private distributors (D. Hall, 2012). The key motive was to break up the existing oligopoly in the electricity market, which was dominated by four corporations, E.ON, RWE, Vattenfall and EnBW, since the liberalisation in 1999. Argentina ended market-based pricing and the gas distributor Metrogas was nationalised in May 2013 (D. Hall et al, 2013). Bolivia nationalised two major electricity distributors in 2013, as well as four generation companies in 2010 (D. Hall et al., 2013). The Dominican Republic nationalised all of its distribution companies in 2003 because of social opposition to increased prices. There were also extensive problems in Brazil, which resulted in a demand crisis and a subsequent reduction programme called Apagão which aimed at reducing the demand by 25% in 2000-2001 (Thomas, 2009). Supply shortages had become an issue for the Brazilian liberalisation experience, because although the demand was growing 5% per year, there was limited new capacity built by the private investors since the privatisation in 1995. After Apagão, nearly all European and US utilities withdrew from Brazil leading the state to repossess some of the distribution facilities. In 2012, the distribution companies owned by Rede Group were taken over by the regulatory body Aneel, as the danger of bankruptcy threatened the power supply in five states (D. Hall et al., 2013).

By the time of the acquisition, the net debts of the Rede companies were amounting to $3.9 billion, owed to both banks and companies. While companies received capital contributions roughly amounting to $1.2 billion, the maturities were lengthened for the rest of the debts.[5] This experience cannot

---

4   See PSIRU website (www.psiru.org) for a full list of publications on privatisation, re-nationalisation/re-municipalisation experiences by PSIRU.

5   See Energisa group website for details of the acquisition process of Rede Group: http://investidores.grupoenergisa.com.br.

be shown as an example for a re-nationalisation tendency, however, as the eight distribution companies owned previously by Rede Group was acquired by Energisa Group in April 2014, making Energisa the sixth largest electricity distribution group in Brazil, with approximately 6.5 million consumers.

As of today, both re-nationalisation and privatisation trends are observed. In some cases, privatisation accelerated. For example, Honduras decided to fully privatise its state-owned distribution company, ENEE, in 2014, because the payment agreements with private producers were taking 90% of its total revenues (D. Hall et al., 2013). Turkey has been one of the countries that privatised both generation and distribution segments gradually on the basis of a mixed regulatory mechanism since 1984. The next section will briefly discuss the changing theoretical debates on privatisation of electricity utilities, the emphasis being on the regulation methods.

2.1   Scholarship on Privatisation of Electricity Provision: How and What to Regulate?

Most of the scholarship on privatisation of electricity and utilities in general has centred upon the choice of principles with respect to regulation: how and what to regulate? Historically, utility regulation has been based upon a rate of return principle. In this mechanism, rate of return objectives is set both on invested capital and sales revenues, allowing investors to recover the costs of their incurred expenses. Starting from 1970s and throughout the 1980s, this structure has been criticized by many from both neoclassical and neo-Austrian schools on the basis of decreased efficiency and excess capacity as it did not include an incentive for investors to reduce costs. Littlechild (1970), Baumol (1975, 1971), Joskow (1976), Joskow and Schmalensee (1986), Kay and Vickers (1988) and Kahn (1988)[6] were among the first to discuss the introduction of marginal cost pricing mechanism in the utilities sector which also formed the theoretical rationale behind the extensive privatisations of the UK utility services during the 1980s. Electricity and telecommunications were given primary importance, as prior to these discussions, these sectors were to be accepted as naturally monopolistic due to the existence of network transmission costs.[7]

---

6 See also Newberry (2001) and (1995) for a detailed discussion of electricity privatisation in the UK.

7 Kay and Vickers (1988) argue that natural monopoly was one reason why they were taken into public ownership in the first place. This argument is criticised by Fine (1990) in the context of British coal industry by showing that there was a fragmented rather than a monopolistic structure prior to privatisation.

The marginal cost pricing mechanism was based on a very simple principle. Given a set of depreciation rules, the cost of added capacity will determine the optimal firm (and market) price for continuation of production. Three sets of magnitudes need to be known in each period: the firm's investment outlays, the prices of production and the depreciation payments on these investments (Baumol, 1971). Like any other cost functions, however, this cost structure corresponds to an implicit production behaviour where it exhibits constant or strict economies of scale, as emphasised by Baumol (1975). A price regulation mechanism where a price cap on the basis of the above criteria adjusts the operators according to the price cap index is believed to reflect the efficiency gains from cost reduction to end user tariffs. The general formula for a price cap is given below:

$$RPI - X + K$$

Where RPI is the retail prices index, X refers to the price decreases stemming from efficiency gains from increased productivity and K refers to price changes due to changes in the prices of inputs. Crudely, the primary advantage of this model over a revenue cap model is that the firms have an incentive to reduce costs where efficiency gains are reflected on end prices, which also benefits the consumers. There is assumed to be a duality between an optimal pricing and optimal investment structure, as over-investment will be punished in such setting where the firms will be forced to reduce prices and end up failing to cover both current and incurred costs. On a revenue-based rate of return regulation mechanism, the duality between optimal pricing and investment is assumed to lead towards excess capacity as there is a monopolistic, non-competitive mark-up incentive for all investments. Throughout the 1980s, regulation discussions have focused on this axis of regulation corresponding to different degrees of competition (Joskow and Schmalansee, 1986; Kay and Vickers, 1988). What was considered important was the extent of competition while regulation being a tool for achieving more competitive market structures by removing the monopolistic incentives such as mark-up. As a result of this, there was a shift in the emphasis from an evaluation of different ownership structures to a comparison of different degrees of competition in privatisation scholarship especially from the 2000s onwards.

How are we to understand these developments with respect to the actual electricity industry privatisation experiences around the world? First of all, it should be noted that the dramatic shifts in the scholarship as well as policy rhetoric does not correspond to the actual practice surrounding the electricity markets, which has been the increasing extent and scope of commodity

relations together with the involvement of the state, which in principle, inter-
fered on behalf and not at the expense of these. Second, the analytical focus on
regulation and the choice between optimal pricing and revenue levels reveals
little about the nature of the organisational relations involved upon which the
levels of inter- and intra-sectoral competition as well as investment depend.
These organisational relations involve the degree of national as well as international cartelisation, the conditions of labour that concerns overall wage levels or sectoral developments, for example whether sub-contracting exists, and
also the impacts of technical progress on competition and sectoral boundaries.
In the context of coal industry privatisation in the UK, Fine (1990) noted that
the rhetoric around privatisation has focused upon power station construction
industries has long being unsatisfactory with substantial cost over-runs and
delays in competition (p. 148). The vertically integrated nature of the industry
was held responsible for the inefficiencies to occur given the naturally monopolistic conditions of competition.[8] It was privatised in 1989, on the basis of the
theoretical rationale explained above, without much attention being paid to
the wider surrounding issues.

   These issues can be summarised as follows. In the process of restructuring
of power station supply in the UK, there were also at least four major industries that were involved, which were defence, electrical consumer durables,
telecommunications and power engineering (Fine, 1990). During the privatisation process, all of these sectors were going through a restructuring in
which the technical progress played a role to lower the boundaries between
the sectors and led to intensified inter-sectoral acquisitions and mergers, as
seen for example in the merger between General Electric Company (GEC)
and Plessey, a British-based international electronics, defence and telecommunications company, in 1988. The issues related to telecommunications
as well as other sectors mentioned above were mostly ignored during the
design of electricity privatisation however important they might be in the

---

8   In the context of coal industry, Fine (1990) shows that it was the absence of these monop-
    olistic conditions, with a fragmented structured of the construction sector depending upon
    sub-contracting and causalised workforce, which prevented firms to enjoy the benefits of
    economies of scale and required the nationalisation of the industry in the first place through-
    out the 1930. The privatisation attempted to reduce the inefficiencies, such as over-capacity
    and limited mechanisation, believed to be created by this structure. Fine (1990) show evidence
    that mechanisation and economies of scale existed in the presence of the state cartel and it
    was the tendency of concentration of production in larger and fewer (core) units that created
    the over-capacity problem. Privatisation came as a political choice to maintain the profitabil-
    ity for larger units arising from economies of scale, as the over-capacity problem could also be
    addressed by increasing investment levels in smaller 'uneconomic' units in the periphery.

implementation, given the close links between the sectors. The other issue, quite independent of the domestic privatisation experiences, was related to international cartelisation closely associated with increasing economies of scale. When privatisation of electricity was in its initial steps in the UK in 1990, there was considerable cartelisation in the international market, with six or seven giant companies including General Electric Company (GEC) of the UK, Alsthom of France and General Electric and Combustion Engineering of the United States dominating the market. Fine (1990) emphasises that this structure is likely to prevail because of an international economy of scale following technical progress, independent of domestic ownership structures. Once it occurs, privatisation might actually contribute to it in the international market, as smaller privatised companies would have more difficulties in enjoying the advantages of economies of scale compared to single state-owned utilities (Fine, 1990). This is especially relevant for lower-income countries.

In line with the methodology outlined in Chapter 1, the world economy develops towards the concentration of capital in fewer and larger units together with the increases in productivity. In this context, a highly concentrated production process in an industry with firms of high levels of productivity and investment is challenged by the smaller units as long as the availability of cheaper labour satisfies profitability for smaller units which have lower levels of productivity as well as investment. In a privatisation experience, these structures play a more important role in addressing the issues of efficiency and competition than the mode of regulation itself, which has been the primary focus in policy making.

Section 3 will address these issues in the context of the electricity privatisation experience in Turkey and will give a general picture of the energy sector, including the electricity industry.

3   Energy Sector Outlook in Turkey

Turkey's total electricity production has doubled in the last ten years in line with growth of the economy. Between 2009-2014, the energy sector received an average of 10% of total public investments. In terms of asset size, the energy sector is the second biggest sector in the real economy after manufacturing with a share of 10% of total assets.[9]

---

9   TURKSTAT (www.tuik.org.tr).

Annual electricity generation is approximately 179.5 billion kWh, with an annual growth rate of approximately 9% in the early 2010s (see Table 2). In 2009, Turkish Electrical Energy 10 Year Generation Capacity Projection Report (2009-2018) published by TEIAS (Turkish Electricity Transmission Company) expected that total electricity demand was to reach 336 TWh with a 6.3% compound annual growth rate in a base scenario in 2018, and 357 TWh with a 7% compound annual growth rate in a high scenario. Although the actual growth in demand stayed lower than projections, in 2016, total gross electricity use has been 278.3 TWh, growing by 3.3% from 2015, and 296.7 TWh in 2017.[10]

As electricity demand is in tight correlation with aggregate demand, the World Bank (2015) warned that the fast growth of the installed capacity could signal an overcapacity problem following the slowing down of the growth levels since 2010. Since 2010, economic growth has settled at 3–4% and electricity demand growth settled at 4-5% annual level (well below the 6–7% annualised rates of the previous decade). Power generation investments have continued, and capacity additions peaked in 2013. Generation capacity margin has reached 70%. The market was going to be over-supplied were it not for the severe drought that affected hydro generation in 2014.

In terms of total energy demand, Turkey is a net energy importer, with approximately 70% of its total energy demand coming from imports of primary resources petroleum, coal and especially natural gas. In 2014, 35% of all energy demand came from natural gas, 28.5% from coal, 27% from petroleum and 7% from hydroelectric sources.[11] The contribution of renewable energy resources to total electricity demand has been rather low, at 3%, although it is increasing. What is striking is the increasing importance of natural gas in terms of contribution to total energy demand, from 5% in 1990. In terms of electricity generation, the share of natural gas also increased from 19.2% in 1995 to 47.9% in 2014.[12] In 2018, the share of natural gas decreased to 40% due to newly established power plants making use of domestic resources.

This rise is important for signalling increasing import dependency, as all natural gas is imported. In 2012, Turkey imported approximately 1.6 Tcf of natural gas, 58% coming from Russia. Another 18% of the total came from Iran, while the rest of was imported from Azerbaijan, Algeria and Nigeria. 91% of the natural gas imported is sold to BOTAS Petroleum Pipeline Corporation,

---

10   All electricity instalment and transmission statistics are from TEIAS (Turkish Electricity Transmission Company) website (www.teias.gov.tr) unless otherwise stated.

11   BOTAS (Petroleum Pipeline Corporation) Annual Sectoral Report, (2014) (www.botas.gov. tr).

12   TEIAS Electricity Statistics (https://www.teias.gov.tr/).

TABLE 2   The development of installed capacity for electricity in Turkey

Year	Thermal	Hydro	Geothermal + Wind + Solar	Total (MW)	Increase
	%	%	%	MW	%
2000	58.8	41	0.1	27264,1	4.4
2001	58.6	41.2	0.1	28332,4	3.9
2002	61.4	38.4	0.1	31845,8	12.4
2003	64.5	35.3	0.1	35587,0	11.7
2004	65.5	34.3	0.1	36824,0	3.5
2005	66.6	33.2	0.1	38843,5	5.5
2006	67.5	32.2	0.2	40564,8	4.4
2007	66.7	32.3	0.4	40835,7	0.7
2008	65.9	33.1	0.9	41817,2	2.4
2009	65.5	32.5	1.9	44761,2	7.0
2010	65.2	32	2.8	49524,1	10.6
2011	64.1	32.4	3.4	52911,1	6.8
2012	61.4	34.4	4.2	57059,4	7.8
2013	60.4	34.5	4.8	64007,5	12.2
2014	60.1	34	5.9	69519,8	8.6
2015	57.3	35.4	7.3	73146,7	5.2
2016	56.6	34	9.4	78497,4	7.3
2017	55.1	32	12.9	85200,0	8.5
2018	52.3	32	15.1	88550,8	3.9

SOURCE: TEIAS, ELECTRICITY GENERATION – TRANSMISSION STATISTICS

which is a state-owned subsidiary operating under TPAO (Turkish Petroleum Corporation). In 2014, 19% of natural gas is directly used by households for heating and other purposes, while 25.4% is used by industry and 48.1% is used for electricity generation. Turkey also imports about 90% of its hard coal consumption mainly from Russia, Australia and United States. In fact, imports of energy products, which account for more than $50 billion in total, has been the largest single item in Turkey's budget deficit during the 2010s (CBRT Turkey, 2014).

Being a net importer of natural gas makes Turkey vulnerable to supply disruptions and pipeline capacity is suspected to be insufficient to keep up with the increasing domestic demand. Moreover, the expansion of natural gas occurred at the expense of coal, fuel oil, and especially hydro facilities that were already in use (Atiyas et al., 2012). In terms of installed capacity, 60% of total electricity installation power is based on thermal plants in 2014, while 34% is based on hydroelectric facilities. Considering that the contribution of hydroelectric facilities to total electricity generation has been 16.1% in the same year, these facilities have provided a contribution below their capacities.

In 2013, The Electricity Market Law (EML) was passed with the aim of decreasing the share of electricity generation based on natural gas to 30%, increasing the share of renewable resources up to 30%, utilising domestic lignite and hard coal resources as well as hydroelectric potential and increasing the share of nuclear power to 5% by 2023.

4   Historical Background and Institutional Framework for Electricity Provision in Turkey

As explained above, electricity generation, transmission and distribution have been traditionally provided by the state in vertically integrated structures, in almost all countries. Turkey has been no exception to that rule. Attempts at privatising the state-owned electricity sector in Turkey started in the 1980s and accelerated in the 1990s. In the beginning of the 2000s, in accordance with the IMF stabilisation programme designed to address the wider macroeconomic instabilities, a full liberalisation package for electricity provision was adopted. By the end of 2014, the privatisation of electricity provision, which included the dismantling of generation from distribution and the privatisation of each, was complete.

Public provision of electricity in Turkey started with the establishment of Etibank in 1935. Starting from the 1950s, construction of thermal and hydro-electric power plants started with collaborative work of the DSI (*The General Directorate of State Hydraulic Works*), the EIE (*The General Directorate of Electric Power*), the MTA (*The General Directorate of Mineral Research and Exploration*), and Iller Bankasi (*Provincial Bank*). According to the First Five Year Development Plan (1963-1967), TEK (*Turkish Electricity Institution*) was established as a vertically integrated state-owned enterprise. Between 1970 and 1993, TEK has been the state monopoly for the generation, transmission and distribution of electricity.

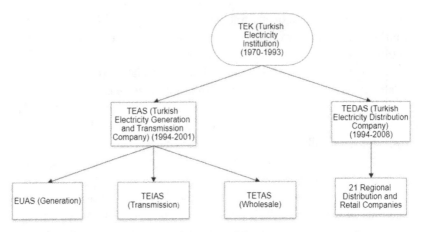

FIGURE 23   The historical institutional structure of electricity provision in Turkey

The first step towards privatisation was in 1984, when actors other than the Turkish Electricity Institution were allowed to enter the market through the Build-Operate-Transfer (BOT) and Transfer of Rights (TOR) schemes. In 1994, TEK was abolished and TEAS (*The Turkish Electricity Generation and Transmission Company*) and TEDAS (*The Turkish Electricity Distribution Company*) were established. During the 1990s, most privatisation legislations concerned generation as the potentially most competitive segment. After the dismantling of the generation and distribution from transmission, which is considered to be unsuitable for privatisation, full privatisation of the electricity provision in Turkey has been one of the steps for the harmonisation with the EU regulations.

In 2001, Electricity Market Law No: 4628 (EML) was prepared in line with the EU Energy Acquis. Within the framework of EML, The Energy Markets Regulatory Authority (EMRA) was established, and TEAS was further unbundled into three companies: EUAS for generation, TEIAS for transmission, and TETAS for wholesale, while TEDAS remaining as the regulatory body for the distribution and retail. The whole electricity market is regulated by EMRA, whose task is to issue licences for all market activities, determine and approve regulated tariffs, monitor market performance, settle the eligibility limits for market access and impose fines and sanctions on the legal entities operating in the market.

Figure 23 displays the unbundling of the institutional structure of electricity provision in Turkey, while Table 3 provides a more detailed timeline for the privatisation process since 1984.

TABLE 3   Privatisation of electricity industry timeline

1984 Law No: 3096, Authorization for Build-Operate-Transfer (BOT) and
Transfer of Rights (TOR)
1994 Law No: 3996, Unbundling of Generation and Transmission from
Distribution and Retail, Introduction of BOT and TOR
1997 Law No: 4283, Introduction of Build-Operate (BO) Scheme
2001 Law No: 4628 (Electricity Market Law), Unbundling of Generation and
Wholesale from Transmission
2004 Privatisation Strategy Paper
2008 Privatisation of Distribution Started
2012 Sector Opennes Reached 84%
2013 Law No: 6446 (New EML), Privatisation of Distribution Completed

---

Turkey has neither signed the Energy Community Treaty of 2005 nor participated in the South East Europe Electricity Market (SEEEM), but it has signalled its intention to participate in the European market for electricity in its
Energy Sector Reform and Privatisation Strategy Paper in 2004, along with
detailed instructions for further liberalisation of the sector (Bagdadioglu and
Odyakmaz, 2009). The Strategy Paper anticipated that the privatisation of
twenty-one distribution and retail companies was to be started by the end of
2006 and completed by 2011.

Although the privatisation of distribution and retail could not start before
2008 due to some financing and implementation problems, which will be discussed in the following sections, it was completed in 2013. In 2013, the new EML
(Law No: 6446) was also amended. In order to complete the liberalisation process of the sector, the new EML changed the licence types, set a pre-licensing
process that has been absent in the previous legislative framework. It also
extended some deadlines set by the previous law, such as the price equalisation mechanism for distribution and supply companies, corporate tax, stamp
tax and VAT exemption, 50% discount on system utilisation fees during investment periods and for five years from the operation start date.

Contrary to the previous law, the new EML is structured around types of
activities rather than licences, and the activities are listed as generation, distribution, wholesale, retail sale, market operation, export and import. Market
operation is a new type of activity that had not been listed in the previous
law and involves the operation of organised wholesale electricity markets and
financial settlements of activities conducted in these markets. The Regulation

on Unlicensed Electricity Production and Electricity Market Licensing Regulation came into force in the same year.

The new Law also enabled share transfers of companies in the energy market. From September 1, 2015 the market regulation for electricity generation is to be carried out by EPIAS (Electricity Market Management Company). EPIAS has been established as a joint stock company to manage and control electricity merchandise nationwide. The main activities and duties of EPIAS are as follows: operating electricity transaction both in day-ahead markets and daily markets, invoicing and other financial activities in the market, operating financial activities in stabilisation and reconciliation market and ancillary services markets together with TEIAS, working through establishing newly organised whole-sale energy markets, if necessary; representing the state as a party in international financial energy conventions or agreements as a member of international energy markets.[13]

Its company shares are divided into three parts: Type A shares are bought by TEIAS and BOTAS (The Petroleum and Pipeline Corporation) making up 30% of the shares, Type B shares are bought by BIST (Istanbul Stock Exchange), 30% while the remaining 40% of shares are bought by private energy companies. Shareholder companies are obliged to obtain supplying or generation licences in the electricity market, a wholesale-retail sale licence or import-export licence. Electricity companies can only engage in activities indicated in their licence and cannot directly become a shareholder in other legal activities in the market. Each company is allowed to obtain 4% of total shares at most in order to avoid monopolisation. A share of profits equal to 10% on capital is to be retained as a reserve fund, with the rest to be paid as dividends to shareholders. A futures exchange option is also being set up. Tariffs on electricity are to be determined transparently in the EPIAS stock market. While transmission, distribution and retail tariffs are still regulated by EMRA, the generation tariff is completely determined by the market.

4.1 Privatisation Process I: Policy Design and Price Regulation

As summarised in the previous section, all public electricity utilities concerning generation and distribution had been corporatised in Turkey, by the end of 2014. It has been one of the first developing countries to finalise the full transition process gradually (Atiyas et al., 2012). The privatisation agenda was inspired by the UK model that was implemented by the legislation of the *Electricity Act*

---

13   EPIAS website (www.epias.gov.tr). EPIAS is also referred to as EXIST (Energy Exchange Istanbul).

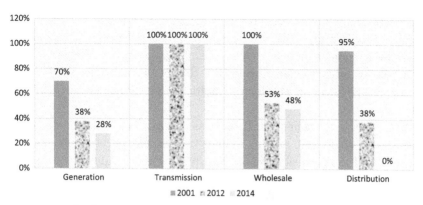

FIGURE 24   The share of the public sector in electricity segments (2001-2014)
SOURCE: TEIAS

of 1989. As discussed briefly with respect to its implementation and outcomes in the previous sections, the privatisation of electricity in the UK aimed at increasing competition through various mechanisms. The most important one was the introduction of a wholesale market, Electricity Pool, which functioned as the unified electricity market for all public and private generators. From that pool, customers with more than 1 MW demand (the threshold to be lowered to zero until 1998) were free to choose their contractors.

The same policy design was implemented in Turkey. First, the areas of generation and transmission were unbundled from distribution and retail, and generation was gradually privatised. Finally, distribution and retail were further unbundled and privatised. There was no privatisation attempt for transmission as it is still classified as naturally monopolistic. Figure 24 shows the declining share of the public sector in generation, wholesale and distribution through the whole privatisation process from 2001 to 2014.

As mentioned in the previous section, Law No: 3096 in 1984 gave authorisation for Build-Operate-Transfer (BOT) scheme for new generation facilities and Transfer of Rights (TOR) scheme for existing facilities. In the beginning, BOT agreements were designed as concessions for companies to build and operate a generation plant for 99 years (it was renegotiated as 49 years in 2013), with transfer of the plant to the state at no cost after the concession period ends.

The World Bank defines the difference between BOT agreements and concessions as follows. In concessions, the concessionaires can operate the existing assets, therefore there will be immediate cash flows from the customers as the main source of revenues. In a BOT Project, on the other hand, there are no immediate cash flows from existing revenue streams and the project company or operator generally obtains its revenues through a fee charged to the utility/government rather than tariffs charged to the consumers. In the power sector, this usually takes the form of a power purchase agreement. In a power purchase agreement, there is likely to be a minimum payment that is required to be paid by the contractor, provided that the operator can deliver the service (availability payment) as well as a volumetric payment for quantities delivered above that level.[14]

Although the BOT scheme in Turkey was arranged as a concession to allow investors to benefit from existing revenue streams, the process was subject to the review of the Council of State (Danistay) under the Administrative Law which involved a lengthy process that discouraged private investors (Atiyas et al., 2012). However, it should be noted that the privatisation also took place at a time of limited primary accumulation in the energy sector, when the firms did not have enough capacity for big infrastructural investments. Therefore, the state has been heavily involved in the financing of the sector before and during the transition phase (Bagdadioglu and Odyakmaz, 2009). In 1994 a Decree was passed to grant tax exemptions and Treasury guarantees for BOT agreements. In 1997, a BO model was also introduced.

The Treasury guarantees were based on a take-or-pay principle. After 1994 until 2001, TEAS bought 85% of the total electricity produced under BOT contracts and 100% of production under BO contracts (Cakarel and House, 2004). In 2000, there were twenty-four power plants under BOT and five plants under BO all of which were all protected by Treasury guarantees. TEAS was responsible for buying all of the produced electricity. Nevertheless, the prices were so high that in 2000 and 2001 it could not pay the full amount and needed a net capital increase from Treasury worth $87 million according to a report prepared by Turkish Court of Accounts in 2004. The same report also revealed that between 2000 and 2004, public losses related to increased Treasury payments to private companies reached $2.3 billion while the profit rate of private firms was over 85%.[15]

The report concluded that BOT and BO agreements overall resulted in increased public losses because of the fallacies in both design and implementation of the scheme. First, auctions were not designed in a competitive way. In many cases, public tenders were not made, and bids were collected from companies operating in the sector, although the design of the scheme held the Ministry of Energy responsible for choosing the location of the plants, in the

14   From World Bank Group Public Private Partnership in Infrastructure Resource Centre website: https://ppp.worldbank.org/public-private-partnership/agreements/concessions-bots-dbos. See the website for more information on the details of concessions, BOT contracts and power purchase agreements.

15   Turkish Court of Accounts, Report on Energy No: 5088/1, (2004).

actual implementation the location of the plants were chosen by the firms. This resulted in excess electricity supply in certain regions which further contributed to public losses due to increased transmission costs and loss ratios in distribution. Third, the prices were predetermined by the firms over the duration of 15-30 years and this resulted in the state buying expensive electricity in dollars. Fourth, some contracts were signed despite having poor feasibility reports according to third party investigations.

Despite substantial efforts by the state to make electricity sector attractive to the private investors, participation of the private sector has remained low until full privatisation (Karahan and Toptas, 2013). When the EML was passed in 2001, the share of the public sector in electricity generation was still over 70%. Attempts were especially unsuccessful in terms of attracting foreign investment, considering the volatile macroeconomic environment of the time. Especially during the 2000s, there is emphasis in the literature on the state's heavy involvement in the sector through its take-or-pay model, which had a limiting impact on competition and the sector remained more or less monopolistic before and after privatisation (Atiyas and Dutz, 2005; Cakarel and House, 2004; Dagdeviren, 2009). Atiyas and Dutz (2005) claim that the existence of take-or-pay agreements created competition not *in* the market but rather *for* the market of which costs are burdened by the public and consumers, while benefits go to the private companies.

Until the amendment of Law No: 4628 in 2001, TEK distributed electricity according to a single tariff system. The tariff reflected the costs of production and the excise and value added taxes, but there was no unbundled tariff system according to different areas of activities. When the EML established electricity markets, the supply side was fully liberalised through a licensing regime. Generated electricity by EUAS and licensed generators could be sold in the market, and auto-producers could also sell surplus. After then, 21 regional distribution companies could also engage in the market and they were allowed to take part in retail supply as long as they had a retail licence. Between 2001 and 2013, while the free consumer limits were decreasing periodically, there was a hybrid system based on a single buyer model. TETAS (Turkish Electricity Trade and Contracting Corporation) has been the state-owned electricity wholesale company responsible as the single buyer from private and public electricity generating companies during the period.

The wholesale market consisted of a bilateral contracting market complemented by a residual balancing market that was launched in 2006. From 2006 onwards, TETAS regulated tariffs according to a price equalisation scheme. It employed bilateral contracts, bought electricity from EUAS, from private companies work under the principles of BO, BOT and TOR, from the settlement

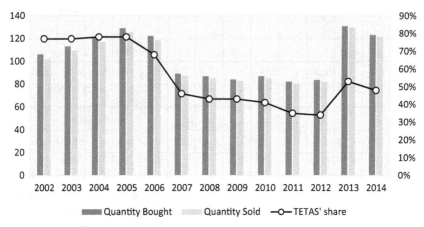

FIGURE 25   Public sector (TETAS) electricity trade
* TETAS' share is shown on the right axis.
SOURCE: TETAS

market that is under the regulation of MFSC (Market Financial Settlement Centre), determined tariffs according in a cost reflective, incentive based pricing mechanism and then sold it to electricity transmission companies, customers that are directly linked to electricity distribution, distribution and retail companies and to the settlement market where any excess supply of electricity can be traded daily (Figure 25). It is also in charge for imports and exports and it is the regulatory body for the Market Financial Settlement Centre (MFSC).

Because TETAS' costs had a large take-or-pay component, the prices of TETAS remained initially very high at a fixed price, so it could not afford a competitive price over the one determined by the market (Atiyas and Dutz, 2005). Figure 26 illustrates the change in TETAS wholesale prices since 2001.

Today, price determination for the wholesale market takes place in the day-ahead market where participation is not compulsory, and any agent can participate by signing an adhesion act. Agents negotiate on the prices for the next day and at the point where demand and supply meets, the Market Exchange Price is determined. Any imbalances that can occur are handled by the Market Financial Settlement Centre (MFSC). The balancing market was introduced as a complementary mechanism but later turned into an electricity spot market. In a balancing market-bilateral contracts model, it is expected that a small portion of electricity (10%-15%) would be traded for balancing purposes, but the balancing market in Turkey attracted almost all electricity generation.[16] This

---

16   Turkish Competition Authority, Electricity Wholesale and Retail Sector Report (2015).

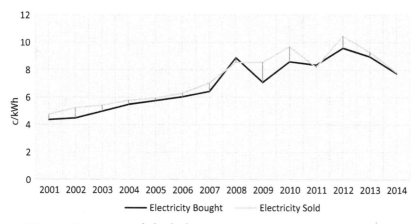

FIGURE 26   TETAS average wholesale electricity prices
              SOURCE: TETAS

was because it reflected better prices for marginal generation capacity and as a result most generators cancelled their bilateral contracts and started selling in the balancing market (Atiyas et al., 2012).

In retail and distribution markets, first, a threshold was put on consumption and consumers exceeding the threshold consumption levels were considered to be eligible to choose their distributors. As of 2014, after privatisation of all 21 retailers was completed, the sector openness ratio has reached 85%, indicating 85% of consumers were eligible to choose their electricity contractors (Figure 27). High sector openness is one of the most important indicators of successfully liberalised markets, but in practice over 40% of free consumers did not use their opportunity to choose their retailers and stayed with their regional distributors.[17]

As mentioned earlier, the regulatory framework for electricity in Turkey is hybrid and it tries to address both revenues and prices, based on rate of return and marginal cost principles, respectively. These principles were adopted prior to privatisation of distribution and retail, in a transition scheme without reflecting the changes on end-user tariffs. According to this scheme, distribution was unbundled into four segments: retail sales, retail services, distribution and transmission. While retail services and distribution segments continued to operate under a revenue cap, a price cap was introduced to retail sales. In

---

17   TEDAS Company Report (2013). See Figure 5-5 for sector openness ratios and free consumer limits since 2003.

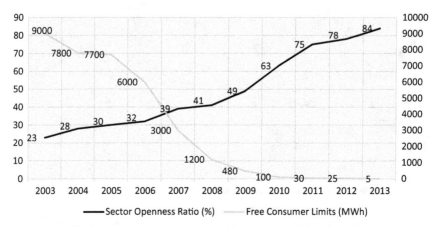

the transmission segments, prices were determined on a cost-plus basis. As 2004 Privatisation Strategy Paper revealed, the recovery of stranded costs has been an important policy consideration and been a determining factor for such a transitionary period.

In the beginning of the privatisation process, Guney (2005, p. 99) laid out that there could be three possible methods for cost recovery in Turkish electricity markets:

1) The state could continue to subsidize BOT and BO contracts via mostly low-cost, state-owned hydroelectric generation,

2) The state could buy out contracts (either at book value or through negotiated securitization, a process in which savings can be obtained on the financing cost of initial generation investments), then release the power and the capacity set forth in the contracts into the market at a price that the market can bear. The resulting costs (the difference between buyout value and market value) can be recovered over time through transition surcharges on customer bills; or

3) The state could release the power and the capacity set forth in the contracts into the market without a buy-out option and levy a transition surcharge on customer bills until the end of the contracts.

The first option would have been the continuation of traditional subsidy scheme through mixing the costs of BOT and BO contracts with the benefits of state-owned, low-cost hydroelectric generation. In a policy paper prepared for Turkey in 2002, the OECD also recommended this option in which the bundling could continue until stranded costs were fully recovered. By this method, the political risk of a transition surcharge on electricity bills would also be avoided.

In fact, Turkey has followed a mixed approach between the first and second options. The state-owned hydro-electric facilities with much lower operating costs than the new facilities were gradually privatised under TOR with a gradual opening of the market. The regulatory mechanism for achieving the gradual liberalisation has been allowing for all stranded costs to be recovered through revenue cap guarantees while there was also a pass-through mechanism to reflect changes in the price cap in case there were improvements in the cost structure. This incentive-based rate of return formulation is applied by EMRA for all segments including storage, transmission, wholesale, distribution and retail. The first implementation period being between 2006-2010, this is a common example of a global public-private partnership practice where if the revenues fall below the minimum revenue guarantees, the government subsidises, and any excess revenue is either retained by the investors or transferred to the public budget.[18]

In terms of the regulatory structure, the Turkish electricity system can be considered to be along the same lines with the rest of the developing world, for which a hybrid system of regulation is encouraged. Among many other examples, India has been one of the countries to adopt an annual revenue and price based regulation mechanism through the unbundling of Delhi's vertically integrated electricity company, Delhi Vidyut Board in 2002 (Pargal and Banerjee, 2014).

As mentioned, the privatisation experience in Turkey has been successful to encourage the private sector participation, especially in generation segment. In less than two decades, the share of the private producers in total generation has increased from less than 20% in 2002 to over 80% by the end of 2016.[19] In 2011, the state's generation company EUAS's share in total installed capacity was 38.3%, while its share in total generation was 32.1%. By the end of 2016, EUAS's market power in total electricity installed power capacity and generation has decreased to 25.7% and 17.1%, respectively.

---

18   In Turkey, the excess revenues are retained by the firms but the excess amounting over 105% of the revenue cap is reduced from the calculations for the following period (EMRA, 2015, Electricity Market Distribution Segment Revenue Regulation http://www.resmi-gazete.gov.tr/eskiler/2015/12/20151219-4.pdf).

19   EUAS, Annual Activity Report (2016).

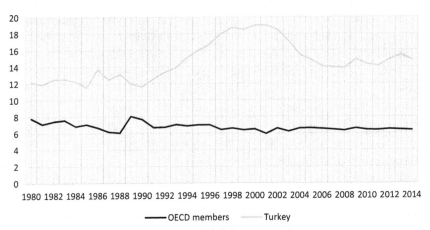

FIGURE 28   Electric power transmission and distribution losses (% of total output)
SOURCE: OECD WORLD DEVELOPMENT INDICATORS

This section explained that the success of the privatisation experience was
due to the choice of regulation mechanisms that reflected the initial costs on
the public budget and consumer bills to encourage the private sector participation. The next section will address how the most important problem in the
Turkish electricity industry, which is losses and theft in transmission and distribution, was handled in the privatisation plan along with other implementation problems.

4.2   Privatisation Process II: Addressing Losses and Theft and Other Problems in Implementation

Prior to privatisation, a major problem of Turkish electricity has been the high
ratio of distribution losses and theft. As a percentage of total consumption, it
has been consistently over the 10% band since the early 1990s, reaching a peak
of 20% in 2000, while the average OECD loss ratio has been at around 7% over
the same period (see Figure 28). Although the reasons behind the losses are
not well known, they are substantially higher in the east and southeast regions
which suggests that the political conflict in these regions could have been a
contributory factor (Atiyas et al., 2012).

To address this problem, instead of offering direct cash subsidies to distribution companies with the highest loss ratios, EMRA introduced a price equalisation scheme in 2006 in accordance with the cost recovery principle. The
scheme is based on a national tariff structure that is uniform across the regions
but differentiated across the consumers. Specific target losses are set for each
distributional company, and any improvement beyond target losses can be

appropriated by the company. If companies make improvements beyond their target losses, the difference is paid by TETAS. If companies' costs stay high due to losses, these costs are directly reflected on end user prices. There is no mechanism however, to reflect the cost improvements on the end user tariffs for ineligible consumers.

According to a Turkish Court of Accounts Report prepared for TEDAS in 2012, the total cost for losses increased to 5.9 billion TRY in 2012,[20] which has been deducted from consumers in the form of a cost item in retail tariffs. The same report also finds that the regional discrepancy is striking with the losses of the company responsible for electricity distribution in the southeast region, Dicle EDAS, amounting to 3.4 billion TRY in 2012, constituting 57.6% of total losses nationwide.[21]

The state's response to the failure in meeting the target losses has been to raise the targets instead of offering a long-term solution for decreasing losses. For example, in the case of Dicle EDAS, the target loss ratios were set at 42.06%, 34.93% and 29.01% for 2013, 2014, respectively, in the initial privatisation plan in 2009 (Table 4). Nevertheless, the actual losses could not be reduced below 70%, putting serious financial constraint on the company. In 2009, Dicle EDAS and Vangolu EDAS, two distributional companies from the southeast and east regions, reported 73% and 55% loss ratios, respectively. The loss ratio has even increased to 75% in 2014[22]. Despite the incentives given by the state for cost reduction in the form of higher loss targets, the distribution company was not able to reduce losses.

An important reason for high loss ratios might be long transmission lines to transfer energy. Private electricity generators are free to choose the geographical locations of their activity, which requires longer transmission lines. This both increases transmission losses and also the transfers from the public budget as the transmission costs are covered by the state-owned company TEIAS. While large industrial cities, such as Istanbul, have excess electricity

---

20 Turkish Court of Accounts, TEDAS Report (2012) (Note: This individual Turkish Court of Accounts Report on TEDAS could not be accessed from Turkish Court of Accounts website (www.sayistay.gov.tr) as of July 2017. Instead, some of its findings are summarised in Turkish Court of Accounts general report on Public Enterprises: T.C. Sayistay Bakanligi Kamu Isletmeleri 2012 Yili Genel Raporu, accessed on 14/07/2017 from https://www.sayistay.gov.tr/tr/Upload/62643830/files/raporlar/genel_raporlar/kit_genel/Kamu%20%C4%B0%C5%9Fletmeleri%202012%20Y%C4%B1l%C4%B1%20Genel%20Raporu.pdf).

21 Turkish Court of Accounts, TEDAS Report (2012).

22 Turkish Court of Accounts, TEDAS Report (2012).

TABLE 4   Loss-theft aim ratios of selected regional distribution-retail companies

Loss-theft aim ratios according to regions	2013	2014	2015
Dicle[a]	(42.06%) 71.07%	(34.93%) 59.03%	(29.01%) 49.03%
Vangolu	52.1%	43.27%	35.94%
Aras	25.7%	21.35%	17.73%
Toroslar	11.8%	11.25%	10.72%
Bogazici	10.76%	10.26%	9.78%
Uludag	6.96%	6.90%	6.90%

SOURCE: TMMOB

[a] The numbers in brackets are the unrevised aim ratios determined by Electricity Sector Reform and Privatisation Strategy Document in 2009 (TMMOB (2012), The Union of Chambers of Turkish Engineers and Architects, The Chamber of Electrical Engineers. Privatisation of Electricity Distribution Report, accessed from http://www.emo.org.tr/ekler/e59e00fdeea8fea_ek.pdf).

demand compared to regionally installed capacity (excess demand for electricity in Istanbul is expected to exceed 8500MW by 2022), some regions such as Eastern Anatolia and Black Sea demand significantly less than they generate. In 2022, excess supply in Cukurova region is expected to increase to 15000MW.[23]

In order to transfer electricity from low demand regions to high demand regions, new investments had to be made to increase the capacity for power distribution units and lengthening transmission lines. As Figure 29 shows, TEIAS's investment costs for the maintenance and improvement of the transmission system has exceeded the projected costs declared by its investment program since 2011, implying that there were unanticipated systemic problems

---

23   TEIAS and TUBITAK MAM Report (2013), "2013-2022 Yillari Turkiye Iletim Sistemi Bolgesel Talep Tahmin ve Sebeke Analiz Calismasi". This report is a 10 year regional demand forecast, which has been replaced in 2017 by TEIAS with a new forecast for 2017-2026 period, can be accessed from https://teias.gov.tr/sites/default/files/2017-06/10Y%C4%B1ll%C4%B1kTalepTahminleriRaporu2016%282%29.pdf.

The reference is made to the previous forecast, as the new forecast only reports expected changes in demand without reference to supply capacity of regions.

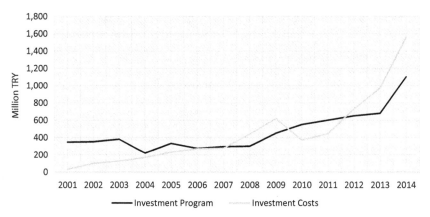

FIGURE 29   TEIAS investment program costs and actual costs
            SOURCE: TEIAS

such as frequent nationwide power outages,[24] as well as extra system requirements such as increased capacity for transmission network.

In addition to the problem of loss and theft, there were also other extensive
financing and malpractice problems in the implementation of the privatisation plan. A report prepared by the Turkish Court of Accounts in 2012 revealed
that there was a malpractice in the handover process of two distribution companies that resulted in a TEDAS loss of 126 million TL.[25] During the handover
process of Meram and Firat distribution companies in 2009 and 2010, respectively, due to miscalculations of company assets, TEDAS's holdings of cash and
cash equivalences worth 14.6 and 7 million TRY were transferred to the private
firms. The same process of illegal cash transfer was also repeated in the privatisation of Baskent, Sakarya, Osmangazi, Camlibel, Uludag, Coruh, Yesilirmak
and Trakya regions. The Ministry of Energy of Natural Resources decided in
2013 that out of the losses reported by the Court of Accounts at 126 million
TRY, there was no mechanism for the retrieval of 82 million TRY, which was cut
from the public budget.[26]

Table 5 displays the actors in electricity distribution, almost all of which
are big conglomerates with substantial investments in other sectors, especially
construction. According to the Competition Law, a single company can hold

---

24   The number of power outages firms in a typical month is 1.7 in 2013, while the num-
      ber is 0.4 for high income OECD countries in the same year (World Bank Data on
      Infrastructure: http://data.worldbank.org).
25   Turkish Court of Accounts (2012).
26   https://www.enerji.gov.tr/

TABLE 5   Actors and tender values in electricity distribution-retail segments

Distribution company	TOR agreement	Tender value (million $)
Baskent	EnerjiSA	1225
Sakarya	Ak Enerji	600
Meram	Alarko-Cengiz	400
Aras	Kiler Holding	128
Coruh	Aksa Enerji	227
Firat	Aksa Enerji	230
Trakya	IC Holding	575
Osmangazi	Yildizlar SSS	485
Yesilirmak	Calik Holding	441
Camlibel	Limak-Kolin-Cengiz	258
Uludag	Limak-Kolin-Cengiz	940
Gediz	Elsan-Tumas-Karacay	1231
Bogazici	Limak-Kolin-Cengiz	1960
Goksu	AKEDAS	60
Akdeniz	Limak-Kolin-Cengiz	546
Menderes	Aydem-Bereket	110
Anadolu Yakasi	EnerjiSA	1227
Dicle	Iskaya Dogu OGG	387
Vangolu	Turkerler Insaat	118
Toroslar	EnerjiSA	1725

up only to 30% of all distribution assets to avoid oligopolisation. Nevertheless, the cross-sectoral linkages are unexamined.[27]

As one of the major goals of a competitive electricity market is reduction of end-user tariffs, the privatisation of retail and distribution companies according to cost recovery principle has been one of the most important steps of the privatisation process. Between 2003 and 2008, prices were kept constant

---

27   Almost all of the actors in electricity distribution displayed in Table 5-4 also have operations in the construction sector. For example, Limak-Kolin-Cengiz consortium was also responsible for the construction of Istanbul Airport by the Black Sea coast from 2014 to 2019. Its tender worth was 22 billion Euros, making it the most expensive single investment project in Turkey until now.

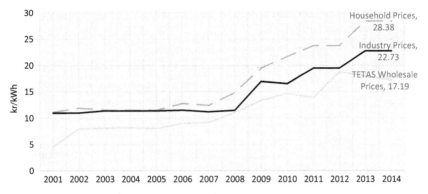

FIGURE 30   Domestic electricity prices according to sectors
            SOURCE: TEDAS

despite the high increase in gas costs. That was mostly for political reasons, as the government did not want to pass increased costs onto consumers before the general elections in 2007 (Atiyas et al., 2012; Bagdadioglu and Odyakmaz, 2009). In January 2008, electricity retail prices were raised by EMRA for the first time for 5 years, and prices almost doubled between 2008 and 2010 (Atiyas et al., 2012). As Figure 30 shows, after the transition to a cost-based pricing regulation in 2006, the electricity tariffs increased substantially both for industry and households.

Among the OECD countries, Turkey has the fourth highest electricity prices for industry, while household prices are only slightly higher than the OECD average. Prices reflect primary product costs such as fuel and natural gas, but also taxes. Taxes on electricity for industry have been traditionally very high in Turkey (18.5%) compared to the OECD average of about 9%, while for households, taxes amounted to 21.5% compared to the OECD average of 19% in during the 2010s.[28]

It should be noted that higher prices are expected to be observed in the beginning of a privatisation period when the initial costs are higher and are not necessarily problematic in and of themselves. What is important, however, is the distributional choice over the reflection of the initial costs on consumer prices in order to enable profitability for the private firms. This section examined some of the problematic features of the Turkish electricity system, such as losses and theft, which have existed prior to privatisation process. The

---

28   OECD.

emphasis is on the fact that although different actors were affected by these problems differentially, the main strategy of the state has always been the reflection of the additional costs on the end tariffs.

The next section will continue discussing the dynamics of the electricity industry more closely through the investigation of importance given to the construction of hydroelectric power plants since the early 2000s.

5   The Case of Hydroelectric Power Plants (HEPPs) in Turkey: How They Are Built and Financed

This section will explain how the privatisation process led to an increasing importance given to the hydroelectric power plant construction since 2003, which contributed to the broader restructuring of the economy that has been discussed in Chapter 4. As explained in Chapter 1, this book locates the devel opments in and around electricity within a broader understanding of capitalist economy with the tendency of increasing capital intensity of production along with the concentration of ownership and the countertendencies at the level of exchange which involve changes in competitiveness and technical change.

Electricity generation is a capital intensive sector with a 50% investment share in total expenditures in 2007 (Bhattacharyya, 2011).[29] Among different technologies, conventional hydropower technology has a higher capital intensity than gas and oil combined cycle thermal plants with a unit variable cost of $2.62 per unit of MWh as opposed to $14.7 fixed operating costs per one MWh (see Table 6).

This section will discuss how the increasing reliance on hydropower is the reflection of the tendency of the sector towards higher capital-intensity at the level of production. As discussed extensively, the Turkish economy was going through a period of restructuring in which new technology became more available facilitating the erosion of the traditional barriers between the sectors in the early 2000s. In that regard, increasing interest in energy production through hydro facilities brought the energy and construction sectors together, which has been made easier through liberalised energy markets. Big-scale investments in hydroelectric facilities increased substantially, which has been made by big conglomerates with joint engagement in both energy and construction sectors. On the other hand, the availability of cheaper new

---

29   The investment share in total expenditures is as high as 91% in coal industry in the same year (Bhattacharya, 2011).

TABLE 6   Fixed and variable cost characteristics of various electricity generation technologies

Technology	Size (MW)	Variable operating & management costs 2015 ($/MWh)	Fixed operating & management costs 2015 ($/MWh)
Coal with 30% carbon sequestration (CCS)	650	6.95	68.49
Conv gas/Oil comb cycle	702	3.42	10.76
Adv gas/Oil comb cycle (CC)	429	1.96	9.78
Adv CC with CCS	340	6.97	32.69
Conv comb turbine	100	3.42	17.12
Adv comb turbine	237	10.46	6.65
Fuel cells	10	44.21	0
Adv nuclear	2234	2.25	98.11
Distributed generation-base	2	7.98	17.94
Distributed generation-peak	1	7.98	17.94
Biomass	50	5.41	108.63
Geothermal	50	0	116.12
MSW landfill gas	50	9	403.97
*Conventional hydropower**	*500*	*2.62*	*14.7*
Wind	100	0	45.98
Wind offshore	400	0	76.1
Solar thermal	100	0	69.17
Photovoltaic	150	0	21.33

SOURCE: EIA (2017), ASSUMPTIONS TO THE ANNUAL ENERGY OUTLOOK

technology was also made profitable for small competitors (mostly operating in run-of-river hydro facilities) given the availability of cheap labour force in an environment of worsening labour conditions.

In 2003, the "Regulation on principles and procedures relating to the signing of water right agreements in the field of electricity production" was put into force, marking an increased importance given to the construction of hydro-electric power plants in Turkey. The Regulation determines the principles and procedures to be implemented by the General Directorate of State Hydraulic Works when signing a water right agreement with corporate bodies operating in hydroelectric energy production. The Regulation also covers the mandatory provisions to be included in such agreements and the principles and procedures of the application process, preparing and delivering feasibility reports, evaluation of the reports, and signing water rights agreements. HEPP licence applications are made to EMRA and licences are issued for 49 years.

Establishment and operation of HEPPs have been one of the main investment areas for big businesses that have already been operating in a variety of other sectors in Turkey after the legislation in 2003. In 2009, the tender process for 52 new small-scale run-of-river hydroelectric power plants has started. The tenders for the privatisation of existing hydro plants were completed by 2011. By 2012, out of 1547 new HEPP applications, 701 were accepted. According to EMRA numbers, 600 HEPP projects have been implemented, 250 of which are concentrated in the Black Sea region.[30] According to DSI reports HEPPs are economically profitable investments and they amortise themselves within 4-9 years. A survey carried out in Marmara region reveals that 45% of the investors have made profits more than they anticipated, while 35% of the investors stated their profit levels matched their expectations (Aktaş and Alioğlu, 2013). In its strategic plan for 2015-2019, The Ministry of Energy and Natural Resources anticipated 36% increase in total capacity of hydro plants through new construction, and 125% increase in total generation through increased efficiency by the end of 2019.[31] The economic rationale behind this strategy is explained as lower operational costs and decreased import dependency, as hydroelectric power units do not depend on fuel which is mostly imported.

The early policy papers by the World Bank (1966; 1957) discuss the choice between hydro and thermal power, which reveal a complicated cost structure. The policy papers state that although the hydro power plants require higher irreversible infrastructure investment in the beginning, they have lower operational costs due to the lack of fuel costs and also because they are relatively simpler in terms of technical design and operating and maintaining requirements once they are constructed (World Bank, 1966; 1957). Although a lot has changed reports were written, dam technology stays more or less similar in terms of its fundamental principles and the choice of inputs.

---

30   EMRA (Republic of Turkey, Energy Market Regulatory Board) website: www.emra.org.tr
31   Ministry of Energy and Natural Resources (2015) "2015-2019 Five Year Strategic Plan" (www.enerji.gov.tr).

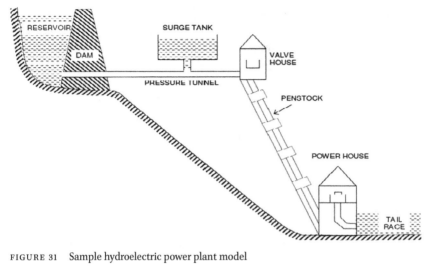

FIGURE 31   Sample hydroelectric power plant model
SOURCE: KHAN ET AL., 2012

The components of a hydroelectric power plant that require the bulk of
investment are the civil works that can be grouped into the following: headworks (extracts water from the river course), waterway (conveys water to
powerhouse), powerhouse (hosts the turbine and generator, converts water
first into mechanical and then into electrical energy) and tailrace (discharges
turbine water into a receiver, lake, river or ocean). Within headworks, there
is the dam and water intake. Waterway consists of headrace (takes the water
from headworks to forebay or the surge tank with minimum head losses),
forebay (connects the headrace with the penstock, preventing air efflux into
penstock), surge chamber (controls pressure in the penstock and headrace),
penstock (pressure pipes, conveys pressurized water from the surge tank to
the turbine). Powerhouse is the segment where the turbine and the generator convert the pressurised water energy into electrical energy (for example, see Figure 31). Tailrace discharges water coming from the powerhouse
(IFC, 2015).
    These units require steel, iron, plastics, concrete/rock or wood as primary
materials, depending on choice. In run-of-river type of hydro plants, where
there is not water storage hence the construction of a dam, the up-front costs
are significantly reduced, and the start-up investment is much smaller. Run-of-
river type hydro projects are classified as 'micro' or 'mini' sized hydroelectric
facilities, their power capacity ranging between 5 kW to 1 MW (as opposed to
small-sized facilities between 1 MW-10 MW, medium-sized facilities between 10
MW-100 MW and large-sized facilities between 100+ MW).

Regardless of the project scale, many hydropower cost components are assumed to be fixed as long as the project includes the construction of a dam. Therefore, the larger facilities have considerably lower costs in the long run. For example, a typical feasibility report might account for 1-2 per cent of total costs of a large hydro facility, while for a small hydro plant the study might account up to 5% (IFC, 2015).[32] In 2009, the run-of-river projects have constituted the largest portion of portfolio of the World Bank hydropower projects in both value and number of projects. In terms of value, run-of-river projects constituted 48% of all the World Bank investment projects in hydro power.[33]

As a crude rule of thumb, in order to cover the early costs that might span through a period of five to fifteen years, a more rapid expansion of the market will favour hydro which might explain its increasing importance in Turkey during a process of macroeconomic expansion which could provide the necessary demand for financing big infrastructural investment. The big infrastructural investments went hand-in-hand with smaller scale investments in run-of-river hydro facilities given the depressed wages which could allow for a high and low productivity investment structures to exist alongside each other.

As explained above, the bulk of investments in hydroelectric facilities require civil work. Therefore, the development of the energy sector in Turkey went hand-in-hand with the developments in the construction sector, which will be discussed more in detail in the following chapter on the political economy of the housing provision.

By 2017, the installed capacity for electricity generation in Turkey reached 79621 MW, 26919 MW of which is based on hydroelectric power plants. Among hydroelectric power plants, 19680 MW worth of power comes from hydroelectric plants with reservation (dam) and 7239 MW comes from hydroelectric plants with no reservation (run-of-the-river electricity). The hydroelectric plants' share in total installed capacity is 33.8%, while its contribution to total generation did not exceed the 20% level band between 2010 and 2015 (see Figure 32).

On the other hand, the investments made in hydroelectric power plants since 2003 increased steadily almost achieving 40% of all investments made in the energy sector in terms of total installed electricity power in 2016

---

32   For more on the cost structures and financing of hydro power facilities, see Head (2000).
33   World Bank Group Report (2009), Directions in Hydropower. Also see World Bank (2013), Toward a Sustainable Energy Future for All: Directions for the World Bank Group's Energy Sector.

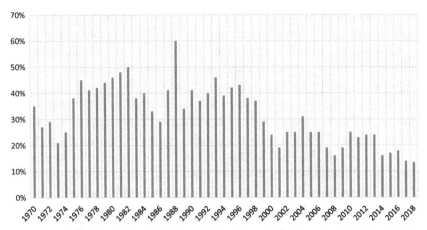

FIGURE 32   The share of electricity generated by HEPPs (including a dam) in Turkey (%)
SOURCE: TEIAS

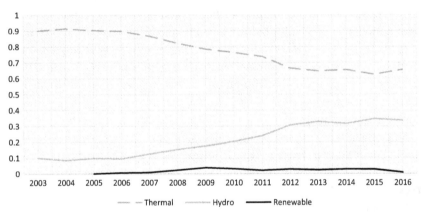

FIGURE 33   The shares of different types of electricity generation facilities in total industry
investments
SOURCE: TEIAS ELECTRICITY STATISTICS

(Figure 33).[34] In 2003, the investments made in thermal power plants contributed to the total installed power capacity by 3241.791 MW, while hydro

---

34   The comparison between different types of investments is made in terms of their contribution to the total installed capacity and not in terms of total value of investment, as there
are considerable cost differences between building thermal and hydro plants. Typically, the
cost of a hydro power plant is 100 to 200 per cent more than a thermal power station (Head,
2000). However, the cost of constructing hydro power plants is only higher in the beginning (if it involves the construction of a dam), and it has much lower long-term operating
costs (the absence of fuel cost being an important factor) (World Bank, 1957).

investments' contribution has stayed at 360.447 MW. From 2003 to 2016, the cumulative investments in hydro plants contributed by 14475.483 MW, growing much faster than investments made in thermal power, which contributed to total installed power by 28276.147 MW during the same time span.

However, despite making important contributions to higher capital-intensity, these investment projects created extensive implementation and financing problems. Among the biggest investment projects in the power sector were the Coruh Development Plan that included the construction of five big scale HEPPs in the Black Sea Region, Ilisu HEPP in the Southeast Region as well as the construction of the first nuclear power plant in Akkuyu, Mersin (Mediterranean Region), all of which were characterised by long-term financing and implementation issues.

Especially during the introduction of build and operate schemes concerning the already operating hydro units that have been under the ownership and management of DSI (State Hydraulic Works), serious financing problems occurred. Seven tenders, notably in Istanbul and Izmir in 2010 and 2011, have been annulled after winning bidders failed to provide the finance to back their high bidding prices (ESMAP, 2015). Second, many projects were implemented despite poor feasibility reports. Third, some of the projects had negative impacts on social life and environment, as their implementation resulted in mass population movements, destruction of agricultural land and permanent environmental damage.

Since the signing of water usage agreement in 2003, 65 lawsuits were filed due to environmental reasons by 2013. In 39 cases, the Council of State decided on the cancellation or suspension of the projects. A report prepared by TMMOB (The Union of Chambers of Engineers and Architects, The Chamber of Mechanical Engineers) in February 2015 reveals that among the projects that obtained licences from EMRA to invest in hydro infrastructure within the last five years, only 14% were able to pass the 70% completion rate (Turkyilmaz, 2015). In order to achieve the target installed capacity determined by the Ministry of Energy's 2015-2019 Strategy Plan, over 60% of the projects were to be completed by 2019, which was not successful. The next two sections will give some details about the financing processes of these big projects.

5.1   *Ilisu Dam: A HEPP Project*
Ilisu Dam is one of the biggest and most controversial HEPP Projects on the Tigris River in the southeast region of Turkey. Its initial design was made by DSI in 1954 as part of the South East Turkey Development Project (GAP). The controversy mostly arose from environmental and cultural concerns; since after its construction a UNESCO protected cultural heritage site, Hasankeyf, would

be flooded also affecting more than 50,000 people living in the area. Despite the government's continual efforts to seek international funding for the huge investment project, the construction process that has started in 2006 has been interrupted several times and it is still has not been completed. The first consortium supplied credit from German, Swiss and Austrian export credit agencies worth $610 million of the project, and the investment was to be completed with 100% foreign credit. In 2000, the British Government declined $236 million funding. In December 2008, the involved European firms suspended funds for the dam and gave Turkey a 180-day period to comply with over 150 international standards.[35] In June 2009, after failing to meet the standards, the European firms officially cut their funding.

Nevertheless, the government was determined to continue with the construction of the dam despite social and economic problems. Shortly after the announcement of the funding loss, the Minister of Environment Veysel Eroğlu said "Let me tell you this, these power plants will be built. No one can stop it. This is the decision of the state and the government."[36] Prime Minister Recep Tayyip Erdoğan stated that necessary funds would be supplied internally in case of loss of international funding. In December 2010, the Ministry of Environment announced that loans had been granted by three Turkish banks, and the project would continue with a new consortium led by Nurol Holding. On 15 July 2010, the Austrian member of the consortium, Andritz Hydro, lifted a temporary suspension on supplying parts to the project and announced it would provide the six 200 MW Francis turbines for the power plant worth $421 million dollars. Its investment is guaranteed by Treasury within the scope of 'Treasury Guaranteed Export Credits' scheme.

5.2   Coruh Development Plan

This plan has been one of the most important comprehensive energy projects in Turkey. The master plan for the project was completed in 1982, including the construction of 10 dams on Coruh River in the Northeast region in a cascade style. It consists of three groups of projects: lower Coruh (Muratli, Borcka and Deriner); middle Coruh (Yusufeli and Artvin); and upper Coruh (Laleli, Ispir, Gullubag, Aksu and Arkun). The preparation of the feasibility report which covers the package of projects was made by the Japan International Cooperation Agency (JICA) between 1986 and 1997. The plan was put into the 1997 Investment Programme by the Turkish government.

---

35   http://www.hydroworld.com/articles/2009/07/european-export-credit.html
36   http://www.radikal.com.tr/turkiye/ilisu-ya-yapilacak-ya-yapilacak-940770/

The individual projects in the Coruh Development Project are as follows. The Deriner HEPP was designed by the original Development Plan (Figure 34) as the highest arch dam in Turkey, of which construction began in 1998. Due to delays in funding, the reservoir began to fill in February 2012 and its power station was completed by February 2013. The consortium was led by ERG Insaat, it included four Swiss and one Russian firm. The construction of the Muratli and Borcka projects started in September 1999, which were undertaken by Turkish and Austrian companies on a full-financing basis with international finance. The consortium of Borcka Dam was led by Yuksel Insaat which has undertaken 15 HEPP projects in total. The construction of Artvin HEPP was started in 2011 by the Dogus Group and completed by the end of 2015. Four domestic banks have supplied long-term project investment credits worth $540 million. The Deriner project being the largest, the second largest project Yusufeli was considered to be the best economically and technically feasible option.

The feasibility study of Japan International Cooperation Agency was based mainly on construction costs and storage parameters (JICA, 1997). The design of the Yusufeli project as a rockfill dam has been calculated to create the highest benefit per cost unit (2.11). The original feasibility report included the cost of the dam and its complementary structures, relocation roads and transmission lines. Nevertheless, the costs of resettlement were excluded. The construction

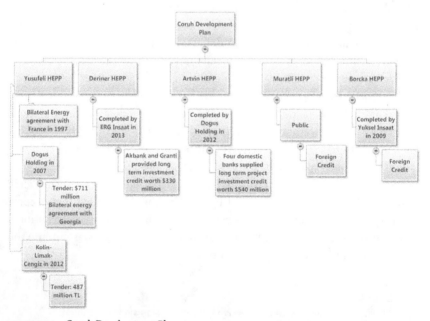

FIGURE 34   Coruh Development Plan

of Yusufeli Dam required the resettlement of the district of Yusufeli, including 19 villages of which the total population is over 15,000 people. In July 2005, a new relocation site for Yusufeli was selected by the Turkish government at Yansiticilar. The resettlement of Yusufeli project included the establishment of new houses by TOKI and the alignment of relocation roads (mainly the Artvin-Bayburt route) which added an additional cost of 427 million USD to the state budget which was not included in the original cost-benefit analysis.[37]

The first tender was made for the Yusufeli project in 1997 and an international consortium was established between Turkey and France under the Bilateral Energy Agreements between the governments. On February 19, 2002 a lawsuit was opened claiming that the project did not follow the tender rules, an environmental report was not prepared, and the social cost of the project would result in the decrease of public welfare. While the lawsuit was continuing, the consortium left the project because it could not supply the necessary international credit according to the framework determined by the Treasury. In 2005, the Council of State decided that the objections were legitimate and stopped the dam construction. In 2007, a change was made to Law No: 4283 and, thanks to the amendment that allowed the transfer of the investment to another consortium without changing the requirements, the project was given to Doğuş, ALSTOM (Switzerland, France, Brazil), Coyneet Bellier (France) and Dolsar (Turkey) for $711 million without announcing a new tender. The consortium obtained its licence from EMRA in 2010 and a bilateral energy agreement was signed with Georgia. Later the project was excluded from the scope of Bilateral Energy Agreements and on 13 August 2012, Kolin-Limak-Cengiz won the new tender for 487 million TRY.

The construction of Yusufeli HEPP was started in 2005 and it still remains under construction in 2020. The design of the project has changed almost entirely. In the original feasibility report, it was designed as a rockfill dam, but later its construction has been started as an arch dam without changing the feasibility report.

It is important to note that these changes were made to reduce costs, alongside transferring the cost of resettlement to the Treasury, including the cost of new road construction worth $250 million. It has been decided that the DSI 26. Regional Directorate was responsible for the expropriation process. In 2009, Turkish Court of Accounts prepared a report revealing that the construction of

---

37   Yusufeli Baraji ve HES "Yeniden Yerlesim Eylem Plani" http://www2.dsi.gov.tr/yusufeli/
      YusufeliProjesi-RevB-Temmuz2006-Bolumler/YusufeliProjesi-RevB-Temmuz2006-
      Bolum3.pdf

Yusufeli and Deriner HEPPs resulted in $461 million public loss due to failures in project management.[38]

The construction of Boyabat HEPP has started in 1998, but due to a lawsuit and failures in obtaining foreign credit, the project has stopped. Samsun 2. Administrative Court halted the project due to the absence of an Environmental Impact Assessment Report (EIA), but later it was decided that the project should be excluded from responsibility for providing one. In 2012, its construction was completed by the Dogus Group (34% partnership) with long-term project investments credits worth $750 million supplied from four domestic banks. The completion of the dam required extra lines for transmission worth 100 million TRY which were supposed to be financed by the investors according to original project, but half of the expenses were paid by the state transmission company, TEIAS.

Today, the biggest HEPP in the Plan, Deriner HEPP is responsible for 0.8% of all electricity produced in Turkey.[39] However, most of these big investment projects could not be completed due to financing and implementation problems. The involvement of the state was indispensable for ensuring the continuation of the projects, given its clear commitment to an establishment of a private energy sector.

It is argued in Chapter 4 that the economy has been going through a restructuring process after the 2001 crisis, increases in the investments in the electricity generation segment constituting an aspect of this. The privatisation experience, within this context, played a role in the changing of organisational relations within the sector at the level of productivity by allowing for loose price targets to be met by both big scale (higher productivity-higher investment) and small scale (lower productivity-lower investment) firms given the depressed level of wages during the period. At this level, the state's involvement mattered only to the extent that the industry stayed profitable enough for commercial relations to exist. The next section will discuss the role of finance within the sector to discuss these issues in greater detail.

6   What Role to the Finance?

This section is about the role of finance within the electricity sector in Turkey. In some core countries, the privatisation of utility sectors has been followed by

---

38   http://www.cumhuriyet.com.tr/haber/diger/191522/Hukumeti_korkutan_rapor.html
39   General Directorate of State Hydraulic Works website (www.dsi.org.tr).

an intense securitisation of assets and debts and the use of such instruments as financial investment tools. This was observed, for example, in water provision in the UK after privatisation of Ofwat in 1989 (Bayliss, 2014b). As argued before, the stable and regular revenue streams in the utilities sectors based on customers' bills contribute to this process. Nevertheless, this phenomenon corresponds to a certain level of development of the commercial relations within the economy and should be understood in relation to the specific depth and nature of the financial system in which such securitisation is taking place. As a financially shallow country, asset market creation within and around the electricity sector is relatively new and underdeveloped in Turkey.

In this context, finance plays a traditional role in the energy sector in Turkey, especially for the electricity generation segments where the most capital-intensive, long-term investments are made. The section will first discuss how the financial expansion contributed to the growth and stability of the sector through the increased availability of long-term project credits. Second, it discusses whether the tendencies outlined by the financialisation literature elaborated in Chapters 2 and 3 are observed.

As Figure 35 illustrates, the total domestic cash loans given to the energy sector has increased substantially from 678,250 thousand TRY (0.6 % of all domestic cash loans) in 2004 to 122,514,120 thousand TRY (6.38% of all domestic cash loans) by the end of first quarter of 2017.

CBRT and BRSA statistics show that although the energy sector receives substantial credit from abroad (Figure 36), it is still primarily financed by equity and by domestic bank credits in foreign exchange, making it vulnerable to foreign exchange shocks. The majority of domestic loans given to the electricity generation, natural gas and hydraulic resources industry were long term FX loans, as illustrated in Figure 37 and 38.[40]

Figure 37 shows that the total cash and non-cash loans given to the energy sector by the domestic banks in Turkey reached $36 billion by the end of 2014, with an annual nominal growth of $6.5 billion. Between 2013 and 2015, the energy sector in total (including the electricity, petroleum and coal and mining industries) used 12.8% of all domestic TRY and FX credits issued on average. It has the second largest share after the manufacturing sector, which has used 42.3% of all domestic TRY and FX credits.

The volume of the Turkish energy sector's long-term loans from abroad also increased substantially by 150 per cent in 12 years, reaching nearly $12.5

---

40   The majority of these long-term loans have medium-term with maturities varying two to
      ten years, as shown in Figure 38 under the classification "Medium- and Long-Term Cash
      Loans" according to BRSA.

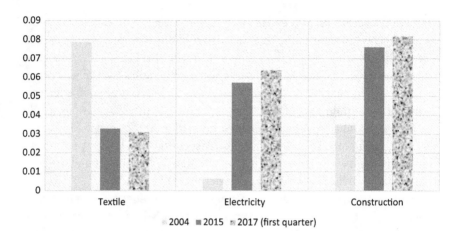

FIGURE 35   Comparison of textiles, electricity and construction industries according to their
shares in total domestic credits
SOURCE: BRSA

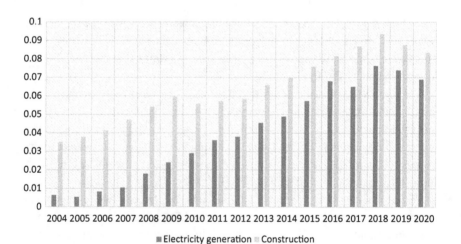

FIGURE 36   Credits given to electricity and construction industries (share of total credit)

billion compared to $5 billion in 2002, according to data released by the
Central Bank in 2015. As Figure 39 shows, the electricity and the natural
gas sector received $9.1 billion from abroad (as opposed to total domestic
bank loans amounting to $36 billion), doubling the amount in 2002, which
was $4.2 billion. Other industries within the energy sector that are closely
in relation with the electricity industry are petroleum and coal industry (production) and mining industry. Loans to the mining and quarrying

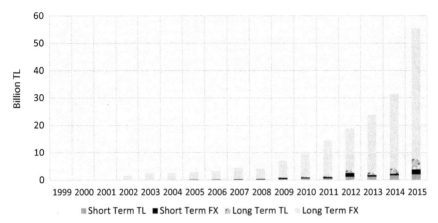

FIGURE 37   The breakdown of total cash loans given to electricity generation, natural gas and
hydraulic resources industry according to maturity and currency type
SOURCE: CBRT COMPANY ACCOUNTS

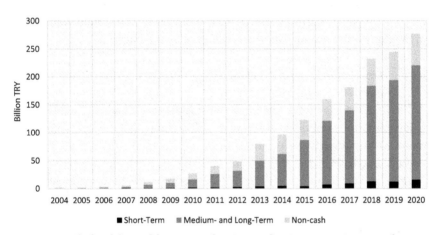

FIGURE 38   The breakdown of domestic credits given to electricity generation, natural gas
and hydraulic resources industry according to maturity and loan type
SOURCE: BRSA

industry increased four times climbing to $2.1 billion (domestic bank loans
were $6.5 billion) from 2002's volume of $439 million. Refined petroleum
products and the coal industry received $1.2 billion worth of loans from
abroad, as opposed to $292 million in 2002 (while the value of domestic
banks loans given to the refined petroleum products and the coal industry were $3.3 billion). Among total foreign credits given to the industry, the

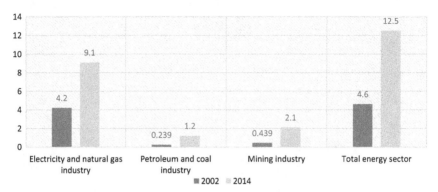

FIGURE 39   Total amount of foreign credits obtained by the energy sector (billion $)
            SOURCE: CBRT

energy sector has the second largest share by 25% after the manufacturing
sector's share of 68%.[41]

The next section will move on to a more detail investigation of financing
practices of electricity firms, by using the corporate financial statements listed
in the Company Accounts Statistics, collected by the CBRT.

6.1   Firm Financing: An Investigation of Corporate Balance Sheets in the Electricity Industry

As discussed in Chapter 2, one of the most well-established arguments of the
financialisation literature is the impacts of increasing shareholder value orientation which moves firms towards short-termist planning practices and a subsequent decrease in real investment (Orhangazi, 2008; Stockhammer, 2005;
Onaran, 2009). Crudely, in a financialised economy, the firms are expected to
rely less on external funding such as bank credits and hold less fixed assets as
opposed to liquid assets and overall have lower levels of gross capital formation (Levy-Orlik, 2012; Tori and Onaran, 2015). This section explores whether
these trends exist in the Turkish electricity generation industry, with the help
of balance sheet information of firms operating in the electricity, natural gas
and hydro resources industry collected by the Central Bank of Turkey between
the years 1999 and 2016.

It should be noted that the analysis is not to provide a perfect representation
of the sector based on a representative firm, but rather to discuss how balance

---

41   CBRT Statistics, Outstanding Loans Received from Abroad by the Private Sector, (www.
      tcmb.gov.tr).

sheet items in aggregate change over time to identify the financing trends within the industry. It has been argued before that the productive capacity within the electricity industry has increased since 2002, in line with the more general capital restructuring process, although the degree and nature of the commercial relations around electricity has changed substantially. This section supports the argument that financialisation trend underlines an increasing depth and extent of commercial relations within the economy which are not necessarily developing at the expense of industrial production.

The balance sheet data for electricity industry come from the financial statements of firms operating in these sectors as aggregated in CBRT Company Accounts statistics, which is the most systematically kept data available for sectoral level developments. Company Accounts statistics are prepared since 1990 by the CBRT based on the voluntary participation and cooperation of firms that send comprehensive and systematic financial statements. The data are released yearly, each year covering the previous three-years. The panel data for the national statistics are unbalanced as not all firms have participated in the survey throughout the 1999-2016 period. Therefore, it should be noted that this dataset cannot present a representative firm, but rather it gives a general picture of the industry with the entry and exit to the survey being compatible with the general development of the sector itself. The first Company Account Statistics report published in 1999 covers the period between 1996-1999, based on the financial statements of 7445 firms 4764 of which are joint stock corporations, 58 are holding companies, 2036 are limited liability corporations, 158 are general partnership corporations, 323 are individually-owned private companies and 84 are state-owned enterprises. The latest statistics, published in 2017 (covering the period between 2014-2016), covers 8721 firms.

Among total firms, the total number of electricity firms is 38 in 1996, while it increases to 319 in 2016 as shown in the Table 7 below. Among total firms operating within the electricity generation, natural gas and hydraulic resources industry, the majority are small and medium-sized.[42]

A closer look into the individual items of these firms' financial statements supports the argument that the industry is traditionally productive, based on bank-based long-term finance. Figure 40 shows that the long-term liabilities increased substantially especially since 2010, exceeding short-term liabilities and shareholders' equity dramatically. It should be noted that this period

---

42   According to the classification of CBRT, small enterprises employ up to 50 employees, while medium-sized enterprises employ between 50 and 500 employees. In the table, most of the firms within the SME category are actually small-sized. In 2016, only 44 firms among 297 SMEs operating within the electricity sector are medium-sized.

TABLE 7   CBRT company account statistics, electricity generation, natural gas and hydraulic resources industry

Years	Total # of firms	Total # of firms in electricity industry	SMEs (<500 employees)	Big (>500 employees)
1999	7445	38	31	7
2000	7604	38	32	6
2001	7537	42	35	7
2002	7729	44	38	6
2003	8007	45	40	5
2004	7507	50	42	8
2005	6667	40	35	5
2006	7103	46	40	6
2007	7308	47	41	6
2008	7249	53	47	6
2009	7352	132	123	9
2010	8080	176	169	7
2011	8576	179	165	14
2012	8925	234	213	21
2013	9468	260	240	20
2014	9115	257	239	18
2015	9341	307	291	16
2016	8721	319	297	22

Electricity industry consists of electricity generation and distribution, natural gas and hydraulic resources.

coincides with the completion of the privatisation process, reflecting the rapid growth of the sector.

Although shareholders' equity increased steadily until 2012, started decreasing after that year until 2015. Short-term liabilities, on the other hand, reached a peak in 2009, most probably due to the global contractionary pressures around that time.

The disaggregated shares of shareholders' equity and bank loans in total liabilities illustrated in Figures 41 and 42 suggest that while there is a cyclical trend in changes in shareholders' equity, the share of short-term and long-term bank loans started to increase steadily as a share of total liabilities after 2010.

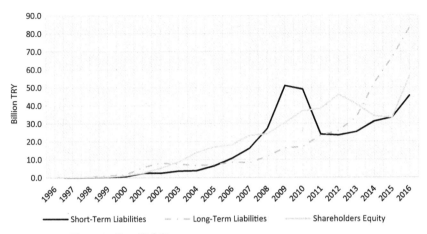

FIGURE 40   Electricity firms' liability structure

Figure 41 shows that between 1996 and 2002, the share of shareholders' equity hovered at around 40%, increased to over 50% after 2003. It dropped to almost 30% of all liabilities in 2009, only to reach a peak at 50% in 2012. Its share decreased to 25% of all liabilities in 2015.

Bank credits, on the other hand, had a share around 35% of total liabilities between 1996 and 2003, then showed a decreasing trend until 2010, as illustrated in Figure 42. After 2010, due to the increased availability of funds, which is discussed in previous chapter, the share of bank loans in total electricity firm liabilities started to increase up to over 40% in 2015. This suggests that firms rely on both internal and external funding resources, although the balance has changed in favour of external funding in the form of long-term foreign exchange credit since 2010-2012. This trend is in line with the increasing private sector indebtedness trend in the same period, as explained and discussed in Chapter 4.

Figure 43 shows that trade finance has improved significantly after 2004. The share of accounts payable increased to 30% of total liabilities from less than 10% in 1996 while accounts receivable followed a similar trend, although slightly higher than accounts payable.

When we look at the asset side, Figure 44 below shows that fixed assets constitute a significantly higher share until 2009. Between 1996 and 2005, the share of fixed assets in total assets has been higher than 70%. Although it has decreased after 2005 until 2009, it increased again to over 70% of all assets in 2016.

Figure 45 shows that the share of total financial assets in total assets has increased substantially between 2004-2010, then decreased after 2010 until

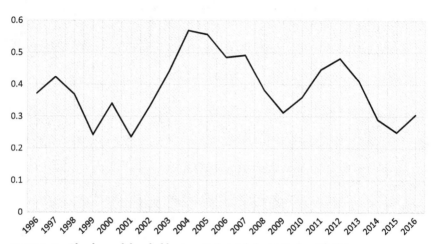

FIGURE 41   The share of shareholders' equity in total electricity firm liabilities

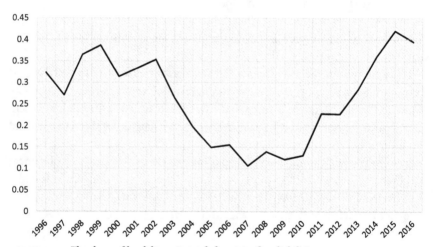

FIGURE 42   The share of bank loans in total electricity firm liabilities

2015. The increase was mostly due to the improvements in the trade accounts receivables as shown in Figure 43. As Figure 46 shows, the share of total cash, cash equivalents and marketable securities in total assets has decreased from an average of 9% between 1996 and 2001 to an average of 5% between 2002 and 2015. Figure 46 also illustrates that the share of marketable securities is negligibly low among total financial assets.

Although the total quantity of securities is negligible, the breakdown of securities in Figure 47 shows an important trend. It seems that the highest

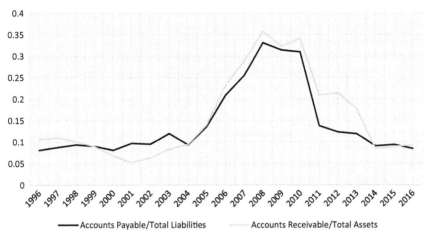

FIGURE 43   Electricity firms trade accounts

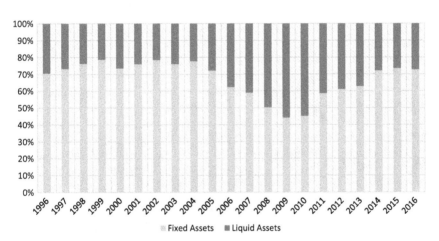

FIGURE 44   The composition of assets according to durability (electricity industry)

share of the public sector bonds and notes is replaced by a higher share of derivative items after 2008, signalling an early emergence of secondary circuit of capital within the industry.

Figure 48 shows a decreasing trend of the share of tangible fixed assets in total assets, which could be indicative of decreasing productive capacity at first glance. However, when the individual items within the total tangible fixed assets are examined, it can be seen that the decrease is mostly due to the decrease in land improvements item until 2001. On the other hand, the share

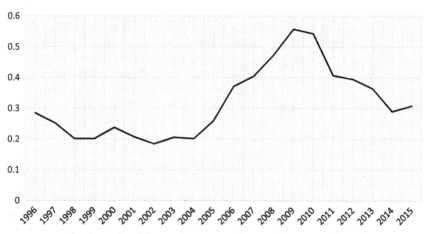

FIGURE 45   The share of total financial assets in total assets (electricity industry)
                        * Total financial assets consist of cash and cash equivalents, marketable
                        securities, trade receivables, other receivables and long-term financial
                        assets items.

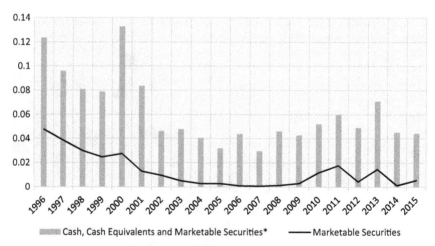

FIGURE 46   The share of total short-term financial assets in total assets (electricity industry)
                        * Trade Account Receivables item is not included in total short-term financial
                        assets item.

of the plant, machinery and equipment item increased dramatically from 13%
to 66%, from 2000 until 2006. As discussed, this period was the beginning
of the privatisation of generation process, when the new investors started to
operate in the industry. After 2006, the share of plant, machinery and equipment in total assets started to decrease down to 30% in 2015. This is line with

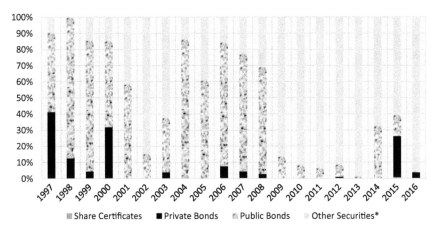

FIGURE 47   The breakdown of marketable securities item according to types (electricity industry)
* Other marketable securities include derivative contracts such as repurchase agreements, profit sharing or investment trust agreements.

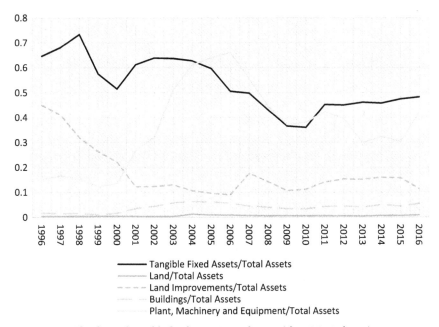

FIGURE 48   The share of tangible fixed assets in total assets (electricity industry)

the pattern of technical progress in the industry, considering that once the initial investments are made, the firms can operate for a long period without requiring new physical investment.

As discussed previously and shown in this section, there were increases in the industrial capacity within the Turkish electricity industry based on a heavy dependence upon long-term bank credits with no evident short-termism in investment practices. Alongside, the market establishment process following the privatisation also enabled the secondary circuits of capital to emerge within the industry. The next section will conclude the chapter by summarising its findings and contributions.

7   Conclusion

This chapter provided a political economy of electricity provision in Turkey since the 1980s. Its first aim was to reflect how the industry has changed through time, with respect to the increasing depth and scope of commercial relations in and around electricity as a wage good. The second aim was to show how these relations, existing along a continuum, could be conducive to the emergence of secondary circuit of capital given the ease of securitisation when there are secure revenue streams based on customer bills.

There is a wide literature on both privatisation and financialisation in economics and human geography with different analytical focus and emphasis. While the discussions on privatisation in the economics discipline changed through time with respect to the impacts of different modes of regulation practices on prices/revenues/investment, recent discussions in human geography focused upon the impacts of 'neoliberalisation' or 'financialisation' on natural resources and the incompatibility of the delivery of human needs with a profit motive. Distinguishing financialisation as such from the increasing degree of market relations within these industries, this chapter provides an interdisciplinary approach for understanding these relations, connecting the increasing marketisation taking place in Turkish electricity industry to the developments taking place in core economies outlined by the financialisation literature, surveyed in Chapter 2.

It suggests that the financialisation process initially involves the extension of commodity relations to a broader base of the population. This is discussed in the context of privatisation process. At a later stage, regular payments from this base contribute to the emergence of a secondary circuit of capital through securitisation of stable revenue streams. This aspect is discussed with the help of electricity industry balance sheets provided by Company Account Statistics by the Central Bank of Turkey between the years 1999-2016. In Turkey, although the securitisation has so far stayed negligible, the process suggested a direction towards increasing commodification, facilitated by the gradual privatisation experience since the early 1980s. These developments went hand-in-hand with the increases in long-term infrastructural investment, especially in traditional hydropower, financed by domestic banks in foreign exchange, indicating that market-based provision might not necessarily be associated with short-termism in investment.

The privatisation of electricity in Turkey presents a mixed picture to interpret. It has been negative in terms of its distributional impacts, given the initial costs were directly reflected on the consumer bills while there were substantial incentives provided for the private sector to operate in the industry. During the transition period from 2001 until 2006, the state-owned wholesale company, TETAS, bought all electricity produced from newly established privately-owned generation companies at high initial costs. TETAS had to combine expensive electricity it bought from private producers with cheaper electricity from public producers in order to sell it to the market at a uniform price. This was reflected, especially for industry, as low levels of competition in the industry and increased end-prices which are among the highest in Europe as emphasised by Atiyas et al. (2012) and Guney (2005).

Although this should be accepted as an expected result of early process of an industrial expansion, it was emphasised that the regulatory choices were made to reflect the additional costs on end prices. For example, the price equalisation mechanism adopted in 2008 to address regional supply-demand imbalances and high loss-theft ratios was designed in a way that while the costs of losses and theft were directly reflected on consumer retail prices, any improvements beyond set targets for losses and theft could be appropriated by the private firms.

Following the privatisation, some structural problems of the industry such as high loss-theft ratios persisted. In 2014, 75% of total electricity sold by the company responsible for the electricity distribution on the southeast region (Dicle EDAS) could not reach final consumers. That is assumed to arise partly from the political conflict in the southeast and east regions and partly from the private companies' investment choices. Although the initial privatisation plan authorised the Ministry of Energy to choose the location of power plant investments, in the actual implementation the private firms were given the freedom to choose their geographical areas of activities which resulted in a supply-demand mismatch across regions. In order to transfer electricity from excess supply to excess demand regions, transmission lines had to be lengthened which contributed to transmission losses and extracted extra funding from the public budget.

Other problems concerning the privatisation were malpractice and financing problems. The promotion of hydropower strategy was challenged by serious financing problems, especially after the withdrawal of international finance institutions due to many projects' poor feasibility and environmental reports. In particular, the implementation of the biggest projects, such as the Ilisu, Yusufeli and Deriner dams, required substantial transfers from the public budget to be completed.

Apart from laying out these problems, the chapter also summarised the positive aspects of privatisation. The first was to show that irrespective of the degree of external support by the state, the market creation was successful in facilitating greater productive investment within the industry. In line with the general restructuring process from labour-intensive to capital-intensive sectors, as discussed in Chapter 4, the productive capacities of the capital-intensive energy sector grew dramatically since the early 2000s. This was visible in the long-term nature of the balance sheets of the firms operating within the sector and the push given to the construction of hydroelectric power plants, which are usually favored during the initial expansion phase of the industry.

Moreover, it was argued theoretically that during a process of intensified reorganisation, the traditional boundaries between the sectors disappear with the impact of technical development. This is reflective of and contributes to the process of concentration of capital in a structure in which while fewer firms engage in more technologically advanced (higher productivity) investments, small firms could compete only given the availability of cheap labour force.

This theoretical tendency was observed in the establishment of close links between the electricity and construction firms in Turkey, facilitated through the construction of big-scale HEPPs across the country. While profitability was maintained for the big firms with the help of the state, small-sized firms could continue operating due to low costs in the construction sector based on low wages and subcontracting practices, which will be discussed in the next chapter.

CHAPTER 6

The Political Economy of Housing Provision in Turkey

1 Introduction

This chapter will provide a political economy of housing provision in Turkey since the 1980s, through investigating both production and consumption dynamics and shedding light on how the sector evolves as a whole. On the basis of the theoretical premises explained before and adopted in the previous chapter on electricity provision, it serves the purposes of this book in two ways. The first is to discuss how the organisational relations in and around housing have changed through time along an increasing scope and depth of commodity relations, without necessarily indicating a withdrawal of the state, similar to the case of electricity. As explained, this concerns in part how labour power is reproduced materially as a use value. Second, it discusses how these relations evolve with respect to the increasing presence of finance in general and interest-bearing capital in particular, further contributing to a financialised accumulation regime through expanding the base for the realisation of circuits of interest-bearing capital created elsewhere, and/or enabling the creation of new circuits through relative ease of securitisation where there are regular payments (i.e., mortgage securitisation). In the context of housing, the continuation of the circuits through revenue generation is deeply connected to the intervention of landed property as a specific commodity form and the social relations that determine the contribution of this commodity form to revenue generation processes as a factor of production.

Financialisation has probably been discussed most extensively in the context of housing, especially with respect to the second aspect mentioned above, following the unfolding of the global financial crisis in 2008 (Aalbers and Christophers, 2014; Dymski, 2010, 2009a, 2009b; Montgomerie and Büdenbender, 2015; Wray, 2008). Mostly, the studies emphasised how the increasing dependence on owner-occupation resulted in excess housing demand with certain repercussions on the macro-determinants of the economy. For example, as discussed in Chapter 2, Toporowski (2009) argued that the owner-occupation created opportunities for asset wealth gains which was ultimately conducive to speculation through borrowing money against rising housing prices and paying the debt when the assets are sold at a higher price. Similarly, from a critical political economy perspective, Montgomerie and Budenbender (2015) emphasise how asset-based welfare systems contributed to increasing household indebtedness and inequality through favouring a minority who could buy property and benefit from welfare gains at the expense of the excluded groups.

Wray (2008, pp. 52–52) explains the establishment of a speculative structure in the housing markets prior to the 2008 mortgage crisis as follows:

> Developers, real estate agents, and appraisers worked together to maximize home prices. Often the developer worked directly with a mortgage broker so that sufficient funding for inflated prices would be forthcoming; this also required complicity of appraisers to ensure home prices would warrant the mortgage foisted on the borrower. The broker also added the first set of enhancements, such as early-payment penalties. Mortgages were then passed along to investment banks that would add further enhancements, such as those provided by credit agencies and insurers. "Trash" was thereby transformed into highly rated securities available for purchase by investors such as pension funds. It was the perfect system to fuel rising home prices, ever-increasing debt ratios, and deteriorating portfolios of unsuspecting investors: the incentives of developers, home sellers, and real estate agents were oriented to maximizing home prices.

It was argued that the incentives to obtain capital gains become conducive to structural instability along the lines of Minsky's hypothesis, triggered by the allocation of debt-associated risks to the balance sheets of the secondary financial institutions such as structured investment vehicles as well as households, which operate in fundamentally different ways from banks (Dymski, 2010; Wray, 2008). However, this mechanism is tightly related to the overall depth of the financial markets in an economy, as Ponzi-financing necessarily follows the shift of the associated risks from the balance sheets of banks to intermediary financial institutions and consumers, which reduces banks' incentives to take action against risky lending (Dymski, 2010; Nesvetailova and Palan, 2013; Tavasci and Toporowski, 2010; Wray, 2008). Cerutti et al. (2015), Bernanke and Gertler (2000) and Borio and Drehmann (2009) also underline that a systemic study of housing markets becomes only relevant for countries where financial and asset markets are well developed and can reflect the underlying inflationary forces, for example in the UK, Netherlands and Switzerland, where mortgage debts reached up to over 80% of GDP immediately after the global financial crisis in 2008.

On the other hand, when the Mortgage Law was passed in Turkey in 2007, the share of mortgages in total GDP did not even reach 1% and it does not exceed 7% by 2020.[1] Instead of suggesting that the housing markets are therefore irrelevant for the Turkish economy, this book shifts the analytical focus and argues that the changes in the housing markets are reflective of the deeper tendency towards commodification of wage goods globally, which can be traced within the housing markets themselves, and not on their possible impacts on the aggregate economy.

As Ball (1983) argued almost three decades ago, the lack of emphasis on the structural dynamics of the housing markets was already present even within the housing studies. By focusing primarily on the consumption dynamics, the studies approached the issue as a primarily distributional one, without placing much emphasis on the production of housing as a commodity with unique characteristics. Dymski (2009a, 2009b) argued the 2008 financial crisis showed that there is also a unique nature of housing due to its geographical aspects. Because the housing market is characterised by unchanging geographical constraints, the process of asset generation is based on a highly risky spatial segmentation through the expansion of mortgage issuance to previously excluded areas, although this was disguised by an apparently homogenous global process of risk distribution prior to the crisis. According to Dymski (2009a, 2009b), the spatial location, informed by each area's historical and institutional background, played an important role in the generation of the crisis, as risk is after all determined by who has access to which financial services at what price, despite being homogenously distributed in return. Similarly, within the discipline of human geography, Harvey (2012, 2003) also emphasised the spatial aspects of housing and argued that the unchanging nature of the location determined the necessary monopoly conditions for centralisation of capital and gave way to a specific accumulation pattern named as 'accumulation by dispossession'.

This chapter claims that in addition to its unique geographical characteristics, the housing system is also unique in its production methods, which facilitates speculation hence disruptive asset price appreciations as a result. It is argued that as the housebuilding industry is structurally unable to move towards high economies of scale due to easy entry and exit conditions and high cyclicality. As a result, combining activities with the land development industry with more capital-intensive characteristics becomes the primary method for sustaining profitability for the housebuilding firms. However, as

---

1 The Banks Association of Turkey (BAT) www.tbb.org.tr

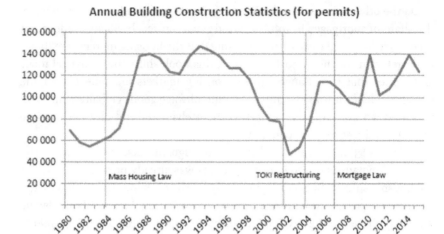

FIGURE 49   Annual building construction permits issued in Turkey
             SOURCE: TURKSTAT

long as landowners hold a monopolistic power over their supply due to the specific "unchanging" nature of land, this can result in output restrictions for the housing industry with an upward pressure on prices (Ball, 2006, 1983).

In Turkey, such disruption was prevented through an equivalent increase in supply due to state ownership in the land markets and strong sectoral inter-linkages with the energy sector. As a result, the housing system developed in a way that, despite substantial increases in speculative activities and intensi-fied securitisation, price appreciations were not observed to a universal extent and contained within the housing market. Figure 49 demonstrates that there was a construction boom in the Turkish housebuilding industry, following the reorganisation of a state institution named TOKI (Housing Development Administration) in 2004. This was a significant turning point, as the reorgani-sation made TOKI the single biggest actor in the land market by authorising it to use, plan and sell public land which constitutes 16-17% of land available for use in Turkey.

This chapter will explain how the historical and institutional development of the housebuilding industry enabled this supply boom, which contributed to stability of the sector alongside the joint investments with the energy sector.

Section 2 will outline the productive characteristics of the housing markets by using the example of Britain in order to locate the Turkish case in a theo-retical and comparative context. Section 3 will introduce Marx's agricultural theory of rent in order to further explain the revenue generation mechanisms within the housing industry. Building upon these, Section 4 will introduce the Turkish case by providing a historical account for the development of the industry, mostly characterised by the state-ownership of land and with strong links to the energy sector which prevented asset price appreciations despite the existence of a speculative structure. Section 5 provides an empirical investigation of the financial statements of the firms operating in the industry to give more detail on their productive and financing characteristics. Section 6 will discuss how housing is consumed as a commodity. Finally, Section 7 will conclude by summarising the findings.

2 Production Matters in a Comparative Context: Housing Provision in Britain

This section discusses the British housing system, to lay out some of the ways in which housing markets function with respect to their structural productive characteristics, and also later to introduce the developments in Turkey in a comparative context. It draws exclusively upon the work of Robertson (2014) and Michael Ball, who studied British housing markets extensively. The emphasis being upon his earlier studies on 'structures of provision', Ball's studies are used in this section to provide the theoretical aspects of housing production in general, such as cyclicality, low economies of scale and high production costs, and the empirical aspects of the British housing system in particular, such as land monopolisation and output restrictions. As Ball (2003, 2006) uses the productive characteristics to explain the limited housing supply in Britain especially since the 1970s, the Turkish case will be later introduced to claim how the same productive characteristics might lead to a housing supply boom given the availability of land. Robertson's (2014) study on British housing markets is introduced, in order to explain how this might relate to an understanding of Marxian theory of rent.

In one of his more recent studies, Ball (2003) although a great variety is observed in different institutional structures across countries, the prime functional aspects of housing development are largely explained by the economic factors such as production characteristics and land supply. The typical production characteristics of the housing industry can be summarised as follows. Usually, labour-intensive techniques prevail in an industry structure consisting of a large number of small firms. The labour-intensive methods make firms 'flexible' to supply shocks. Together with high competition and the relative ease of entry and exit into and out of the industry, these production aspects give the industry a strongly cyclical characteristic with low economies of scale, possibly explaining the small size of firms. Profitability is mostly tied to supply constraints, with long-run risk-adjusted returns closely reflecting the improvements in the marginal costs of inputs. Construction inputs play a great role in determining the input costs and backward linkages, for example while timber-rich countries in North America and Scandinavia developed industries with timber-framing systems and extensively use pre-assembled internal house fittings, the Netherlands and France rely more on concrete off-site house structures, which determined their backward linkages of the sector accordingly (Ball, 1983).

While the cyclical effects push the mark-ups during the boom and lower them during the busts, technological advancement towards capital-intensive structures is prevented through easy entry and exit, as long as there are suppliers who are willing to cut prices during the periods of busts further contributing to the cyclical nature of demand. During the 1950s and the 1970s, the extensive social housing building in Europe increased housing demand and smoothed output fluctuations, resulting in the emergence of large housing suppliers. Nevertheless, scale economies stayed at low levels and the large suppliers disappeared as soon as public funding ceased (Ball, 2003). Thus, while in many industries international differences in macroeconomic cycles have encouraged firms to globalise, this has not occurred in housebuilding because of the low scale economies and the importance of local information in land and housing markets. As a result, the cycles of housing investment in each country have tended not to coincide (Ball and Wood, 1999). In his later studies, Ball (2006, 2003) emphasises that it is such cyclicality and low scale economies (together with the regulation principles, land planning and labour practices) that can to a large extent create flexibility in stock adjustment practices and explain the great variety of institutional settings across countries despite the highly competitive characteristic of the industry.

Here, land planning practices require special emphasis as planning regulations have significant impacts on the overall housing supply (Ball, 2011, 1999). This is mostly because in contrast to the labour-intensive characteristics of the housebuilding industry described above, land development and planning require substantial capital investment, therefore the returns in the land development industry should be correspondingly higher in order to compensate for costs and uncertainty. Moreover, these initial investments tend to be risky due to the commodity (-form) characteristics of land. The specific, 'unchanging' location of land makes the land plots imperfect substitutes for each other and ties the investments to the location of particular land plots, for which the demand depends upon a wide range of determinants incorporating non-market elements, and making capital investments on land riskier, especially in the urban context. The theoretical significance of the particular characteristics of land markets will be discussed in greater detail in the next section on the theory of rent.

The crucial point is that the differences in relative risks and returns in these two markets create a simple division between land planning and housebuilding industries, characterised by riskier and higher capital investments in the former and lower returns, lower risks and more competition in the latter (Ball, 2003, 1983). This simple division is, however, altered significantly when land supply is restricted, as in the case of Britain. When landowners hold significant market power and are not in a position to be 'forced' by the market to sell their properties, housebuilders who have their own land banks gain advantage in terms of determining the timing of land development to be followed by housing construction and then sell it at a time of boom (Ball, 1983). This gives rise to a "speculative" housing market structure with output-restricting characteristics, which has been a defining aspect of the British housing market especially since the 1970s. When this speculative structure was established in Britain in the 1970s, output restriction was so severe that new construction constituted only 14% of all houses sold in the market in 1978 (Ball, 1983, p. 50). Ball (1983, pp. 50-51) explains the speculative formation as follows:

> In speculative building, the profit-making process is different and in it development profit predominates. Development profit is achieved by a judicious purchase of land and conceiving of the appropriate residential scheme for the site. The predominant risks to assess are the marketability of houses built on a site, the price paid for the land, the timing of the development, and the overall scale of housebuilding appropriate for the firm's resources in the context of the current state of the market. This is a very different management function from that of the contractor.

Ball (1983) argues that the main reason for the establishment of a speculative industry was the centralisation of the ownership of land in the hands of few large housebuilders with access to their own land banks, especially after a bust of the market in 1973. During market upswings, acquiring land banks gives advantages to large firms, as it is not possible to respond to the rapid fluctuations in the demand through an expansion of output without a large selection of land plots. However, as the holders of residential land sites develop a degree of monopoly power through the land they own, which functions as a debt-free wealth source during housing market upswings, firms find it cheaper and quicker to acquire land by taking over another builder and its land bank than through direct purchase in the land market itself, which reinforces centralisation (Ball, 1983.

Once the centralised structure is established, it reinforces itself through output restricting decisions of large owners during busts, which places serious constraints for smaller firms in terms of increasing costs, as observed in a bust in the British market in 1973. In other words, when the landowners have a certain degree of control over the timing of their market activities, speculative housebuilders with sufficient land banks gain advantage over other firms, in terms of responding appropriately to the fluctuations of the market. Once a speculative formation occurs, it reinforces itself through obstructing cost decreases.

The productive characteristics of speculative building are found to be significantly different than 'productive' housebuilding. First of all, the turnover of capital is much longer as the capital for development has to be invested in land many years in advance of construction. Second, a larger quantity of capital has to be sunk into infrastructure, with no revenues flowing until houses are built and sold. Last but not least, in addition to the structural characteristics of land development as an industry, planning and development in Britain is empirically a very lengthy and bureaucratic experience with significant delays. In an empirical study based on a sample of 180 construction sites, Ball (2011, p. 358) finds that despite the government data suggesting that almost 70 per cent of all major planning application are processed within thirteen weeks, only 40 per cent of the sample was approved on the first application and the average time of processing after the approval was substantially higher, 41% of the sites taking over a year, 17% taking over 100 weeks and 6% over 150 weeks.

As a result, building costs increase substantially, and Ball (1983, p. 18) finds the origins of many periods of rapid housing price inflation as a consequence of the attempts of housebuilders to raise their profits and to minimise the conversion of land development gain into land rent appropriated by others. He uses a global construction cost index for Cost of New Construction (CNC), based on changes in wages, the price of materials and labour, the ratios in which those materials are used, productivity in the building process and the size of building firms' mark-ups, to show that there were not cost improvements in the speculative housing markets (1983, p. 122). A fixed bundle of labour and materials was assumed and price variations for each component of the bundle fed into the index with periodic crude adjustments made for changes in productivity, overheads and profits. He finds that there were no cost improvements, simply because productivity improvements were almost non-existent in speculative housebuilding. This was also empirically observable in the fact that while in the mid-1950s the average house took eight months to build, it took twenty months in the 1980s due to much higher costs. In his own words (1983, p. 100):

The sharp rise in construction costs explains why the output of new owner-occupied housing has slumped so dramatically over the past fifteen years [...] Large increases in house prices are now needed to induce any substantial new housing output. The inter-linkage between rising housing prices, escalating building costs and declining housebuilding is a key indication of a growing crisis in the present structure of owner-occupied housing provision. All three elements feed off each other. Cost increases lower the profitability of house building so housebuilders cut back on their output; over time that increases the shortage of housing which forces up prices; and from the demand side the instability of demand creates production problems for housebuilding which gradually pushes up building costs. There is no single cause for these factors; the problem is a structural one inherent in the present form of owner-occupied provision.

Overall, Ball's analysis of the housing system emphasises that the most crucial aspects which move the industries towards technical change, which are first, standardisation and continuity of production and second, economies of scale, are structurally absent in the housebuilding industry in Britain, which might explain the housing crisis that still prevails today.

Robertson (2014), on the other hand, argues that although the speculative housebuilding emerged in Britain due to the structural inability of the industry to move towards economies of scale, this does not lead to the conclusion that the output restriction is the necessary outcome of the speculative process. In a PhD study, Robertson (2014) finds that although the contemporary housing system in Britain continues to preserve its output-restricting character, this should be interpreted as a contingent development. It is striking that between 2000 and 2007, when housing prices reached a peak before the crisis, while housing prices and mortgage credits increased by 173% and 182% respectively, housing completions only increased by 17% in Britain (Robertson, 2014). Immediately after the crisis, by early 2010, house prices had recovered to roughly 11% below their previous peak and have since begun to rise again.

Robertson (2014) argues that the critical aspect of that development has been the scarcity of land, which is strictly contingent. The impact of land scarcity on price determination could be observed directly and simply in the regional mismatch of prices: while the average house price in London was £362,699 in early 2014, it was £119,702 in the North of England (Robertson, 2014). Because housing production was low and outer city expansion was limited due to restricted land availability, monopoly rent was generated by the excess of demand in the metropolitan areas, contributing to overall surplus to be appropriated both in the form of profits for the housebuilders, as well as capital gains for the consumers.

For producers, the channel for rent appropriation is mercantile capital activities such as speculative housing trading based on potential profit expectations from land price increases. For consumers, appropriation from monopoly rent takes the form of capital gains incorporated into sales prices or future rental streams. Indirectly, monopoly rent increases also contributes to aggregate capital gains from secondary markets by generating extra sources of revenue within the sector. According to Robertson (2014), these developments are directly related to the incorporation of land at the level of production, before revenues are distributed in the form of profits, wages and rent. The next section will introduce Marx's theory of agricultural rent in order to discuss these issues in greater theoretical detail.

3   Production upon Landed Property: Marx's Agricultural Rent Theory

This section provides a theoretical discussion of Marx's agricultural rent theory. As many have questioned, including Ball (1980), whether rent is a theoretically distinguishable category from profits has been subject to debate since Jevons suggested that Ricardo's intensive margin theory offered a general theory of price. As a theoretical category, rent has been an exclusive product of political economy, as in neoclassical theory land is not treated differently than any other fixed capital input. The theoretical framework adopted in this chapter relies heavily upon the interpretation of Marxian rent developed by Fine (1982b, 1980, 1979) including the responses to the concerns raised by Ball (1980).[2] According to that interpretation, surplus generation and distribution mechanisms in agriculture are different from those of industry which might impede (or contribute to) the accumulation of capital through land. This has implications for capital restructuring through housing as it is strictly tied to land.

The classical Ricardian interpretation of rent is based on the assumption that the hierarchy in land fertility is given and is 'independent of capital' because of the indestructibility of land as a fixed capital input (Kurz, 1978; Fine, 1982). In Marx, however, rent is a separate category not because land has special characteristics as a means of production, although such characteristics further determine the nature of production with landed property, but because

---

2   For more details within the context of an extensive debate: see Fine (1979), Ball (1980), Fine (1980). For a neo-Ricardian partial equilibrium in a multi-sectoral model interpretation, see Kurz (1978). For a neoclassical critique of the category of rent, see Samuelson (1992).

it is extracted by landlords at the expense of industrial capitalists. It should be noted that this process does not refer to a "cause of the creation of such surplus profit, but is the cause of its transformation into the form of ground-rent" (cited in Fine, 1986, p. 123).

From that perspective, the source of rent is the historical development of agricultural production within the capitalist economy that tended to rest upon land commodification through private ownership as one of the prerequisites for capitalist production in agriculture. Once capitalist production in agriculture emerges, rent relations reproduce themselves through the class division between landowners and industrial capitalists:

> [T]he form of the landed property which we shall consider is a specifically historical one, a form transformed through the influence of capital and of the capitalist mode of production, either of feudal landownership, or of small-peasant agriculture as a means of livelihood, in which the possession of the land and the soil constitutes one of the prerequisites of production for the direct producer, and in which his ownership of land appears as the most advantageous condition for the prosperity of his mode of production.
>
> MARX, cited in FINE, 1986, pp. 121-122

In that sense, Marx's starting point for theorising rent is its historical nature and his emphasis is on the implications of such a historically determined category for capitalist accumulation compared to Ricardo's emphasis on rent as a technical category. In other words, Marxian rent is not a theory of soil but of relations of production attached to soil. Nevertheless, in addition to historical grounding, Marx also acknowledges land as a means of production with some peculiar characteristics in the sense that it cannot be capitalistically reproduced, and some of the material properties that go into production of agricultural goods (such as fertility and location) are naturally conditioned and cannot be readily replicated elsewhere. Together with the social relations of landed property in capitalism, the relatively permanent technical properties of land have an impact upon both the determination of market values and prices of production and the four different categories of rent, as listed below. These distinct categories arise from unique intra- and inter-sectoral competition dynamics at different stages of accumulation (Fine, 1979):[3]

---

3   Please note that these distinctions are made for expositional purposes to explain the distinction of AR from simple monopoly price conditions at the level of entry, and DRI and DRII exist independently of these qualifications.

1) Differential Rent I (DRI): Extensive rent, arises from equal applications of capital to lands of different quality (in terms of fertility, location),

2) Differential Rent II (DRII): Intensity rent, arises from different applications of capital to lands of same quality,

3) Absolute Rent (AR): Arises from the barrier of landed property to inter-sectoral competition, depending exclusively upon the flow of capital onto new lands.

During the normal course of capitalist production, market values are established through simultaneous determination of average productivity (determined through intra-sectoral competition) and normal size of capital invested (determined through inter-sectoral competition). In agricultural production however, because each land has its own individual characteristics, it is not possible to determine simultaneously both average productivity and normal size of capital. Because a payment must be made to the landowner at all times, agricultural capitalists must be able to create surplus value which might explain why even the worst land in cultivation is able to appropriate surplus in the form of rent.

According to Ricardian intensive margin theory, the existence of rent payments gives rise to an undifferentiated technical rent category arising from the difference between productivity of different lands and that of marginal investment. In the analyses of Marx, however, it is well known that it is the average production technique that determines the market values, and not the marginal unit of investment. The procedure for determining the average production technique, however, is distinct from the averaging of most and least favourable techniques, and rather it refers to the sufficiently weighty technique in the industry. In the context of agricultural rent, the historical underpinnings for determining the most common production technique are revealed, as it is not possible to follow the same procedure due to the intervention of landed property that obstructs the simultaneous determination of average production technique (and size of the capital) in the industry.

The process of accumulation in agriculture can be explained as follows. In abstract, producers can extract surplus either through application of equal size of capital to lands of different quality, which gives rise to the deduction in the surplus in the form of DRI, or through application of different sizes of capital to lands of same quality, which gives rise to DRII. As mentioned before, these two categories are not simply empirically additive but qualitatively different, because DRII never exists in its pure form, but always exists given the basis of DRI. Because of the indestructible nature of the soil, technical improvements that alter the normal size of capital on a given land, can *also* improve the quality of land, destroying the equal quality assumption. In other words, if more capital giving rise to DRII improves land quality permanently, it is also a differential improvement, determining new conditions for DRI.[4] Nevertheless, the equal quality assumption is made to qualitatively determine the source of a different category of rent that is necessarily a product of improved production conditions. Because DRII also permanently alters DRI, producers' avoidance of DRII would mean they would prefer investing extensively rather than intensively. As a result, this would reduce the incentives for technical change. In other words, the existence of DRI and DRII does not only imply a transfer of the surplus produced to landlords in the form of rent, but also a distortion in the formation of market value (Fine and Saad-Filho, 2010).

The distinct categories of differential rent correspond to differences in the mechanism of surplus generation in relation to technical properties of land. If DRII impedes, or modifies, the pace of accumulation, or the technical progress in agriculture, the organic composition of capital (OCC) in agriculture would be systematically low in relation to industry, as agricultural production expands extensively rather than intensively. In a dynamic economy, where the pace of accumulation is slower in agriculture in relation to industry, there is a separate category of absolute rent (AR) which implies, in addition to distortion of the flows between individual capitalists in agriculture, the flow of capital into agriculture is further distorted at the level of inter-sectoral competition (for capital to flow onto new lands) by the impact of landed property.

Because the OCC is systematically lower in agriculture, to the extent that accumulation is impeded by the relations of land, agriculture produces more surplus value compared to industry, where there are equal profit rates across sectors. Therefore, the prices of production would be lower than the value in the absence of landed property. However, landed property charges a rent and increases the prices of production above value. In the limit, that difference between values and prices of production in agriculture corresponds to AR. As Fine (1979) shows this limit is not arbitrary but the extent to which the lower OCC reflects the choice of pursuing profit through accumulation on new (DRI) as opposed to existing (DRII) lands.

Nevertheless, this would appear be a static interpretation which would imply any industry with a lower OCC or monopolistic entry conditions would be able

---

4   Harvey (1982, p. 356) claims, "in the case of a relatively permanent improvement that change the equal fertility assumption, DRII is converted directly into DRI". This would be a misleading interpretation of DRII, as its existence already presupposes improved conditions of technical change.

to generate rent. It is important to emphasise the source of AR is the low OCC in agriculture, dynamically determined by the existence of DRII. Agriculture necessarily produces more value the excess of which can be appropriated as rent at the level of determination of prices of production. But this is not a disproportionate monopoly excess as AR cannot exceed DRII and disappears if all land were leased or the composition of capital in agriculture were equal to that in industry (i.e., if land did not intervene in the accumulation process). In other words, *"if all land suitable for agriculture in a certain country were leased"* landed property would have ceased to act as a barrier for entry for capital and AR would disappear. Similarly, *"if the average composition of agricultural capital were equal to, or higher than that of the average social capital, then absolute rent would disappear."* (Marx, cited in Fine, 1986, p.133).

The conditions for the disappearance of absolute rent indicate that absolute rent is not solely the static difference between value and prices as the result of monopolistic entry conditions to the land markets, but the dynamic result of the intervention of landed property to accumulation by changing the technical conditions of production and potentially reducing the incentives for technical change. In that sense, the basis of AR comes from the extension of capital onto new lands rather than intensive cultivation of existing lands which would form the basis for surplus appropriation for DRII (Fine, 1980). AR cannot exceed DRII, because DRII is necessarily a product of rising OCC in agriculture and if AR exceeds DRII, intensive cultivation replaces extensive cultivation, leading to a rising OCC in agriculture.

Nevertheless, because of the permanency of production conditions, and the social relations surrounding landed property, such differentiation is primarily made not to imply the existence of a general theory of rent, but to trace the sources of rent and show the impact of landed property on capitalist accumulation for agricultural production. In principle, there cannot be a general theory of rent as there is not a simultaneous determination of DRI and DRII on the basis of normal capital size and average productivity in agriculture as this is contingent on how landed property intervenes in capital accumulation within and on the land. In other words, unlike industry, it is not pre-determined in agriculture whether intra- and inter-sectoral competition will lead to the determination of market values on the basis of the application of average size of capital with average productivity, as these do not exist. Instead, the prices of production will correspond to either the total application of capital to the worst land (least productive), while at other times it will correspond to the productivity of an additional unit of investment (Fine, 1980).

In addition to the three rent categories discussed above, there is an additional rent category described as "determined by neither the price of production of the commodities nor by their value, but rather by the demand of the purchasers and their ability to pay" by Marx (cited in Robertson, 2014, p. 104). This is monopoly rent, which is a price category whose source lies in the circulation of revenues rather than the circulation of capital. In other words, monopoly rent is not a value, but a pure price category, and hence, instead of being price-determining, it is price-determined. Still, it is treated within the category of rent as, although its relation to production differs from other rent categories, its recipient is still the owner of land as such, which has been the primary pre-occupation of Marx's treatment of landed property. Monopoly rent plays a crucial role in urban settings as will be discussed in the next section.

3.1   *Rent in Urban Settings*

When rent is conceptualised in an urban setting, it requires a separate theorisation as the range of activities conducted on urban land varies widely potentially exceeding the technical determinants of production associated with landed property in agricultural production. This is, for example, acknowledged by the prominent Marxist scholar Harvey (2012, 2003) who conceptualised a specific contemporary capitalist accumulation pattern based on rent appropriation through urban transformation: namely 'accumulation by dispossession'. In it, he referred to a relatively undifferentiated nature of rent relations in the urban context on the basis of land use for the sake of financial gains as accumulation proceeds. His theorisation of urban transformation is based upon his interpretation of rent theory developed in *Limits to Capital* (1982) where he claims, with the increasing pace of accumulation, as monopolisation obscures supply and demand dynamics, land starts to be traded as a pure financial asset, and "[a]ny stream of revenue (such as an annual rent) can be considered as the interest on some imaginary, fictitious capital. For the buyer, the rent figures in his accounts as the interest on the money laid out on land purchase and is in principle no different from similar investments in government debt, stocks and shares of enterprises, consumer debt and so on. The money laid out is interest bearing capital in every case" (p. 347). Although this would be a theoretically misleading analogy, it emphasises a crucial aspect of the land markets by revealing the monopolistic elements in the rent creation processes especially within the urban context.

The monopoly elements in the urban land markets have been acknowledged by many others, including Neil Smith (1987, 1979) who explains the process of gentrification on the basis of a 'rent gap' that is created by the mismatch of supply and demand in expanding cities. The rent gap theory claims that the durability of fixed capital on land 'locks' the intensity and type of land use over years as the city expands and creates a rent gap that 'forces' cities towards gentrification. In an expanding city, potential land rent for a given piece of land will increase over the long run. Initial development will involve an intensity of fixed capital investment and a land use appropriate for the procurement of potential land rent i.e., actual land rent will equal to potential land rent. Nevertheless, with increasing intensity of fixed capital, potential land rent is likely to rise above current rent given the durability of fixed capital. Clark (1988) claims such demand corresponds to an overall rent category which is not limited to actual payments to separate landowners, but an extraction from all actors undertaking all types of activities over land in the form of increased land prices. It should be noted that, similar to Harvey's theorisation, 'rent gap' theory by Smith (1987, 1979) refers to a monopoly price formation due to a restriction of access to entry, and as such is not specific to the intervention of landed property as a special factor of production.

The processes through which landed property obscures capitalist accumulation in agricultural production were discussed in the previous section. Agricultural rent arises partly because landed property exists as an obstacle to entry by setting monopolistic entry conditions, but also because rent categories in the agricultural context have the capacity to distort both market values and processes of production as they determine the basis for the technical conditions of agricultural production. In an urban setting, the sources of rent might be located differently as the technical qualities of land itself do not always go into the production conditions of the commodities produced on urban land. For example, although the location of a land plot has a role in determining the price of the dwellings built on it, location itself does not generate differential rent in an urban setting unless production of buildings is cheaper because of spatial characteristics of that particular land i.e., closeness to a train station that makes transportation of inputs easier. Second, in an urban context, conditions that determine land quality are not contingent upon the indestructible properties of land such as fertility, but rather upon demand (Robertson, 2014).

At this point, it is necessary to re-emphasise that rent appears as a distinct category from profits, not because of the necessity of permanent surplus profits or technical qualities unique to land, but because rent is appropriated by landowners instead of the industrial capitalists. There cannot be a general theory of rent with pre-determined impacts on accumulation as any analysis regarding the relations of landed property should be conceptualised within the specific historical conditions of landed property as well as in relation to the activities conducted on that land. This context-specificity is the reason why Ball (1979) argues that rent relations cannot form a separate category to discuss the developments within a theoretical context. As explained in Chapter 1, however, theoretical categories of Marxist political economy are formed incorporating the empirical elements, and the discussion on the category of rent is a good exercise to emphasise this aspect. It is exactly because of this aspect of the theory itself, rent appears to be separate theoretical category that can be either price-determining or price-determined, or some combination of the two, depending on the context.

The differentiation occurs at two stages as first, access of capital to land is differentiated from access to industry. Second, there is a further differentiation over the range of activities that can be conducted on land, because whether naturally given or not, how technical qualities of land affect surplus creation and appropriation is also contingent upon the form of activities. For example, the use of land by capital for mining purposes refers to a process of intervention of landed property in a significantly different way, as the 'indestructible' qualities of land are not observed, which raises questions over whether royalties paid for the mining industry should be classified as rent or not (Fine, 1982). Leaving these wide-ranging issues aside, this section emphasises that how landed property actually intervenes in the accumulation process is an empirical question and should be answered as such.

It is within that empirical context rent relations are discussed, even more so in an urban environment as the range of activities upon urban land varies greatly. Here, it is useful to discuss David Harvey's 'accumulation by dispossession' concept based on urban rent. In his conceptualisation, there are two situations in which the category of monopoly rent comes to the fore. The first arises because social actors control some special quality resource, commodity or location which, in relation to a certain kind of activity, enables them to set monopoly prices. In the realm of production, the most obvious example is the vineyard that produces wine of extraordinary quality that can be sold at a monopoly price. In this case, monopoly price creates the monopoly rent. The spatial version of that would be the proximity to some highly concentrated activity (such as a financial centre). In the second case, the land or resource is directly traded upon and scarcity is created by withholding the land or resource from current uses and speculating on future values. Monopoly rents are both created and reduced by competition at the same time. The more commodification leads to less monopoly power, nevertheless, at the same time, the fiercer the competition, the faster the trend towards monopoly because of the tendency of centralisation of capital (Harvey, 2002).

Because globalisation has significantly diminished the monopoly protections given historically by high transport and communication costs, Harvey (2012) claims that spatial competition provides the monopoly conditions necessary for a secure base for centralisation as it has always included some natural monopolistic elements within it. While mobile capitals (financial, commercial and productive capital with different surplus appropriation capacities) were engaging in a 'race to the bottom' in which the cheapest and most easily exploited labour power drives the capital mobility and investment decisions, the competitive power of spatial investments has depended on factors such as long-term investments in built environments which are by definition geographically immobile. For Harvey, urbanisation further commodifies urban land because the relatively permanent fixed capital assets associated with it are highly localised in their distribution, creating scarcity. He then claims, "[b]ecause rent is a transfer payment to a scarce factor of production, then the urbanisation process also multiplies the opportunities for realising rent" which creates a basis for rent-seeking activities associated with urban transformation as a general method for overcoming the overcapacity crises of capitalism (1982, p. 64). As posed by Engels' in his famous series of articles regarding the 'housing question' in 1872, this refers to an ever-expanding urban transformation: "[t]he breeding places of disease, the infamous holes and cellars in which the capitalist mode of production confines our workers night after night, are not abolished; they are merely shifted elsewhere! The same economic necessity that produced them in the first place, produces them in the next place." (quoted in Harvey, 2012, pp. 16-17).

Like absolute rent, monopoly rent depends upon the barrier of landed property at the level of inter-sectoral competition arising purely from supply and demand interactions. Nevertheless, it is also distinct from absolute rent that its formation depends purely upon supply and demand conditions, with no relation to the composition of capital in production upon landed property. Contrary to what Harvey suggests, this book argues that the theoretical significance of monopoly rent is not universal, but arises only under specific historical contexts in which there are *development gains*; and such gains contribute to the restructuring of productive and other types of capitals through the incorporation of landed property, or when there are more generalised monopoly rent increases due to demand-side factors such as ease of regulation and mortgage expansion.

Development gains occur when a new investment on a specific land improves the quality of surrounding land plots. Ball (1983, p. 143) defines development gain "as the difference between house price and the cost of constructing the dwelling (including site servicing)". The gain is divided between the landowner and the builder: while the former gets a price for their land, the latter appropriates profit from housing development on that land. By giving the example of a train station construction, Robertson (2014) argues that there might be two reasons why a train construction might increase the prices of land plots in the surrounding area. The first is that it makes the area more desirable and the demand increases accordingly. Nevertheless, this would ultimately be limited, creating a contingent imbalance between demand and supply. A permanent change would occur only under the conditions when the train station contributes to the increases in productivity in the surrounding plots by lowering the costs of production, for example, through reducing the transportation costs for capitalists producing in the vicinity. As a result, above normal surplus value is produced on the land surrounding the train station, some of which is appropriated as development gain (Robertson, 2014, p. 119). Development gains are important to emphasise how the productive conditions surrounding landed property are context-specific, and despite the tendency, organic composition of capital in production through landed property might increase on new or existing land to pursue development gains.

As suggested, development gains provide localised monopoly rent increases due to increases in demand following land development in a specific area. Nevertheless, these gains could also be generalised if they are incorporated into circuits that affect the demand on a sectoral level, such as through ease of land planning and development regulation or the increased availability of finance through mortgage expansion. While the revenue increases as a result of these factors accrue as capital gains to certain actors, they partly contribute to rent revenues in the form of monopoly rents, not only to be extracted by landlords, but to be extracted from the social pool of revenues.

This is not to reject Ball's (1980) claim that the impacts of the intervention of the landed property are in the end contingent. On the contrary, Marx's theory of agricultural rent is exactly about how the intervention of landed property is contingently incorporated into the theory as a unique factor of production. In that sense, David Harvey's (2003) accumulation by dispossession theory is criticised for offering a generalised revenue generation process on the basis of rent as monopoly price, despite its many insights. Instead, it is argued that how rent relations (universally to a certain extent in creation of AR, and both generalised and localised in the creation of monopoly rent) might contribute to overall revenues which might in turn contribute to the realisation of circuits of interest-bearing capital.

The following sections will seek the presence of this phenomenon in the context of Turkey, with the help of focusing on a state institution, TOKI (Housing Development Administration). TOKI has absolute monopoly control over public land in Turkey, which constitutes more than half of all land, and approximately 16-17% of all land available for use. Following its restructuring during the period 2002-2004, which gave it exclusive ownership rights on the

Treasury estates along with planning and zoning authorities, TOKI adopted a revenue-sharing strategy that provided high value inner city land for lower than market prices to the private developers. This structure was favourable for larger firms with strong links to the energy sector to engage in housebuilding activities, as they could enjoy monopoly profits gained through a merger of housebuilding and land development activities in a land-constrained environment, especially in the metropolitan urban areas that would otherwise be unavailable for housebuilding. As a result, development gains could be made, giving rise to a 'speculative' housebuilding industry with joint activities of mercantile and productive capital, as was the case in Britain.

The next section will give a general account of the industry in the current period and describe how it relates to the rest of the economy. The following sections will describe how this process unfolded, locating it within the historical context of urbanisation.

4   The Dynamics of Housing Production in Turkey: A Construction
         Boom Facilitated through State Institutions

As mentioned previously, the construction sector has been considered as one of the 'driving engines' of accumulation during the post-2001 period in Turkey. (Karatepe, 2016; KPMG, 2017). It should be noted that the sector constituting approximately 8% of the GDP cannot alone account for the success of the accumulation in that period, especially considering that the majority of investments by the sector were in residential housing, characterised by low-scale economies. Nevertheless, it is also characterised by strong inter-sectoral linkages, among the highest compared to other sectors, especially through its contribution to infrastructure (World Bank, 1984). Therefore, not surprisingly, the developments within the housing (hence construction) industry have been closely linked to the developments in other sectors, especially within the energy sector in Turkey.

In earlier studies, inspired by Kuznet's (1952) pioneering study on the comparison of the role of different industries in the formation of gross capital formation, the relationship between overall economic development and the corresponding contribution of the construction sector has been examined. In a global study including countries with a population over one million, Strassmann (1970) found that the contribution of the construction sector to GDP changes significantly according to the country's development level, increasing from an average of 4.6% in lower-income countries to over 7% in middle-income countries (See Table 8). That is because, while the

TABLE 8   Strassmann's findings regarding the relationship between construction and
economic development

Income per capita ($)	Contribution of construction to GDP (%)	Employment in construction in total labour participation (%)
80-350	4.6	3.9
350-900	7.1	6.7
over 900	7.1	7.2

SOURCE: STRASSMANN (1978)

manufacturing sector was given a boost during the early stages of development, construction follows to keep up with the infrastructural needs of industry when countries experience rapid industrialisation at the middle-income
level. Low productivity and higher wages, however, slow down the growth of
industry as the economy advances, which is why the rapid expansion of the
construction sector is famously described by Strassman (1970) as a "middle-
income country bulge".

Ball (2003) also confirmed that between 1956 and 2000, for Germany, France,
Canada, the USA and the UK, housing investment shares have never risen above
7-8% of GDP even when there were chronic shortages. The typical share of
housing investment in the annual national income of an advanced economy
with a moderately expanding population would seem to be around 4-5% with
the extra percentage point depending on the social attitude to the housing conditions of lower-income groups (Ball, 2003). Ofori (1990) points to possible areas
for improvement through globalisation, in which housebuilding industries can
contribute more to overall development through benefiting from internationalisation of production. As mentioned before, however, internationalisation in the
housebuilding industry remains limited due to its informal, local-information
driven and low economies of scale character (Ball and Wood, 1999).

Turkey has been no exception to this rule, and the share of the construction
sector in total GDP rose from 4.6% in 2000 to 8% in 2016, while its contribution
to employment increased from to 6.3% to 7.3% (TURKSTAT). Figure 50 shows
that the changes in the construction sector growth patterns were very much
in line with the changes in overall GDP. The average growth rate of the sector
reached a peak in 2010 at 18%. After that peak, it has started to decline. In the
first three quarters of 2014, the growth rate each year has been 5.1 per cent, 2.8
per cent and 1 per cent, respectively.

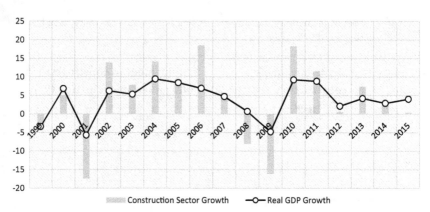

FIGURE 50   Comparison of construction sector growth and real GDP growth in Turkey
SOURCE: TURKSTAT

As mentioned throughout the book, the Turkish economy has entered a new, volatile macroeconomic phase since 2018, which has affected the construction sector deeply. In the third quarter of 2018, the construction sector has contracted by 5.7%, which shows that the sector is being affected by the volatility. As discussed before, this book is primarily interested in the long-term evolution of the sector as a whole and its specific place in the economy, therefore the focus will be placed on the period between 2004-2017, which shows continuity to reveal long-term trends in the absence of external shocks.

As Figure 51 illustrates, the credits given to the sector also increased significantly in line with sector growth, from 13,228,670 thousand TRY in January 2005 (6.3% of all domestic credits) to 286,790,800 thousand TRY (the amount of cash-credits has been 164,707,410 thousand TRY) in June 2017. While the share of cash-loans given to the sector constituted 8.4% of all cash loans in June 2017, its share increased to 10.6% when non-cash loans were also included. Among its total credits, non-cash loans constituted a significant portion, as 42.6% of all credits were non-cash loans in the same period.

Table 9 shows that although its contribution to overall GDP has stayed moderate, the construction sector's share in total fixed capital investment has been very high, trailing the manufacturing and transportation sectors, at 13.2% in 2015 and 14.3% in 2016.

In that overall picture, the most striking aspect of the construction sector growth has been the housing supply boom, as discussed in the introduction and indicated by Figure 49. Although disaggregated data for credits extended for the purpose of construction of residential buildings do not exist, as over

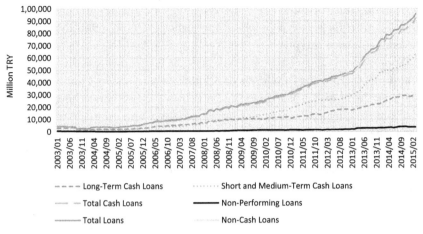

FIGURE 51   Domestic bank credits given to construction sector in Turkey
SOURCE: BAT

TABLE 9   Fixed capital investments made by different sectors

Sectors	Fixed capital investment (nominal prices, million TRY)			Percentage share		
	2015	2016	2017	2015	2016	2017
Agriculture	14,814	15,713	18,823	3.7	3.6	3.8
Mining	11,701	11,086	12,844	2.9	2.5	2.6
Manufacturing	119,478	131,573	145,720	29.6	29.9	29.3
Energy	13,040	12,929	14,818	3.2	2.9	3.0
Transportation	90,285	100,407	112,888	22.3	22.8	22.7
Tourism	19,183	14,051	13,751	4.7	3.2	2.8
Construction	53,222	63,175	73,068	13.2	14.3	14.7
Education	23,976	25,187	29,377	5.9	5.7	5.9
Health	20,543	21,614	25,271	5.1	4.9	5.1
Other	37,865	45,024	50,575	9.4	10.2	10.2

SOURCE: REPUBLIC OF TURKEY, MINISTRY OF DEVELOPMENT

70% of the construction sector is based on housing,[5] the developments within the construction sector as a whole can signal the production dynamics of housing to a large extent.

Supply boom was substantial visible after the restructuring of the state institution, TOKI (Housing Development Administration) between 2002-2004 and the enactment of the Mortgage Law in 2007 which exempted housing credits from banking and insurance transactions tax worth up to 5% of the total loan. The state's involvement in the sector as a whole has been significant and, during the period when public investment in construction has stayed considerably low between 1993 and 2003, the share of the sector decreased from 6.7% to 4% of GDP and the construction sector shrank by 22.4% cumulatively (Coşkun, 2015).

Nevertheless, more than 70% of all investments are made by the private sector and TOKI's contribution the industry is not primarily through its construction activities, but rather through incorporating land markets into the circuits of productive and mercantile (as well as interest-bearing) capital and facilitating a more effective land planning process. More precisely, its impacts on the housing system were through four channels. First, its direct housing supply for low- and middle-income households smoothed the supply in an industry that is structurally cyclical. Second, it facilitated demand (and contributed to the creation of monopoly rent in the form of development gains) through its large-scale urban regeneration projects, especially in inner city areas. Third, it also contributed to the generation of development gains through its large-scale revenue-sharing projects which provided high value urban land to private developers who could enjoy localised monopoly profits in a highly competitive industry characterised by low economies of scale. Last but not least, it expanded capital markets through establishing real estate investment trusts, and acting as a 'state-owned securitisation agent', similar to the case of the National Mortgage Corporation, Cagamas, in Malaysia (Rethel, 2010). The next two sections will explain these channels in detail within a historical context.

4.1 A History of Housing Provision in Turkey within the Context of Urbanisation

This section will discuss how the housing system developed in Turkey within the wider context of urbanisation. The first mass housing construction programmes for low- and middle-income groups in Turkey date back to the early

---

5 TURKSTAT Annual Construction Statistics (http://www.tuik.gov.tr/PreHaberBultenleri. do?id=21759). All sectoral statistics are from TURKSTAT, unless otherwise stated.

1950s, when urbanisation accelerated after the end of World War II.[6] Prior to that period, the spatial setting had remained almost the same since the fall of the Ottoman Empire, which was shaped on the basis of ethnicity with strict segregation among neighbourhoods with no central organisation (Faroqhi, 1984). There was a lack of well-developed transportation and road systems, which also contributed to the lack of central control over urban spaces especially over the outlying parts of the cities. When the nation-state emerged, one of its key strategies was to establish an urban structure based on centralisation. Especially with the étatist policies after 1930, there was a conscious effort for urbanisation based on expanding the railway network to the neglected parts of the country; a strategy pursued through the selection policy of location for state economic enterprises.

In a peasant economy mostly based on cereal products produced in the vast farms of inner Anatolia with extremely limited transportation links and a limited workforce due to war losses and population exchanges, the state's industrialisation attempts in the early years of the Republic focused on opening factories in medium-sized Anatolian cities that were along the existing railway links to create a better functioning transportation system, but also a more homogenised nation-state with the help of urbanisation (Chaudhry, 1993). As a result, urbanisation developed in a centrally organised way, based on the choice of location of state enterprises.[7] Given the limited infrastructural capacity of big cities, migration especially to Istanbul was not wanted by the state authorities and such enterprises facilitated the organisation of social life around factories in inner Anatolia, which also had the purpose of creating an industrial labour-force based on a nation-state citizenship identity (Arnold, 2012).

After World War II, there was shift in both the motives and experiences of urbanisation as the étatist policies declined in importance under the open

---

6   Three million people migrated to urban areas between 1950 and 1960 increasing the urbanisation rate from 25% to 34% (http://www.tuik.gov.tr).

7   As also mentioned in Chapter 4, Arnold (2012) argues that this choice was primarily political, without much attention being paid to economic feasibility. The Thornburg Report in 1949 stated that economic considerations have played little or almost no role in selecting sites of state enterprises, which led to a geographical development that was difficult to sustain. For example, the report defined the Karabuk Iron and Steel Plant, which is the first iron and steel factory of the Republic, as an 'economic monstrosity' which had neither the necessary labour supply nor the technical equipment to transfer iron from iron ore deposits. When Karabuk Iron and Steel Factory was built in 1938, Karabuk city was an incredibly small village with less than twenty households with no railway or any other transport connections, but it was relatively close to Zonguldak coal mines and railway station. As the city was located away from the coast, it was decided that it would be a good strategic point in terms of protecting the factory from future military attacks.

economy conditions of the 1950s. Şengül (2003) claims that the second distinct phase of urbanisation between 1950 and 1980 was characterised by rapid migration from rural to urban areas in order to sustain a labour-intensive import-substitution accumulation system. In accordance with the principles of the Marshall Plan, modernisation was promoted in agriculture, leading to the first massive influx of rural population to cities at the end of the Second World War. During this period, the state made minimum investment in the built environment, and the newcomers in the cities transformed the urban space towards an expansion of illegal squatter housing (*gecekondus*).[8]

Gecekondus played an important role in determining the housing consumption culture in Turkey as, during the 1960s, urban areas were characterised by the intensity of unplanned squatter neighbourhoods. By the time the Squatter Law was passed in 1966, squatter settlements contained more than half of the total population of the large cities (Şengül, 2003). Bugra (1998) states that 59% of the population in Ankara, 45% in Istanbul and 33% in Izmir lived in squatter settlements in the first half of the 1960s. In the 1980s, these percentages were 55%, 70% and 50%, respectively. This was also the period when an urban middle class was emerging, increasing the housing demand in inner urban areas.

The mass housing need emerged in this period, in the context of increasing polarisation and fragmentation between the middle-income inner urban areas and the peripheries characterised by the low-income squatter settlements. The first period of mass housing projects was initiated by the economically liberal government of Adnan Menderes, in collaboration with housing co-operatives and municipalities in the early 1950s. In 1952, the Social Security Organisation (SSO) began to provide housing credits for low- and middle-income households. Between 1950 and 1965, a total of 374 co-operatives produced 32,862 dwellings, 25,000 of which were financed by the SSO. Later, the legal framework for mass housing by co-operatives was first set by the Co-operative Law in 1969 and later by Mass Housing Law (Law No: 2985) in 1984.

Home-ownership has traditionally been the primary tenure culture in Turkey, as there has been no official state support for rental social housing provision as in the housing allowances to lower income renters such as in the UK, France or the Netherlands (Sarioglu-Erdogdu et al., 2012). 2011 census data show that 68% of all households owned their own homes. In the absence of such rental mechanisms that would require a limited amount of monthly

---

8 These illegal squatter dwellings of the 1950s were unofficially named as 'gecekondu' in the media, which means 'built in one night' in Turkish. Today, the term is still used not only to describe the rapid urbanisation movement in the 1950s, but also to refer to illegally built dwellings in general.

payments instead of savings, legalising unauthorised land appropriations was the only way for mass housing provision for the poor (Oncu, 1988; Tekeli, 1982), while the legal framework for occupation was mostly aimed at benefiting the urban middle class rather than the urban poor by extending home-ownership to new households through increased credit availability. During the 1980s and 1990s, membership of co-operatives has been an important means of access to ownership, as the number of dwelling units provided by cooperatives has risen from 8.7% of all dwelling units according to occupancy permits in 1980 to 25-30% during the second half of the 1980s and 1990s (TURKSTAT). Nevertheless, homeownership through membership of cooperatives was an opportunity only for households with permanent employment in the formal sector (Bugra, 1998). For the lower income groups, ownership came through illegal channels where the occupiers were allowed the property rights of lands, they 'enclosed' through a series of amnesty laws in a quasi-legal market (Bugra, 1998).

It is important to note that it was the high percentage of urban public land that enabled ownership through 'enclosures', because in contexts where the land belongs to private individuals, property owners can often take measures against illegal occupying, as argued by Keleş (1990, 1972). In line with this argument, Bugra (1998) remarks that 75% of illegal settlements in Istanbul, 88% in Ankara and 80% in Izmir were made on enclosed urban public land, which could not have been possible in the presence of private landownership. Although the property right distribution to illegal settlers through quasi-legal ways created an unusual opportunity for clientelistic and populist policies and contributed to a fragmented urban structure in the absence of socio-political mechanisms to integrate the urban poor (Oncu, 1988), this practice had some redistributive impacts with the active involvement of the state albeit indirectly given the lack of legal framework.

In line with the change of accumulation strategy from domestic import substitution to export orientation on the basis of wage suppression in the 1980s, the central state body further withdrew from direct engagement in housing policies. During the 1980s, the primary built-in investments of the state have tended to be more in infrastructure, especially communication and transportation, while the housing need was satisfied through a combination of market and quasi-market arrangements as mentioned above.

Municipalities became one of the most important actors after the establishment of metropolitan municipalities and the enactment of the Law on Land Development, Planning and Control (Law No: 3194) in 1985, which empowered them with plan making, subdivision and approval on public land. The Mass Housing Law established a Housing Development Fund and also The Housing Development Administration (TOKI). Initially, the primary role of TOKI was to provide housing supply and housing loans. Each year 5% of the Treasury budget was allocated to the Housing Development Fund that was to be used by The Housing Development Administration (TOKI) for that purpose.

However, the duties and responsibilities of that institution have changed dramatically following a reorganisation in 2004, which transferred all public land in Turkey to its land bank. The next section will discuss the significance of that development for the housebuilding industry.

4.2 The Rise of a State Institution in the Transition towards Market-based Provision: TOKI (Housing Development Administration)

Without a doubt, TOKI is the most important actor in the Turkish housebuilding industry today, through a variety of different channels: engaging in direct land sale; creating development gains through public-private partnerships and big-scale urban transformation projects; and lastly, smoothing the supply through engaging in direct housing supply for low- and middle-income groups. Today, among TOKI's total housing projects, 40% is addressed for middle-income families, 23% is for low-income families, 6% is housing in risk-prone zones and 15% for urban development projects. 85% of urban regeneration projects consist of affordable housing, while 15% of funds are used for luxury housing.[9] Its sales alone, worth 4.8 billion TRY, constituted 86.3% of all sales of state-owned institutions in 2015.[10] While 92.8% of its sales revenues come from direct land sales, 6.5% comes from its revenue-sharing programmes.

As mentioned, between 1984 and 2003, the primary aim of the Housing Development Fund and the Administration has been to facilitate homeownership for lower- and middle-income segments through direct construction or low interest rate housing credits. During this period, 5% of the state budget was transferred to the Housing Development Fund each year. In total, 940,000 housing units were financed through TOKI's loan originator banks, Emlak Bank, Pamuk Bank and Vakif Bank. During the late 1980s and the early 1990s, commercial banks also started issuing mortgage loans, mostly denominated in foreign currency. Nevertheless, the extent of mortgage issuance remained limited, as the macroeconomic environment was very volatile, and it was difficult to protect the value of the loans in a highly inflationary environment (tilt effect), given the devaluation of the Turkish Lira in 1994, when inflation also reached a peak level at 119% (Erol and Patel, 2004).

9   TOKI website (www.toki.gov.tr).
10   https://www.sayistay.gov.tr/tr/Upload/62643830/files/raporlar/genel_raporlar/kit_genel/2015_Ki2.pdf

After the crisis in 1994, all private mortgage lending activities came to a halt in 1995. As a result, Emlak Bank (The Real Estate Bank of Turkey) continued its activities as the leading housing credit lending institution through TOKI. In 1998, it also introduced an index-linked programme (wage-indexed and consumer price-indexed) besides a traditional fixed rate mortgage programme (Erol and Patel, 2004). Between 1984 and 2002, 43,145 housing units were produced by TOKI, while credit support was provided for 940,000 dwellings.[11] Approximately 90% of total loans were given to the housing co-operatives. As mentioned, the co-operatives have played an important role in providing housing supply through membership, reaching a peak during the 1992-1993 period, by providing just over 30% of all dwellings according to occupancy permits.[12]

In the 2000s,[13] the previous methods of housing provision stopped being satisfactory given the pace of urbanisation. Moreover, given the decentralised nature of housing construction, urban planning and land subdivision were not firmly regulated. The Urban Development Law stated that the municipalities were responsible for land provision through public subdivision up to 40 per cent of the city land. Nevertheless, some municipalities did not want to engage in parcel creation as it was costly, and left the task of plan making to landowners and house-builders (Turel and Koc, 2015). As a result, the land development process in Turkey has not been uniform and shows great variety according to bureaucratic and financial choices of individual municipalities.

The creation of larger urban plots was necessary to facilitate a less costly and faster method for housing construction. For this purpose, the Housing Development Fund was abolished in 2001, along with Emlak Bankasi (The Real Estate Bank of Turkey), of which real estate operations and assets transferred to TOKI. The tasks and assets of the Urban Land Office were also transferred to TOKI. In 2003, The Emergency Action Plan for Housing and Urban Development was passed, giving TOKI more responsibilities and liabilities. The goal of the plan was set to build 250,000 housing units through renovation, transformation and production by the end of 2007. In 2004, the Law No: 5162 and the Law No: 5273 were enacted, which amended the duties and responsibilities of the Administration extensively. In 2007, Mortgage Law No: 5582 was

---

11   TOKI website (Twww.toki.gov.tr).

12   This ratio decreased to 5.6% in 2011 (TURKSTAT).

13   The Association of Real Estate and Real Investment Companies (GYODER) estimates an urbanization rate of 78% in 2015 compared to 44% in 1980, indicating that the population of urban areas will increase to 71 million in 2023 from 60 million in 2015. In the last decade, Turkey's urban population has grown three times faster than its overall population.

passed. Following the legislation, TOKI stopped providing housing credits, but its other activities continued.

Among the extensive regulatory changes, two amendments in particular were significant. First was the amendment made in Article 4 of Law No: 1164. The amendment stated that except for estates that were allocated to public institutions, all Treasury estates could in principle be transferred to TOKI at no cost, upon TOKI's request to the Ministry of Finance and Ministry of Environment and Urban Planning. As a result, TOKI has effectively increased its land bank from 16.5 million m² to 65 million m² (approximately 16-17% of total land available for use), following the first five years of the regulation.[14]

The second important amendment was made in Law No: 2985, which authorised TOKI to conduct planning and zoning activities on Treasury estates, without requiring further permission from local or central governing bodies, as long as the plans were not in conflict with the activities of municipalities within their jurisdiction. As the Chamber of City Planners declared in a press release in 2008, this development gave TOKI exclusive land planning authority, without proper checks and balances.[15] Indeed, the Ministry of Finance Turkish Court of Accounts Audit Report in 2015 revealed that there were some breaches of the legislation in the practice of estate transfers as, although the Law only allowed for the transfer of the estates that had not undergone land development, some land plots that were already suitable for housebuilding were also transferred.[16]

During the 2000s, 78 laws and 10 by-laws were made concerning the production of the built environment most of which were aimed at making urban planning more flexible and removing obstacles created by land for both private and public sector actors (Balaban, cited in Topal et al., 2015, p. 43). When TOKI started to build on and provide public land in the early 2000s, the previous actors such as co-operatives and many small private land-owners were unable to compete as the private land market had become functionally ineffective (Turel, 2010).

As discussed previously, the cooperation of land development and housebuilding industries is crucial for maintaining profitability for the

---

14   http://www.radikal.com.tr/ekonomi/toki-5-yilda-65-milyon-808-metrekare-lik-alani-mulkiyetine-gecirdi-879732/

15   https://www.tmmob.org.tr/icerik/spo-butun-planlama-yetkileri-hukumetin-ozel-kurumlarina

16   https://www.sayistay.gov.tr/tr/Upload/62643830/files/raporlar/kid/2015/Genel_B%C3%BCt%C3%A7e_Kapsam%C4%B1ndaki_%20Kamu_%C4%B0dareleri/MAL%C4%B0YE%20BAKANLI%C4%9EI.pdf

labour-intensive housing industry. In Turkey, the regulations concerning TOKI consolidated the market power of the state within the land markets, which contributed to the profitability of the housing market within a dual structure. In that structure, while the availability of land attracted many small competitive housebuilding firms, profitability was also maintained for a small number of large firms with strong links to the energy sector, especially through monopoly profits of 'development gains'.

Development gains were mostly made through a revenue-sharing programme that started in 2006, based on TOKI's public land sale to private developers. TOKI explains the system as a build-and-sell model which is adopted to close the gap between its short-term investment expenses and long-term receivables.[17] The mechanism can be summarised as follows. First, TOKI calls for an open tender that is not regulated within the legal framework of Public Procurements and Tender Laws. While TOKI provides the land subject to tender, bidders offer a ratio of total probable revenue of the project and are responsible for construction, infrastructure, marketing and sales upon the land. Usually, high value inner city public land is offered below its market value, so that the extra revenues generated can be shared among the private investors and TOKI participant companies (the share of the private sector usually has been around 30-40% of total revenue). As a result, while the participation of private developers is facilitated through the provision of valuable metropolitan land at lower than market prices, TOKI can cross-subsidise affordable mass housing to lower income segments (Topal et al., 2015).

Table 10 below shows some examples of the highest-value revenue-sharing projects of TOKI in collaboration with private sector developers.[18]

In total, forty-one revenue-sharing projects were approved some of which are still under construction by 2020. The process is carried out by TOKI itself, and its participation companies, Real Estate Investment Trusts (REITs), which were first established between 1996-1998.

---

17   See TOKI website (www.toki.org.tr).

18   To emphasise the inter-linkages between the construction and energy sector, Soyak Holding that undertook the Istanbul Kucukcekmece projects shown in Table 6-3, also made substantial investments in electricity generation between 2008-2011. Among these projects were Bayramhacili HEPP in Nevsehir, Gullubag HEPP in Erzurum province, Hasanlar HEPP in Duzce, with a total capacity of 152 MW, worth $350 million in total. Similarly, among Nurol Holding's electricity investments were Nurol Goksu HEPP located in Konya province, with a capacity of 10.8 MW, as well as the TOR license for Ceyhan HEPP for 49 years, with a capacity of 63 MW installed power. Nurol Holding also owns one of the thirty-one real estate investment trusts in Turkey, named Nurol Real Estate Investment Trust.

TABLE 10   Selected revenue-sharing projects of TOKI according to tender values

Revenue-sharing projects	Responsible company	Tender value (TRY)	Number of dwellings
Istanbul Kucukcekmece Halkali (Olympiakent)	Soyak Insaat JSC	59,678,946,00	1364
Istanbul Kucukcekmece Halkali Stage II	Soyak Insaat JSC	96,772,432,00	2228
Istanbul Kucukcekmece Halkali Zone IV.	Ozsaya Ins. JSC & Guner Ltd. Co.	78,857,100,00	1368
Istanbul Kozyatagi	Baytur Ins. JSC	56,760,000,00	800
Istanbul Halkali Mass Housing Project	Artas JSC & Gun-erLLC	87,000,500,00	1044
Istanbul Atakoy Zone VI	Mutlu Insaat JSC	223,692,204,00	950
Istanbul Bahcesehir (UpHillCourt)	Varyap Varlibaslar Teknik Co.	118,944,000,00	682
Istanbul Bahcesehir Zone T2	Gulkelesoglu Insaat & Ifas Yapi & Ar-Ke Insaat & 2M Insaat & Gul Insaat Joint Project	180,510,000,00	600
Istanbul Bakirkoy Zeytinlik	Ozyazici Ins. Elekt. Mak. Ltd. Co. & Karadeniz Orme Joint project	447,150,000,00	527
Istanbul Sisli Mecidiyekoy	Nurol REIT & Nurol Insaat JSC	111,800,000,00	
Ankara Cankaya Beytepe	Turkerler Insaat JSC	397,000,000,00	800
Ankara Cankaya Dikmen	Meka Mesken JSC & Akturk Yapi JSC & Emlak Paz. Joint project	304,500,000,00	1832

SOURCE: TOKI

TOKI also generates development gains through its large-scale urban regeneration projects. From 2003 to 2014, it delivered 88,593 units under its shanty transformation programme.[19] By 2020, 233 urban regeneration projects have been undertaken by TOKI, 115 of which are still under construction.

Among these projects are the *Basibuyuk Project* that covered an area with approximately 20,000 lower-income *gecekondu* inhabitants on the Asian part of Istanbul and *Tarlabasi Renewal Project* covering 20,000 m² of land with 278 certified historical buildings (Kuyucu and Unsal, 2010). Located at the very centre of Istanbul, the *Tarlabasi Project* has been the symbol for the rapid urban transformation process taking place in Turkey since the early 2000s, with a tender worth $500 million won by Calik Holding in collaboration with Beyoglu Municipality in 2007.[20] Implemented in 2006-2007, both projects have encountered significant resistance from inhabitants and legal problems. Although the Administrative Court reversed the judgment for expropriation in the area for not being in accordance with the public interest in 2014, the process still continues.[21] Another contested urban regeneration project has been *Sulukule*, located on the border of the historical peninsula of Istanbul, with an area of 8000 m² with 571 households. Its regeneration has been a joint project of The Istanbul Metropolitan Municipality, The Fatih Municipality and TOKI. The tender was won by Ozkar Insaat in 2006, worth 62,675 thousand TRY.[22] These projects are significant to reflect TOKI's ability to generate localised monopoly profits on high-demand metropolitan land through expropriation, which would otherwise be unavailable for the private sector.

---

19   TOKI website (www.toki.gov.tr).
20   The CEO of Calik Holding in 2007 was Berat Albayrak, the son-in-law of President Tayyip Erdogan, who has been an MP since June 2015 and currently serves as the Minister of Finance and Treasury since July 2018. Calik Holding also has substantial investments in the energy sector including electricity generation and distribution and established international collaboration with companies such as Rosneft, General Electric, Qatar Holdings and Mitsubishi. It owns Aras EDAS (Eastern Anatolia) and Yesilirmak EDAS (Northeastern Anatolia) electricity distribution companies and has been involved in the construction and management of eight power plants in Turkey; including Cankiri Thermal Power Plant (TPP), Yatagan TPP, Kizkayasi Hydroelectric Power Plant (HPP), Adacami HPP, and four other power plants based on renewable (solar and wind) energy (www.calikenerji.com). It also has electricity generation investments abroad, including the construction of eleven simple cycle power plants in Turkmenistan.
21   Decree: 6. Daire 2011/7160 E., 2014/2910 K. http://emsal.danistay.uyap.gov.tr.
22   Similarly, Ozkar Insaat operates under the umbrella of Ozdogan Group, which also has multiple investments in energy. Among them, the biggest is the Ayvali Dam and HEPP project, located on Coruh River in Erzurum, with an installed capacity of 135 MW. It also completed the Ankara-Sivas High-Speed Railway project in 2017, which is to start its service soon.

Alongside these projects, TOKI continues to provide direct housing supply for low- and middle-income groups, which fulfils another stabilising function for the industry. Prior to its reorganisation, between 1984 and 2002, the total supply of TOKI was 43,145, which is 2% of total housing starts according to permits. After the restructuring, this picture changed drastically, as Turel and Koc (2015) state that during the period from 2003 to 2012, housing starts by TOKI increased to nearly 11% of all national starts, which was the reason why Turkey had the highest volume of housing production in Europe. From 2003 to 2014, 392,327 units were built for low- and middle-income groups in total.[23]

The housebuilding industry also benefits from TOKI's social housing provision, as direct supply can contribute to smoothing supply fluctuations especially during downturns, which can protect profitability for the other firms in the market, as exemplified in Britain in the early 1970s. Another important function of social housing construction has been the expansion of cities towards peripheries as the majority of these projects were undertaken in these areas, which further contributed to the stabilisation of the market by diversifying localised demand. As discussed previously in the context of agricultural land, price structures of production upon land strictly depend on the availability of new land for expansion. Although housing production is structurally different than agricultural production in the sense that the properties of land do not directly play a role in price determination (i.e. they do not alter the cost of production for housing), the availability of land can significantly contribute to the stability of the market by reducing the monopoly power of large firms.

Last but not least, another important function of TOKI has been to facilitate securitisation through its REITs, of which total value on the Istanbul Stock Exchange (BIST) has increased from $1.84 billion in 2009 to $8.33 billion in 2013.[24] There are 31 REITs in total, seven of which are participation companies of TOKI. Among them, Emlak Konut REIT is the largest subsidiary, funded by the assets transferred from the liquidated Emlak Bank in 2002. It is among the thirty largest companies (sixth place) listed on the Istanbul Stock Exchange with a market value just over $3 billion in July 2017 (BIST).

As Erol and Tirtiroglu (2011) note, REITs must invest a minimum of 50% of their portfolios in real estate asset-backed securities. This is an important development, signalling an entrance of interest-bearing capital into the housebuilding industry, albeit to a limited degree which will be discussed in Section 6.6. As discussed by Rethel (2010), a similar process was observed in Malaysia,

---

23   World Bank Report (2014) Turkey's Transition. (www.toki.gov.tr).
24   BIST website http://www.borsaistanbul.com/docs/default-source/research/orhan-erdem .pdf?sfvrsn=0

where a quasi-public agency, Cagamas (National Mortgage Corporation), did not only establish a primary mortgage market, but also contributed significantly to the corporate bond market through issuing mortgage-backed securities. Although established privately, its biggest shareholder remains Malaysia's Central Bank with a share of 20%, Cagamas was founded to become a "credible issuer of secondary mortgage securities" and became the largest issuer of asset-backed securities in Malaysia with a market share more than 50% (Rethel, 2010, p. 499). Although the aggregate extent of secondary mortgage issuance in Turkey is extremely limited (the value of these securities does not exceed 1% of GDP), the establishment of REITs signals the direction of the industry towards intensified securitisation as exemplified by Malaysia before.

In conclusion, the functions of TOKI within the Turkish housing market are several, which can be summarised as follows. First, it facilitated demand and generated monopoly profits for the private developers through its urban regeneration and revenue-sharing projects by providing metropolitan public land which would otherwise be unavailable. Second, through its social housing activities it smoothed supply fluctuations and diversified demand in a highly competitive, cyclical industry with easy entry and exit conditions. Finally, it contributed to the securitisation process through its REITs. As a result, the state's involvement in the sector has worked in a way to facilitate accumulation through the incorporation of the land market into the circuits of capital, engaging in productive, mercantile and interest-bearing activities. The next section will provide an empirical investigation of the firms' financial statements to answer whether such changes in the production patterns were reflected on the corporate balance sheets accordingly.

5   An Empirical Investigation of the Construction Sector Firms' Financial Statements

This section will investigate the financial statements of the firms operating in the construction sector, based on annual data released by Central Bank of Turkey Company Account Statistics.[25] Table 11 below shows disaggregation of the firms listed in the CBRT Company Account Statistics according to size, between 1999 and 2016. It should be noted that this is a sectoral level dataset, which is not restricted to residential housing, but considering 70% of all

---

25   See the previous chapter on electricity for details on the collection of Company Accounts Statistics by CBRT. All descriptive statistics provided in this section are my own calculations based on Company Accounts Statistics, unless otherwise stated.

TABLE 11   CBRT company account statistics
              construction sector firms

Years	Small	Medium	Big
1999	576	288	66
2000	689	264	40
2001	653	311	40
2002	662	296	27
2003	623	267	32
2004	498	236	28
2005	438	236	27
2006	428	259	32
2007	398	269	43
2008	388	271	41
2009	392	298	43
2010	428	330	40
2011	468	389	44
2012	492	409	39
2013	570	389	35
2014	479	453	30
2015	649	528	30
2016	549	361	35

construction is made for residential purposes, the sectoral level developments
also give an indication for the housing system. In line with the general characteristics of the industry, the great majority of the firms operating in the industry and listed by the CBRT are small- (549 firms in 2016) and medium-sized (361
firms in 2016), as opposed to big (35 firms in 2016).

The purpose of this section is to show that the impacts of the supply boom
were also reflected on the balance sheet of the firms[26] operating in the sector
as increasing production, despite the increasing prevalence of mercantile and
interest-bearing activities. During the period between 1998 and 2014, annual
construction investments increased cumulatively by 80.6% (Erol and Unal,
2015). The number of total housing unit starts by permits increased to 878,490

---

26   Please note that the 'firms' refer to the firms listed in the Company Account Statistics
      throughout the chapter.

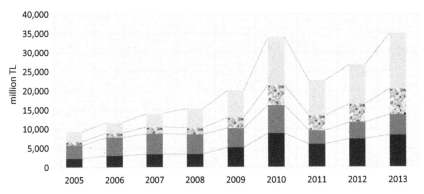

FIGURE 52   Credits held by construction sector firms
           SOURCE: BRSA

(803,507 of which were given to the private sector) in 2015, from 161,920 in 2002. The share of the private sector in total housing starts increased from 70 per cent in 2000 to 92 per cent in 2015.

As a result, in 2016, the sector received the second biggest share from the total credits given to the real sector at just above 8 per cent, after trade and retail. As Figure 52 shows, these credits were mostly FX short-term credits between 2005 and 2007. After 2008, long-term foreign exchange credits constituted the biggest share in total domestic credits given to the sector (Figure 53).

On the liabilities side, this development was reflected as the increase of the share of long-term credits in total liabilities from just below 5% between 2003-2007 to above 20% in 2015. Figure 54 demonstrates that the long-term liabilities including bank credits increased its share substantially from less than 20% in 2002 to almost 40% in 2016.

Similar developments were observed on the asset side. Figure 55 shows that although the share of liquid assets in total assets is still significantly higher than the fixed assets, reflecting the labour-intensive character of the sector, it decreased from just above 70% in 2007 to below 60% in 2016. On the other hand, the share of Plant, Machinery and Equipment decreased from above 9% of all assets in 2004 to below 4% in 2015, while the share of land stayed more or less at the same level, fluctuating between 4-6% of all assets (Figure 56). The share of the buildings item increased from below 5% in 2005 to 8%, contributing to the increase in the share of fixed assets in total assets.

The decrease in the plant, machinery and equipment item might be accepted as a reflection of the housebuilding sector's structural inability to move towards higher economies of scale in a competitive environment, as explained

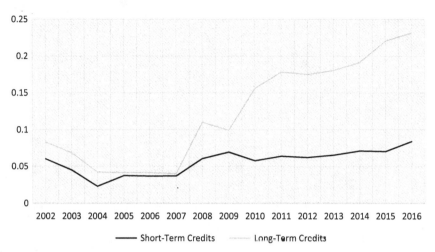

FIGURE 53   Construction sector firms short-term and long-term bank credits as a share of
total liabilities

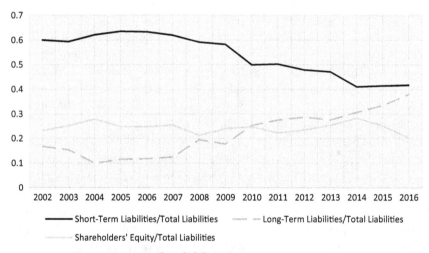

FIGURE 54   Construction sector firms liability structure

previously. In a competitive industry, the growth of the sector could attract
more and more firms with smaller size, which could result in the protection of
the labour-intensive character of the industry. As discussed in the previous section, a quasi-market intervention of the state provided stability for the housebuilding industry, which could continue attracting small-sized firms through
the availability of land, while also supporting a small number of larger firms
with links to the energy sector, through the generation of monopoly profits.

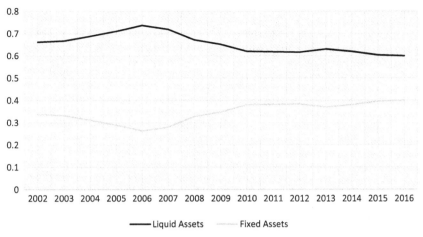

FIGURE 55   Construction sector firms asset structure (share of total assets)

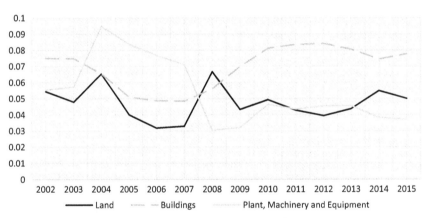

FIGURE 56   Share of land, buildings and plant, machinery and equipment items in
total assets

Below are the seasonally and calendar adjusted turnover and production indices prepared by TURKSTAT, showing an almost secular increase in both except for a short period during the 2009 financial crisis (Tables 12 and 13).

It could be suggested that the supply boom was made possible by a decrease in the costs through suppression of wages and increase of working hours. Although formal employment statistics cannot reflect the labour characteristics of the sector, as it is highly informal and depends heavily on subcontracting practices, Table 14 shows that, while the hours worked in total decreased substantially gross wages and salaries increased substantially. It

TABLE 12   Construction seasonally and calendar adjusted turnover index

Years	Seasonally and calendar adjusted turnover index (2010=100)				Annual average
	Q-I	Q-II	Q-III	Q-IV	
2005	70.1	72.3	76.0	80.6	74.7
2006	89.6	94.8	103.5	105.0	98.2
2007	107.8	108.6	109.1	116.1	110.4
2008	117.7	120.5	126.3	119.6	121.0
2009	113.7	109.4	99.8	101.9	106.2
2010	95.6	101.7	101.3	99.2	99.4
2011	105.0	105.5	104.8	108.3	105.9
2012	105.0	109.2	114.1	122.6	112.7
2013	127.2	127.3	132.6	125.6	128.2
2014	163.2	128.6	130.5	127.2	137.4
2015	136.9	126.1	135.4	138.4	134.2
2016	141.9	152.9	143.9	152.4	147.8

SOURCE: TURKSTAT CONSTRUCTION TURNOVER AND PRODUCTION INDICES

is not, however, possible to find a better proxy for employment characteristics, without a thorough list of subcontractors. Sozen and Kucuk (1999) find that there are about 20,000 subcontractors in the industry which is twice the number of the registered contractors. In an empirical study they conducted with 33 subcontractor organisations operating under the Istanbul Chamber of Commerce, in addition to primary subcontracting, the practice of secondary subcontracting was also found prevalent, further complicating the labour relationships within the industry and indicating the high degree of informality.

In summary, this section further emphasised that the increasing housing demand in Turkey resulted in a supply boom as reflected on the balance sheets of the firms, which prevented the industry from generating disruptive boom-bust cycles. The core of the Turkish construction sector is a typical, competitive housebuilding industry with easy entry and exit conditions especially due to the availability of public land. Within that structure, profitability could be protected through increasing informalisation for smaller enterprises and intersectoral linkages with the energy industry for larger enterprises. There was also

TABLE 13   Construction seasonally and calendar adjusted production index

Years	Seasonally and calendar adjusted production index (2010=100)				Annual average
	Q-I	Q-II	Q-III	Q-IV	
2005	86.6	83.9	87.0	91.4	87.2
2006	97.4	102.3	106.0	107.6	103.3
2007	107.2	109.8	111.3	108.5	109.2
2008	104.4	103.9	99.6	95.1	100.7
2009	88.3	80.3	80.6	88.1	84.3
2010	95.6	98.1	101.4	104.8	99.9
2011	108.5	110.7	112.5	113.2	111.2
2012	110.5	110.7	112.5	115.5	112.3
2013	118.8	119.9	121.7	122.9	120.8
2014	126.5	125.3	124.8	121.5	124.5
2015	123.5	127.1	129.0	126.1	126.4
2016	131.4	134.9	128.3	126.5	130.2

SOURCE: TURKSTAT CONSTRUCTION TURNOVER AND PRODUCTION INDICES

TABLE 14   Construction total hours worked and gross wages and salaries indices

Years	Hours worked index (2010=100)	Gross wages and salaries index (2010=100)
2010	100	100
2011	101.6	114.2
2012	102.1	131.7
2013	95.8	144.4
2014	84.3	148
2015	76.3	153.1
2016	69.5	173.6

SOURCE: TURKSTAT

the contribution of monopoly rent gains to profitability, facilitated through quasi-market state interventions such as its revenue-sharing and urban regeneration programmes since 2006. These findings support the argument that the outcomes of the culture of owner-occupation are highly contingent, and that the emergence of a "speculative" housing industry is not necessarily indicative of excess demand and decreased production given the necessary conditions such as the availability of land and sustained profitability of production for the firms.

6   The Dynamics of Housing Consumption in Turkey

Until now, this chapter has focused on the supply side and did not discuss how housing is consumed as a commodity in Turkey. This book argues that the most important feature of financialisation is not necessarily the declining productive capacities of the firms, but rather the commodification of wage goods such as housing in line with the tendency of the value of the labour power to decrease. Therefore, this section will explore how the dependence on individual homeownership gained crucial importance in Turkey since the early 2000s, which resulted in increasing housing demand.

As this process was heavily affected by the active presence of the state in Turkey, it is crucial to emphasise that the commodification of housing does not necessarily mean the withdrawal of the state, but rather the contribution of the state towards the efficiency of the markets. This emphasis can be seen in the World Bank documents, in which the policy rhetoric for housing has changed substantially from the withdrawal of the state in the 1980s-1990s to the participation of the state as the market facilitator in the 2000s. As Van Waeyenberge (2015) finds, in 1993, the World Bank's advice for governments in that regard had been "to abandon their earlier role as producers of housing and to adopt an enabling role of managing the housing sector as a whole" (p. 1).

In this World Bank document, the objective being the elimination of public subsidies in housing provisioning and creating replicability by the private sector in order to target efficiency and profitability in housing markets, the most important pillar for the strategy of enabling markets was defined as supporting the inclusion of intermediary financial institutions within housing systems that could issue long-term mortgage loans to low- and moderate-income households (pp. 55-56). As a result, during the 1990s, the Bank's housing loans increased fourfold in constant terms, to account for 15 per cent of the Bank's housing portfolio, up from 2 per cent during the 1980s (Van Waeyenberge,

2015).[27] Later, the state's direct involvement was encouraged through public-private partnerships, similar to the rhetoric around electricity privatisation policies.

As the book discussed within the context of electricity in the previous chapter, the state has always been involved in social provision in Turkey, irrespective of the shifts in scholarship and policy rhetoric. This does not contradict with the global trends, as although the forms and means of intervention have changed through time, commodification processes especially after the late 1990s went hand-in-hand with the increasing involvement of the state in social provision globally (Fine and Saad-Filho, 2016). The same trend is observed within the housing industry in Turkey, in which individual homeownership was facilitated through a supply boom, owing much to the state for the creation and the sustainability of the markets.

The increasing commodification of housing inevitably resulted in higher consumption, as reflected in the sudden spike of housing credits in 2014 (Figure 57). As discussed more in detail in Chapter 4, amendments were made in the Consumer Protection Act (Law No: 4077) in 2003, easing the regulations for consumer loans and credit cards. As a result, household debt increased sevenfold reaching 49 per cent of disposable personal income in 2012 (Karacimen, 2014). Among total consumption credits, the share of housing credits increased substantially from below 5% in 2001 to 34.4% by March 2017.[28] Nevertheless, as Figure 57 shows, the share of the number of housing loan borrowers in total consumer loan borrowers stayed more or less the same, which indicates that the increasing share of the housing credits is reflective of the general increase in consumption credits, rather than vice-versa.

In a comparative context, the housing credit growth also has been high, and as Figure 58 shows, Turkey experienced the globe's fastest real credit growth in 2015, by 17%. In 2016, the real credit growth has decreased to 9%, following the fastest growth rates in Mexico, Philippines, Slovak Republic and China.[29] In 2019, the annual credit growth rate further decreased to 1.9%, indicating that the market had stabilised after an initial boom.

It's been mentioned before that although the credit growth is fast, the share of mortgage credits in Turkey does not exceed 7% of total GDP even in 2020.

---

27 For World Bank policy documents on housing see World Bank (1993), "Housing: Enabling Markets to Work"; World Bank (2006), "Thirty Years of Shelter Lending: What Have We Learned?", World Bank (2009), "Housing Finance Policy in Emerging Markets".

28 BAT (The Banks Association of Turkey) consumer and housing credits statistics (www.tbb.org.tr). Also see Figure 57.

29 IMF Global Housing Watch (http://www.imf.org/external/research/housing).

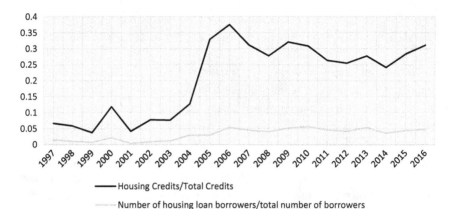

FIGURE 57   Housing credits as a share of total household credits and number of housing loan
borrowers as a share of total loan borrowers in Turkey
SOURCE: BAT (THE BANKS ASSOCIATION OF TURKEY)

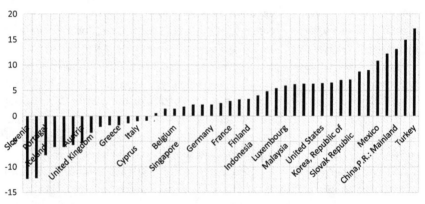

FIGURE 58   Real credit growth in housing in 2015 (annual percentage change)
SOURCE: IMF GLOBAL HOUSING WATCH

Compared to many developed countries, mortgage markets in Turkey still are
underdeveloped especially considering that the risk accumulation is low and
the sector is not heavily reliant on secondary mortgage markets through the
issuance and trade of collateralised debt obligations that practically did not
exist until recently (Erol, 2015; Erol and Çetinkaya, 2009).

    As a result, although residential prices are showing an increasing trend in
Turkey (Figure 59), it is unlikely that even a total breakdown in the revenues
will generate a systemic crisis for the economy, given the size of the housing
market. Moreover, the upward pressure on residential prices is not unique,

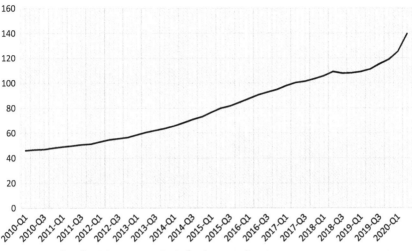

FIGURE 59   Residential property price index (2017=100)
SOURCE: CBRT

given similar trends were observed in almost all developing countries, including Brazil and India, where residential housing prices increased by more than
76% and 50% from end-2007 to end-2014, respectively.[30] In 2014, residential
prices in Turkey increased annually by 6% in real terms,[31] which could indicate
the early stages of an access problem according to Coskun and Watkins (2014).
Price to rent ratio also increased from the base in 2010 (=100) to 139 by the second quarter of 2015, indicating that the asset prices increased faster than rents
(Figure 60). The increase in this ratio has been the highest among OECD countries in 2015, as the average OECD average price to rent ratio has only risen to
103 in 2015 from the base in 2010. However, this ratio for Turkey decreased to 98
in 2019 with the same base year, while the ratios for the US and the UK stayed
almost the same (108 and 112, respectively). The drop further signals that after
the initial boom of the market following the demand spike, price increases
were stabilised within the market itself.

Erol (2015) also finds that most of the price changes in the residential properties in Turkey can be explained by endogenous factors and do not signal a
speculative boom, although the increasing trend in prices since 2010 cannot
be denied. There are a number of factors that could have contributed to such

30   BIS Residential Property Price Statistics. Detailed dataset can be retrieved from http://
      www.bis.org/statistics/.
31   BIS Residential Property price Statistics.

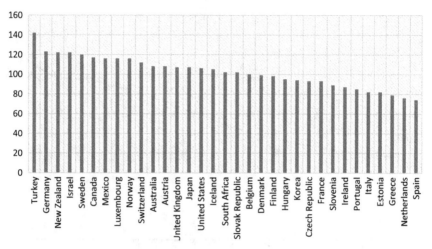

FIGURE 60   Price-to-rent ratio in housing (2015: index 2010=100)
SOURCE: IMF GLOBAL HOUSING WATCH

an increase, easier access to housing credit being one of the primary factors as discussed extensively. Topal et al. (2015) also point to the increasing presence of foreign investors, as real estate sales to foreigners were made possible with an amendment of the Land Register Law (Article 35) in 2003. Between 2003 and 2013, the property sales to foreigners reached 25 billion USD, corresponding to 13% of the tourism revenue earned in the same period (Topal et al., 2015). Yirmibesoglu (2008) claims that the declining household size from 4.14 in 1990 to 3.85 in 2000 was another factor behind the growing housing demand.

In summary, there were substantial increases in housing demand following the credit supply boom especially since the 2000s in Turkey. However, due to equivalent increases in the housing supply, the demand growth was contained within the markets themselves. Moreover, the relatively small size of the housing market prevents the fluctuations of the industry to become too risky for the aggregate economy. This does not suggest a 'financialised' housing industry in a traditional sense. Nevertheless, as discussed, the industry is subject to considerable change, due to increasing dependence on owner-occupation, which resulted in a housing supply boom to match the increases in housing demand. This chapter in particular, and the book in general, is interested in the investigation of this multifaceted process of change *in its own right*, without giving exclusive attention to its possible destabilising impacts, which may or may not be present. The next section will investigate whether another financialisation argument, which is the increasing dependence upon 'predatory lending' to the poor, is present in the Turkish context.

6.1   *Housing Consumption: Who Consumes How Much?*

As discussed in Chapter 2, a particular stream in the financialisation literature claims that in many countries, maintaining relative levels of consumption
by means of borrowing when real wages have stagnated has been an integral
macroeconomic factor to sustain aggregate demand (Dos Santos, 2013). In that
sense, the market-based provision of health, education and most commonly
housing, has been an important demand strategy, which incorporates lower-
income households through 'predatory lending' (Dymski, 2009a, 2009b). Dos
Santos (2013) claims that credit extension to lower-income group segments has
replaced the initial expansion of credit to middle-income groups, and in some
middle-income countries, for example in Brazil and Malaysia, the commercial banks were specifically required to meet targets of high-interest mortgage
loans to lower income households.

Karacimen (2015, 2014) supports this argument in the context of Turkey,
and finds that predatory lending practices were prevalent (see Table 15) as
around 42 per cent of all household credits were given to people below median
monthly income level (earning less than 1000 TRY a month) during 2009-2011.
In 2010 and 2011, the amounts of loans borrowed by the lower income half of
the population constituted almost 60 per cent of their income (Karacimen,
2014). In 2014, 27% of all household credits were given to households below
1000 TRY monthly income level while their share in total credits was 18%.[32]
Considering these groups are the most vulnerable at times of crisis, Karacimen
(2015) argues that the increasing indebtedness of the lowest income groups
increases social vulnerability in the presence of financial volatility, to which
deteriorating labour market conditions have been conducive.

Given the assumption households spend up to 30% of their income on housing credits, Turhan (2008), however, predicted that only the top 10% would be
able to use mortgage credit given interest rates of 1.5% a month and typical
maturity of 7-10 years. Topal et al. (2015) also claim that 44% of mortgaged purchases were made in the biggest four cities, indicating mortgages were mostly
accessible by the metropolitan elite.

Figure 61 shows that although the share of low-income group households in
total number of credits increased, the amount of credits given to households
below median income level decreased. In fact, after 2004, the average share of
the lower-income half of the population from total credits decreased from well
above 60% of all household credits to 20% in 2016. 2004 was the year when

---

32   27% of all household credits were given to households between 1000TRY-2000TRY
income level, constituting more than half of all household credits together with the lowest income group (their share in total credits was 40%).

TABLE 15   Percentage of household credit borrowers according to income groups

Percentage of loan borrowers by income groups

Years	0-1000TRY	1001-2000TRY	2001-3000TRY	3001-5000TRY	5000TRY +	Unspecified
2010	41.6	27.9	11.4	6	6.3	6.5
2011	42.9	25.8	11.7	5.6	5.4	8.5
2012	38.1	25.1	13.1	6.4	6.6	10.5
2013	32.7	27.6	14.5	7.4	9	8.5
2014	27.4	27.2	13.1	7.3	14.8	9.8

SOURCE: KARACIMEN, 2014

there was rapid demand-driven increase in total housing credits because of an extension of maturities and a rapid drop in the monthly interest rate from 2.57 per cent in mid-2004 to 0.99 by the end of 2005 (Karacimen, 2014). Although disaggregated data on housing credits according to income groups do not exist, the decreasing share of credit given to households below the median income level suggests that credits given to below median income households are more likely to be lower-value personal finance credits, which constitute the highest share in total household credits, at 63.5% in March 2017, instead of housing credits.

The statistics collected by The Banks Association in Turkey in March 2017 show in Table 16 that among total household credits worth 54,645 million TRY, 16,171 million TRY (29.6% of all household credits) was given to the upper-income group earning 5000 TRY and above, as opposed to 11,135 million TRY (20.3%) given to the income group earning up to 1000 TRY a month, and 6,980 million TRY (12.7%) to the income group earning between 1000-2000 TRY a month. Table 17, however, shows that among the total number of credits issued, the lowest-income group below the median income level receives the highest share. Among 2,533,205 credits issued, 712,725 are undertaken by the income group earning below 1000 TRY a month, which constitutes the highest share according to the numbers of loans issues, as opposed to the amount. As mentioned, this probably reflects an increase in personal rather than housing credits. The next section will give a brief summary of the findings and conclude the chapter.

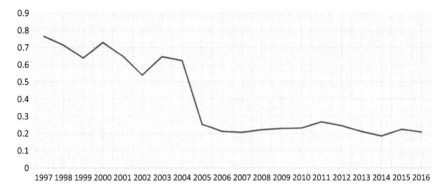

—— The amount of credits given to households below median income credits as a share of total household credits

FIGURE 61   The amount of credits given to households below median income level (as a share of total household credits)
SOURCE: BAT

7   Conclusion

This chapter provided a political economy of housing provision in Turkey in a historical context, along the increasing scope and depth of commodity relations in the chain of activities from production to consumption. As mentioned, this investigation has a theoretical relevance for investigating the tendency of capitalism towards lowering the value of labour power in the abstract (while money wages' capacity to buy wage goods increase due to necessarily cheapening wage goods, or through increased availability of credit as in the case of cheapening mortgages, for example), which is partly constituted by the consumption of housing as a use value. As such, the significance of housing commodification for the study of financialisation is twofold: while the existence of regular revenue streams through consumption provides the necessary base for the attachment of the circuits of interest-bearing capital through the provisioning of wage goods, this in turn decreases the simple value embodied in these commodities. As discussed in the earlier chapters, however, this process refers to a simple abstract tendency, which is never observed directly on an empirical level, but rather through mediations due to the presence of countertendencies as well as contingencies. In other words, the impacts of financialisation become an empirical question to be contextually investigated for each different wage good across different countries.

TABLE 16   Amount of credits issued according to income groups (million TRY)

		Amount of credits given according to income groups, million TRY					
Period		0-1.000	1.001-2.000	2.001-3.000	3.001-5.000	5.001 +	Un-classified	Total
2016	TRY	7,781	6,790	5,361	6,012	8,150	3,851	37,945
March	FX	2	0	0	1	2	0	5
	Total	7,783	6,790	5,361	6,013	8,152	3,851	37,949
2016	TRY	8,861	7,243	6,188	7,820	9,777	4,046	43,935
June	FX	0	0	0	0	6	0	7
	Total	8,861	7,243	6,188	7,821	9,783	4,046	43,942
2016	TRY	8,654	6,550	5,710	7,337	8,490	4,358	41,099
Sept	FX	0	0	0	0	3	0	4
	Total	8,654	6,550	5,710	7,337	8,493	4,358	41,103
2016	TRY	13,009	8,946	8,299	11,573	12,739	6,054	60,621
Dec	FX	0	0	0	1	4	0	5
	Total	13,010	8,946	8,299	11,574	12,743	6,054	60,626
2017	TRY	11,305	6,980	6,044	8,402	16,173	5,740	54,645
March	FX	0	0	0	1	4	0	5
	Total	11,306	6,980	6,044	8,403	16,178	5,740	54,650

Housing provides a good case for further explaining why this is the case, due to the intervention of landed property which is absent as a factor of production in other wage goods, such as electricity. Within the housing studies literature and the financialisation literature in particular, the analytical focus has traditionally been on the mechanisms through which a transition towards market-based provision could affect the macro determinants, as in the case of an asset price inflation scenario. Most of these studies are interested in locating housing within a systemic context, but without treating housing as a unique industry with its own revenue-generating mechanisms. In that sense, for many of these studies, the relevance of the housing markets is strictly limited to their ability to reflect the underlying inflationary forces within the economy.

In line with the principles of the 'systems of provision approach', which is partly inspired by Ball's (1983) studies of the housing markets, this chapter argued that the housebuilding industry is characterised by some structural features regarding its production methods, which in turn determine

TABLE 17   Number of loans issued according to income groups (million TRY)

Number of loans issued according to income groups							
Period	0-1.000	1.001-2.000	2.001-3.000	3.001-5.000	5.001 +	Un-classified	Total
2016 TRY	616,693	590,824	305,761	244,472	347,149	226,248	2,331,147
March FX	12	2	2	9	23	0	48
Total	616,705	590,826	305,763	244,481	347,172	226,248	2,331,195
2016 TRY	660,599	598,679	346,536	302,337	378,090	250,234	2,536,475
June FX	0	0	3	11	40	1	55
Total	660,599	598,679	346,539	302,348	378,130	250,235	2,536,530
2016 TRY	656,515	532,515	308,975	272,800	308,639	247,781	2,327,225
Sept FX	1	1	3	3	32	1	41
Total	656,516	532,516	308,978	272,803	308,671	247,782	2,327,266
2016 TRY	772,820	585,245	365,122	358,202	377,143	299,840	2,758,372
Dec FX	3	0	1	18	33	1	56
Total	772,823	585,245	365,123	358,220	377,176	299,841	2,758,428
2017 TRY	712,724	477,929	278,634	261,097	499,863	302,915	2,533,162
March FX	1	1	0	8	33	0	43
Total	712,725	477,930	278,634	261,105	499,896	302,915	2,533,205

SOURCE: BAT

the price dynamics within the housing markets, irrespective of the degree of commodification.

Specifically, it explained how housebuilding and land development develop as two structurally distinctive industries due to significant differences in risk and return structures: while the former is a low-scale labour-intensive industry with lower risks and lower returns, the latter is characterised by significantly higher risks and higher returns, making the industry more capital-intensive. In this context, a 'speculative' housebuilding industry emerges in countries where land supply is limited, and landowners have a degree of monopoly power in their decisions to sell; such as in the UK, where bigger firms with sufficient land stocks could engage in stock-adjustment against increasing costs arising from failure to facilitate productivity increases, and adopt an output-restricting character in order to protect profitability through buying and selling (Ball, 1983, 2003).

The chapter argued that the output-restriction is not a necessary outcome of this structure, as long as the intervention of landed property could generate extra rent revenues, which could attract a wide pool of actors to the industry. Indeed, the historical development of the Turkish construction industry since the 2000s suggests that the speculative elements were incorporated without obstructing supply, after the restructuring of a state institution, the Housing Development Administration (TOKI) during 2002-2004 and the dramatic decline in the monthly interest rates in mortgages from around 2.5% to 1% in 2004. As a result, a housing supply boom followed, and the construction sector investments increased cumulatively by more than 80% between 1998-2014 (Erol and Unal, 2015), over 60% of which was made for residential purposes.

The supply boom was made possible with the help of this state institution, named TOKI. As TOKI is the single biggest actor which owns 16-17% of all land available for use and it has absolute control over its land bank, it could contribute to the emergence of a housebuilding industry, which was both output-facilitating and speculative, through various channels. First, it smoothed the fluctuations in supply through engaging in low- and middle-income housing production especially in the outer areas of cities where housing demand is low. Second, it facilitated demand through large-scale urban transformation and regeneration projects especially in Istanbul and Ankara. Third, given that the firms in Turkey did not have large land banks, as the sector's development prior to the post-2001 crisis period had been limited by the absence of an established land market, TOKI's revenue-sharing projects on high-demand inner city state estates have provided localised development gains that could contribute to higher-than-average profits appropriated as rent by all actors in the industry. This strategy was particularly in favour of the bigger firms with sufficient capital to engage in riskier land development investments, especially with inter-linkages to the energy sector. Another strategic importance of TOKI has been the introduction of real estate investment trusts operating under its umbrella, which contributed to the deepening of capital markets, albeit from a very low base compared to many other countries.

In short, a speculative housebuilding industry was established, without this being reflected as disruptive price appreciations, partly due to the availability of landed property to enable new housing supply. Moreover, the inter-sectoral linkages with the energy sector also helped larger firms to protect profitability without output-restricting and continue operating within a highly competitive and low-economies of scale industry.

Therefore, the book argues that the real significance of the housing markets for the economy does not arise from their ability to reflect the underlying inflationary forces as any other asset market could, but rather from the use value of housing as a wage good to reproduce the workforce. Despite the great differences between the British and Turkish housing systems, there is a common element in both countries, which is the commodification of housing through the promotion of individual home-ownership. From its peak at 31% in 1981, the percentage of households in social housing in Britain fell to 19% in 2001, while owner-occupation, by contrast, reached above 70% (Robertson, 2014). Similarly, the homeownership level reached 68% in Turkey in 2011 (TURK-STAT), which traditionally did not accommodate a social housing system. This chapter is organised around the investigation of housing as an increasingly commodified use value in line with the widening discrepancy between means of production and items of consumption, which is itself a reflection of broader value relations of the economy along with financialisation. The next and final chapter will further emphasise this aspect in light of what has been discussed throughout and conclude the book.

CHAPTER 7

Conclusion

1   Introduction

This book provided a political economy of electricity and housing provision in Turkey, in light of the financialisation literature. Its purpose is to establish a theoretical link between the commodification of wage goods and the financialisation processes since the late 1970s and early 1980s that have been widely associated with a diverse range of empirical processes such as intensified debt and equity-based securitisation and financial profit seeking, slowing down of real accumulation, stagnant wages and widening income inequality, and/or a set of policies such as deregulation in labour and financial markets. By theorising financialisation as the material base for a distinct phase in mature capitalism when money capital acquires a distinct quality (use value) to expand itself independently from the processes of production (as interest-bearing capital) and investigating this contextually in the provisioning of wage goods, it was concerned with two interrelated issues. First was to locate the developments within the electricity and housing markets in Turkey within a systemic theoretical framework through the use of the concept of financialisation. Second, and more broadly, the book investigated how the individual cases from Turkey provided insight for an understanding of financialisation in particular and the workings of the economy in general. This chapter will conclude the book in light of these primary concerns, which will be discussed once again in Section 2 through a brief summary of the book's main findings and contribution. Section 3 will conclude by identifying some further issues for future research.

2   Main Findings and Contribution

As mentioned above, this book had two interrelated concerns, the first of which was to understand how the organisational relations with respect to the production and consumption of electricity and housing in Turkey have changed over time, by making use of the concept of financialisation as the increasing presence of interest-bearing capital as self-expanding money capital (or more widely referred to as the emergence of the secondary circuit of capital).

This first concern is more or less straightforward and self-explanatory, and it seeks to address the individual cases through the use of concepts employed in

Marxist political economy, the emphasis being upon a specific interpretation of financialisation. In that respect, the empirical cases of electricity and housing provisioning in Turkey were discussed in Chapters 5 and 6 with respect to their move towards market-based forms of provisioning, reflected in the increasing scope and depth of commodity relations across the vertical chain of activities from production to consumption. As emphasised, the commodification process was readily associated with the promotion of individual final consumption of these goods, without this necessarily being accompanied by the withdrawal of the state. In contrast, the book provided empirical evidence that both electricity and housing were increasingly produced (and consumed) through the market as items of final consumption in Turkey since the 1980s, together with an active involvement of the state. The involvement of the state was evident in the increased budget transfers during and after electricity privatisation and the choice of cost recovery regulation mechanisms to favour private enterprises over end-users in the electricity system.

In the housing system, the state was heavily involved in the promotion of a private housebuilding industry through the establishment of primary (and later secondary) mortgage markets, directly through the restructuring of a state institution during 2002-2004, the Housing Development Administration (TOKI) which had a monopolistic position in the land markets in terms of ownership and access, and indirectly through easing land development and planning regulations. It was argued that although the commodification process does not directly suggest a financialised structure, in which revenues are securitised and bought and sold without a direct relationship to the processes of production, it contributes to it by expanding the base of consumer revenues with significant regularity as well as contributing to the realisation of circuits by generating consumption demand.

The book aimed at understanding these processes empirically at their early stages in Turkey, in line with the specific development trajectory of Turkey as a transition economy. Chapter 4 on the political economy of Turkey emphasised that, in line with its specific stage of development, the trajectory of financialised accumulation in Turkey has followed a different path than developed economies. As discussed in Chapter 2, financialisation is mostly discussed within the context of developed economies with respect to its destabilising impacts on production, growth and distribution. As a result, financialisation in developing and emerging economies emerged as a separate literature, as discussed in Chapter 3, by emphasising how the depth and scope of financial markets are themselves responsible for the emergence of developed country cases of financialisation, which is absent in developing countries. Instead, the developing country financialisation literature focuses upon how the destabilising impacts of the primary financialisation processes in the core are 'imported' by the developing countries through capital account liberalisation and monetary policy, which restrain the policy choice of developing countries and reinforce and reproduce the uneven and dependent nature of international development.

Drawing upon the empirical evidence for the manufacturing sector restructuring from low-technology labour-intensive sectors towards higher-technology capital-intensive sectors after the 2001 crisis, the book argued that there was a national economy level structural change in Turkey since 1980. This contrasted with the prediction of the literature on financialisation towards global managerial short-termism and impatient finance, as the increases in productive capacity went hand-in-hand with the increasing commodification of electricity and housing and the emergence of secondary circuits of capital in Turkey, especially after a typical foreign exchange induced developing country crisis in 2000/2001. In other words, while the maintenance of capital inflows through high interest rates and their channelling into domestic borrowing through new issuance of government debt instruments during the 1990s signalled an increase in speculative activities, this was not necessarily strictly hampering for productive investment throughout the 2000s, until 2017. Instead, as labour productivity and capital-intensive production techniques increased across the economy (counterbalanced with increasing informalisation in more traditional sectors), along with increasing household and private sector indebtedness, the private sector's heavy reliance on government securities during the 1990s could also reflect domestic producers' attempts to protect the value of their capital in a macroeconomic environment characterised by chronically high levels of inflation.

In that process, the crisis of 2001 and the subsequent financial sector restructuring has been a crucial turning point, in terms of eliminating small banks engaging in riskier borrowing and lending activities with weak balance sheet structures. The crisis had differentiated impacts on different actors in the economy, as while the larger actors with tight links to the financial sector were not affected, the access to credit for smaller enterprises became severely restricted. As a result, profitability was maintained across the economy in a dual structure, in which considerably bigger medium-low and medium-high technology sectors had to channel their production into exports through external borrowing, in the face of shrinking domestic demand, given their less flexible production conditions to keep up existing production levels (and adopt technologically more advanced techniques), while the smaller low technology industries turned towards increasing informalisation and subcontracting practices. In this respect, the macroeconomic trajectory was favourable for the growth of the capital-intensive energy sector together with horizontal inter-sectoral linkages to the highly cyclical and informal construction sector that was facilitated by, and further facilitated, commodification of electricity and housing as discussed in Chapters 5 and 6. These findings contributed to an understanding of the individual cases of electricity and housing provisioning in Turkey in terms of placing them within the overall accumulation.

As mentioned above, the second concern of the book is to understand how the individual cases provide insight for an understanding of financiali-sation in particular and the workings of the economy in general. As empha-sised throughout, irrespective of the result of (but causal in the emergence of) these sectors' overall contribution to successful accumulation, this concern is located at a deeper level of analysis and reflects some methodological prin-ciples outlined in Chapter 1. First of all, these principles are based upon the conceptualisation of the categories of exchange to reflect the simultaneous circulation of use values as the concrete material commodities (or commodity forms) and values as the abstract labour time embodied in (and necessary to reproduce) these commodities.

Distinct from the ahistorical concept of utility employed in contemporary economics, the concept of use value emerges when commodities reflect the underlying social relations through their material properties. This aspect first appears in Marx's analysis of money acquiring a 'universal' use value to monop-olise exchangeability. Apart from its particular use values to satisfy human needs and provide utility, it is this universal aspect of money that separates it aside from the mass of commodities, as acknowledged widely within the tradi-tion of Marxist political economy. Many of the theorists suggest, however, use values lie outside the scope of political economy as once commodities leave the sphere of the unity of production and circulation, they are no longer gov-erned by its laws. Among these are Hilferding as one of the most well-known theorists of Marxist political economy, who claimed "[t]o be a use value is evi-dently a necessary prerequisite of the commodity, but it is immaterial to the use value whether it is a commodity. Use value as such, since it is independent of the determinate economic form, lies outside the sphere of investigation of political economy. It belongs in this sphere only when is itself a determinate form." (cited in Rosdolsky, 1977, p. 74).

For others, including Rosdolsky (1977), Weeks (1983) and Fine (1994), on the other hand, although it is true that individual use values are no longer deter-mined by the laws of capitalist accumulation once they leave the circuit of capital as commodities, the use value investigation is indispensable for the analysis of capitalist exchange in general. For Rosdolsky (1977, p. 84), "the most important determinations of the exchange value derive precisely from use value and from the relation between the two of them: for instance, ground rent [deriving from the use value of landed property], the minimum level of wages, and the distinction between fixed and circulating capital" which have the most direct influence on the determination of the exchange categories, such as prices.

At the most general level, the distinction between fixed and circulating capital is crucial as capitalist exchange concerns how the mass of value of capital grows not only in absolute terms, but also how the mass of value of capital (embodied in the production process as constant capital) grows in relation to the variable capital as living labour, (re)produced through the individual consumption of use values outside the circuit. Indeed, one of the primary distinctive characteristics of capitalism from the previous modes of production is the structural separation between the means of production produced and owned by the capitalists as constant capital and the items of final consumption which constitute the labour power as the variable capital. While the value of constant capital in relation to variable capital grows as accumulation proceeds, it means that the items of productive consumption dominate the circulation quantitatively, although the majority of net income is consumed through wages (Fine and Leopold, 1993).

In addition, this process is far from arbitrary, and the increasing production of items of consumption as commodities and their subsequent removal from the circuit of capital is proportional to the extent of the expulsion of living labour from the production process (Fine, 1994; Fine and Leopold, 1993; Rosdolsky, 1977; Weeks, 1983). Meanwhile, the social reproduction of labour power through individual consumption of wage goods represents an inversion of the logic of value, where exchange relations are represented as undifferentiated relations between money wages and use values, without reflecting the underlying social relations that govern who consumes what and how much.

As summarised in Chapter 1, 'the systems of provision' approach to social reproduction draws upon such fundamental principles. It concerns how specific use values as final consumption items are produced increasingly through the market as commodities, reflecting the tendency of capitalist accumulation to reduce the value of labour power. Meanwhile, however, the items of final consumption necessarily cheapen and money wages (despite stagnant in the recent period) can buy more commodities, helping satisfy a minimum living standard. Nevertheless, as the final consumption is maintained outside the circuit of capital, the previously established norms of consumption gradually disappear, most visible in the erosion of public services as necessary constituents for the functioning of the society as whole, of which the economy is a part.

As suggested however, by no means this tendency suggests a linear process, as the tendencies and countertendencies exist in contradiction and the success of accumulation depends whether these can co-exist simultaneously as the realm of commodity production necessarily expands itself. As such, the investigation of tendencies and countertendencies in the actual operation of the economies becomes an empirical question, conducted contextually through how the balances between value magnitudes and use values are maintained. In maintaining such balances, not only the laws of capitalist production, exchange and distribution play a role, but the intervention of the state, the extent of domestic labour and the socially-constructed meanings attached to the consumption of specific use values are determining.

Apart from its empirical contribution, the most important contribution of this book is to provide a theoretical alternative to study financialisation through a simultaneous investigation of use values and values. This preoccupation is made explicit whenever possible, for example in the distinction of the approach adopted in this book from Keynesian analyses in general, with respect to the latter's not assigning a separate use value for the labour power and treating the product of living labour as the revenue share of workers. Similarly, the emergence of IBC as a logically distinct category is emphasised in Chapter 2, only once money acquires a specific use value to expand itself as money capital.

In Chapter 6 on agricultural rent, the use value of landed property to be used by landowners to appropriate a part of social surplus without landed property being produced by capital relation was mentioned. In that respect, Chapter 6 on the political economy of housing provision in Turkey explained how the existence of rent revenues in the housebuilding industry could be conducive to revenue generation, through creating above-average monopoly profits appropriated in the form of rent, especially in the urban context through 'development gains', without necessarily resulting in universal price appreciations and output restriction, as in the case of many developed countries within the context of which housing markets are mostly discussed. Chapter 6 found evidence for the emergence of a speculative housebuilding industry in Turkey, following the increasing dependence on owner-occupation since the early 1980s. It found that some new actors such as the real estate investment trusts and other secondary financial institutions entered the industry, with extra rent revenues being facilitated through the state's active involvement in the land markets.

It is crucial to note that the land markets are characterised by the heavy presence of state ownership in Turkey, and therefore the state's active involvement significantly shaped the productive characteristics of the industry. Its involvement took various forms. First, it smoothed supply fluctuations in a highly cyclical industry through engaging in direct housebuilding for low- and middle-income groups. Second, it facilitated land development for all actors by easing regulation and planning. Third, it provided Treasury estates and contributed to rent revenues especially in central urban areas through the creation of development gains based on revenue-sharing programmes and large-scale urban regeneration projects since 2006. Fourth, it established Real Estate Investment Trusts (REITs) under its umbrella, which facilitated the formation of secondary mortgage markets based on asset-backed securities, albeit from a low base.

In a comparative context, it was found that the state-ownership of land (hence the relative absence of impediment through) the intervention of landed property in Turkey contributed to the stability of the housebuilding industry despite an increasing trend in prices. These developments were investigated in comparison to the developed country case of Britain, in which in addition to the depth of financial markets, the output restricting character of the housing industry due to monopolisation in the land markets resulted in disruptive asset price boom-bust cycles.

The developments within the housebuilding industry are also discussed in relation to the developments within the electricity industry, discussed in Chapter 5. In that respect, although electricity is not only a final item of consumption, but also an intermediary product, Chapter 5 firstly discussed the commodification of electricity as a use value within the context of gradual privatisation since 1984. It argued that the experience has been mixed in terms of its results for the industry as well as consumers. It was negative in terms of its distributional impacts, given the initial costs were directly reflected on consumer bills, whereas there was no regulation mechanism to include the cost improvements on retail prices despite the substantial incentives provided for the private investors. During the transition period from 2001 until 2006, the state-owned wholesale company, TETAS, bought all electricity produced from newly-established privately-owned generation companies at high initial costs and sold it to the market at a uniform price. This was reflected as low levels of competition in the industry and increased end-prices, for both consumers and the industry, which were among the highest in Europe during the period. Although this was a result of an early process of industrial expansion, the chapter emphasised the state's favoured the private sector participation at the expense of increasing end-user prices. There were also substantial public budget transfers, particularly in the implementation of the biggest projects, such as the Ilisu Hydroelectric Power Plant (HEPP) in Southeastern Anatolia, and Yusufeli and Deriner HEPPs in Northern Anatolia.

Nevertheless, another important finding of the chapter on electricity provision in Turkey was that during the process of intensified re-organisation of
capital as discussed in Chapter 4, the horizontal links between different sectors have been strengthened, signaling that the economy was moving towards
intensified centralisation of capital and economies of scope. In the case of
Turkey, both economies of scale and scope were evident in the energy sector; reflected respectively in the intensified energy production through greater
competition while fewer firms engaged larger scale higher-productivity
investments through combining operations in energy and construction sectors. Profitability was also maintained for smaller firms, as long as they could
compete given the availability of a cheap labour force and casualised subcontracting arrangements especially in the construction sector. From that perspective, the organisational relations within these sectors were in line with the
findings of Chapter 4, which suggested that the capital restructuring from low-
capital intensity to higher-capital intensity within manufacturing signalled an
easier adoption of new technologies and erosion of the traditional boundaries
between the sectors at an overall economy level.

The next section will discuss further issues arising from the findings and
conclude the book.

3   Further Issues and Concluding Remarks

As mentioned in the introduction, the theoretical approach adopted in this
book necessitated a highly abstract methodological and theoretical discussion in early chapters to derive the categories employed in the highly concrete
empirical analyses of Chapters 5 and 6. This meant that the book had to deal
with many issues to cover a broad scope. As a result, the coverage was highly
selective to provide the necessary analytical framework within the limits of
a book, and some aspects that could be valuable for the individual analyses
of housing and electricity systems, and financialisation, as well as their inter-
relations, were left behind or investigated only cursorily.

In a very interesting article, Milor (1990) discusses the state planning exper-
iment of Turkey during the early 1960s, inspired by French indicative planning.
Despite the political suspicions arising with the connotations of planning, the
Dutch economist Tinbergen and his assistant Koopman were invited to Turkey
in April 1960, the latter to stay further to conduct preliminary research for a
five-year development plan. In May 1960, the Democrat Party (DP) government
of Adnan Menderes was thrown out by a military coup, and the young techno-
crats who worked with Tinbergen and Koopman were appointed to create the

State Planning Organisation (SPO) in September 1960. The members of SPO continued to work along Tinbergen's suggestions, which aimed at introducing a type of planning that would not interfere extensively but enable the private sector through the promotion of capital-intensive techniques and maximisation of labour productivity. During the two-year process of plan preparation, Nicholas Kaldor was also invited to Turkey, who proposed a comprehensive agricultural taxation reform which would put incentives for farmers towards mechanisation. He suggested that because taxation on agricultural products was very low, and farmers did not basically pay any taxes for products above average, there were no incentives towards mechanisation and as a result, land was underutilised which prevented the sector from developing (Milor, 1990).

The agricultural reform package and the promotion of capital-intensive techniques in a systemic manner were not met with enthusiasm by the military officials, due to concerns over job losses as well as migration movements especially from the agricultural Eastern provinces. There were also pressures on planners to arbitrarily change and manage their calculations, for example to increase the growth expectations for the first year of the plan from 6.5 per cent to 7.6 per cent of GNP for reasons of optimism. As a result of the tensions that arose between the planners and the military officials, the founders of the SPO resigned collectively, right after the adoption of the First Five-Year Development Plan (1963-1967) in 1962, signalling that the planning experience did not go according to the initial expectations. Milor (1990) questions whether the development trajectory in Turkey could have been different given the extensive state interventionism during the period of import substitution of 1960s could achieve sufficient quality in terms of institutional coherence and coordination among state organisations as well as selectivity of policies that focused upon strategic sectors and industries. He states that given 60 per cent of all industrial investments were made by State-Owned Enterprises, their inefficiency in terms of lacking selectivity played an important role for the overall state of the economy in the following decades. However, the book also argued that although the industrial policy programme may have looked incoherent from a macroeconomic perspective in retrospect, there was a consistent tendency across time towards the establishment of markets for social provisioning when each of these sectors are investigated individually. In that sense, a macroeconomic perspective might not fully reveal the purpose of seemingly incoherent and irrelevant set of policies.

Indeed, the issue of macroeconomic coherence has also been discussed extensively within the context of formerly planned economies especially in Central and Eastern Europe (Kornai, 2000, 1986). For the Hungarian economist Kornai (1986), who wrote extensively on the issue, the Soviet State-Owned

Enterprises were structurally inefficient due to their 'soft-budget constraints' and detachment from cost considerations which led to the emergence of chronic shortage economies in the region. Following the collapse of the Soviet Union, Gabor (2012b) explains that these countries went through a substantial transition in two phases, first between 1989 and 1994, when the planned economies shifted their production strategies from a strictly vertically-integrated structure to a market-driven system, and then a seemingly successful integration into the global economy from 1995 onwards, on the basis of fighting against the inherited repressed inflation. She argues that the chronic shortage narrative advocated by Kornai (1986) and others, supported by the IMF's monetarist policy suggestions based on income policies and devaluations, was far from reflecting the structural character of the planned economies based on the benefits of vertical integration.

In transition to financialised accumulation, Gabor (2012b) suggests that the failure of the transition policies based on the "soft-budget constraint" approach was that these policies could not address the absence of commodified social provisioning in planned economies, which made income policies redundant as wages only represented a small proportion of the production costs (they were not contained enough in the costs of production). Therefore, as the costs of imported intermediate goods increased through repeated devaluations during the transition process, hampering production, creating markets for social provisioning emerged as a highly difficult task. A meaningful further research is to discuss how the establishment of strong private markets for social provision has been one of the primary accumulation channels for Turkey in its transition process within a comparative context.

Another important extension of the book would obviously involve the impacts of the Covid-19 crisis on the economy, and especially the construction and energy sectors. As disclosed in the introduction, I have chosen to exclude this discussion out of the scope of this book, as the crisis is still ongoing at the time of writing this book in 2020. Covid-19 has brought an almost unprecedented level of uncertainty to the global economy, the repercussions of which will be felt deeply in the years ahead. In the case of Turkey, given its macroeconomic fragilities and high levels of foreign indebtedness, alongside the deepening of some macroeconomic problems such as unemployment and high inflation, especially the energy firms might be facing some serious default risks in the future, while the construction sector firms could be expected to adjust more flexibly to external shocks given the cyclical, labour-intensive nature of the industry.

I will conclude by repeating the main argument of the book. Commodified social provisioning indeed represents a detachment of (re)production of labour power as a commodity from the production process and is in line with intensified financialised accumulation. Nevertheless, the outcomes of this process remain highly historical and contingent, depending upon a collection of policy choices and contextual elements, as the book explored. The reader might have noticed that the book never explicitly discusses the 'impacts' of the social and political elements in the maintenance of this process. That is because by conceptualising the economy as a structurally contextual entity, it reasserts the argument that the discussion of the impacts of the political choices upon the economy is not meaningful as long as the economy is a social and political entity in itself. In that respect, Milor's question whether things could have been different also remains unanswered in retrospect.

Bibliography

Aalbers, M.B., Christophers, B., 2014. Centring Housing in Political Economy. Hous. Theory Soc. 31, 373–394. https://doi.org/10.1080/14036096.2014.947082.

Acar, O., Caglar, E., 2012. Yeni Tesvik Paketi Uzerine Bir Degerlendirme (Politika Notu No. 201221). TEPAV, Ankara.

Adelman, I., 2000. Redrafting the Architecture of the Global Financial System-Editor's Introduction. World Dev. 28, 1053–1060.

Aglietta, M., 1976. A Theory of Capitalist Regulation: The US Experience, English Translation. ed, Verso classics. Verso Books, London; New York.

Aglietta, M., Breton, R., 2001. Financial Systems, Corporate Control and Capital Accumulation. Econ. Soc. 30, 433–466.

Aglietta, M., Rebérioux, A., 2005. Corporate Governance Adrift: A Critique of Shareholder Value. Edward Elgar, Cheltenham.

Aktaş, E., Alioğlu, O., 2013. Türkiye'de Enerji Sektörü Analizi: Marmara Bölgesi Termik Santraller Örneği. Çukurova Üniversitesi Sos. Bilim. Enstitüsü Derg. 21, 281–297.

Akyuz, Y., 1993. Financial Liberalization: The Key Issues (Discussion Paper No. 56). UNCTAD, Geneva.

Akyuz, Y., Boratav, K., 2003. The Making of the Turkish Financial Crisis. World Dev. 31, 1549–1566. https://doi.org/10.1016/S0305-750X(03)00108-6.

Alper, C.E., 2001. The Turkish Liquidity Crisis of 2000: What Went Wrong. Russ. East Eur. Finance Trade 37, 51–71.

Alper, C.E., Onis, Z., 2003. Emerging Market Crises and the IMF: Rethinking the Role of the IMF in the Light of Turkey's 2000-2001 Financial Crises. Can. J. Dev. Stud. 24, 255–272.

Arestis, P., 1996. Post-Keynesian Economics: Towards Coherence. Camb. J. Econ. 20, 111–135.

Argitis, G., Evans, T., Michell, J., Toporowski, J., 2014. Finance and Crisis: Marxian, Institutionalist and Circuitist Approaches (FESSUD Working Paper Series No. 39).

Arnold, C.E., 2012. In the Service of Industrialization: Etatism, Social Services and the Construction of Industrial Labour Forces in Turkey (1930-50). Middle East. Stud. 48, 363–385.

Arrighi, G., 1994. The Long Twentieth Century: Money, Power and the Origins of our Times. Verso Books, London.

Arthur, C.J., 2002. Capital in General and Marx's Capital, in: Campbell, M., Reuten (Eds.), The Culmination of Capital: Essays on Volume III of Marx's Capital. Palgrave Macmillan, New York, pp. 42–64.

Arthur, C.J., 1998. Systematic Dialectic. Sci. Soc. 62, 447–459.

Ashman, S., Fine, B., 2013. Neo-liberalism, Varieties of Capitalism, and the Shifting Contours of South Africa's Financial System. Transform. Crit. Perspect. South. Afr. 81/82, 144–178.

Atiyas, I., Bakis, O., 2013. Structural Change and Industrial Policy in Turkey (Working Paper No. 3), REF. TUSIAD.

Atiyas, I., Cetin, T., Gulen, G., 2012. Reforming Turkish Energy Markets: Political Economy, Regulation and Competition in the Search for Energy Policy. Springer, New York.

Atiyas, I., Dutz, M., 2005. Competition and Regulatory Reform in Turkey's Electricity Industry, in: Togan, S., Hoekman, B. (Eds.), Turkey: Economic Reforms and Accession to the European Union, Papers in Conference Proceedings. World Bank, Washington D.C., pp. 187–208.

Aybar, S., Lapavitsas, C., 2001a. Financial System Design and the Post-Washington Consensus, in: Fine, B., Lapavitsas, C., Pincus, J. (Eds.), Development Policy in the Twenty-First Century. Routledge, London & New York, pp. 28–52.

Aybar, S., Lapavitsas, C., 2001b. The Recent Turkish Crisis: Another Step Toward Free Market Authoritarianism. Hist. Mater. 8, 297–308.

Bagdadioglu, N., Odyakmaz, N., 2009. Turkish Electricity Reform. Util. Policy 17, 144–152.

Bakker, K., 2007. The "Commons" Versus the "Commodity": Alter-globalization, Anti-privatization and the Human Right to Water in the Global South. Antipode 39, 430–455. https://doi.org/10.1111/j.1467-8330.2007.00534.x.

Bakker, K., 2005. Neoliberalizing Nature? Market Environmentalism in Water Supply in England and Wales. Ann. Assoc. Am. Geogr. 95, 542–565. https://doi.org/10.1111/j.1467-8306.2005.00474.x.

Bakker, K., 2004. An Uncooperative Commodity: Privatizing Water in England and Wales, Oxford Geographical and Environmental Studies Series. Oxford University Press.

Balibar, E., 1995. The Philosophy of Marx. Verso Books, London.

Ball, M., 2011. Planning Delay and the Responsiveness of English Housing Supply. Urban Stud. 48, 349–362. https://doi.org/10.1177/0042098010363499.

Ball, M., 2006. Markets & Institutions in Real Estate & Construction. Blackwell, Oxford.

Ball, M., 2003. Markets and the Structure of the Housebuilding Industry: An International Perspective. Urban Stud. 40, 897–916.

Ball, M., 1999. Chasing a Snail: Innovation and Housebuilding Firms' Strategies. Hous. Stud. 14, 9–22. https://doi.org/10.1080/02673039982975.

Ball, M., 1983. Housing Policy and Economic Power: The Political Economy of Owner Occupation. Methuen, London & New York.

Ball, M., 1980. On Marx's Theory of Agricultural Rent: A reply to Ben Fine. Econ. Soc. 9, 304–326. https://doi.org/10.1080/03085148008538599.

Ball, M., Wood, A., 1999. Housing Investment: Long Run International Trends and Volatility. Hous. Stud. 14, 185–209. https://doi.org/10.1080/02673039982911.

Barba, A., Pivetti, M., 2009. Rising Household Debt: Its Causes and Macroeconomic Implications – a long-period analysis. Camb. J. Econ. 33, 113–137.

Baumol, W., 1975. Scale Economies, Average Cost and the Profitability of Marginal Cost Pricing (Working Papers). C.V. Starr Center for Applied Economics, New York University.

Baumol, W., 1971. Optimal Depreciation Policy: Pricing the Products of Durable Assets. Bell J. Econ. Manag. Sci. 2, 638–656.

Bayliss, K., 2014a. The Financialization of Water. Rev. Radic. Polit. Econ. 46, 292–307. https://doi.org/10.1177/0486613413506076.

Bayliss, K., 2014b. The Financialisation of Water in England and Wales (FESSUD Working Paper Series No. 52).

Bayliss, K., 2008. Water and Electricity in Sub-Saharan Africa, in: Bayliss, K., Fine, B. (Eds.), Privatization and Alternative Public Sector Reform in Sub-Saharan Africa: Delivering on Electricity and Water. Palgrave Macmillan, Basingstoke, pp. 88–122.

Bayliss, K., Fine, B., 2008. Privatisation and Alternative Public Sector Reform in Sub-Saharan Africa: Delivering on Electricity and Water. Palgrave Macmillan, Basingstoke.

Bayliss, K., Fine, B., Robertson, M., 2013. From Financialisation to Consumption: The Systems of Provision Approach Applied to Housing and Water (FESSUD Working Paper Series No. 2), Financialisation, Economy, Society and Sustainable Development.

Bernanke, B., Gertler, M., 2000. Monetary Policy and Asset Price Volatility. NBER Work. Pap. No. 7559.

Bhattacharyya, S.C., 2011. Energy Economics: Concepts, Issues, Markets and Governance. Springer.

BIS, 2009. Capital Flows and Emerging Market Economies (No. 33), Committee on the Global Financial System (CGFS) Papers. Bank for International Settlements, Basel.

BIS, 2007. Financial Stability and Local Currency Bond Markets (Committee on the Global Financial System (CGFS) Paper No. 28). Bank for International Settlements, Basel.

BIS, 2002. The Development of Bond Markets in Emerging Economies (BIS Papers No. 11). Bank for International Settlements, Basel.

Blaug, M., 2003. The Formalist Revolution of the 1950s. J. Hist. Econ. Thought 25, 145–156. https://doi.org/10.1080/104277103200083309.

Bonizzi, B., 2013. Financialization in Developing and Emerging Countries. Int. J. Polit. Econ. 42, 83–107. https://doi.org/10.2753/IJP0891-1916420405.

Boratav, K., 2012. Türkiye İktisat Tarihi 1908-2009, 16th ed. Imge Kitabevi, Ankara.

Boratav, K., 1981. Kemalist Economic Policies and Étatism, in: Kazancigil, A., Ozbudun, E. (Eds.), Ataturk: Founder of a Modern State. C. Hurst & Company, London, pp. 165–190.

Boratav, K., Yeldan, E., 2006. Turkey, 1980-2000: Financial Liberalization, Macroeconomic (In)Stability, and Patterns of Distribution, in: Taylor, L. (Ed.), External Liberalization in Asia, Post-Socialist Europe and Brazil. Oxford University Press, pp. 417–455.

Boratav, K., Yeldan, E., Kose, A.H., 2000. Globalization, Distribution and Social Policy: Turkey, 1980-1998 (SCEPA Working Paper No. 2000–10). Schwartz Center for Economic Policy Analysis (SCEPA), The New School.

Borio, C., Drehmann, M., 2009. Assessing the Risk of Banking Crises – revisited. BIS Q. Rev. March 2009.

Borio, C., Lowe, P., 2002. Asset Prices, Financial and Monetary Stability: Exploring the Nexus. BIS Work. Pap. No 114.

BOTAS, 2014. 2014 Annual Report. BOTAS (Petroleum Pipeline Corporation Turkey).

Boyer, R., 2005. How and Why Capitalisms Differ. Econ. Soc. 34, 509–557.

Boyer, R., 2000. Is a Finance-led growth regime a viable alternative to Fordism? A preliminary analysis. Econ. Soc. 29, 111–145. https://doi.org/10.1080/030851400360587.

Boyer, R., 1990. The Regulation School: A Critical Introduction. Columbia University Press.

BRSA, 2014. Türk Bankacılık Sektörü Genel Görünümü. BRSA (Banking Regulation and Supervision Agency of Turkey), Ankara.

Bryan, D., Rafferty, M. 2006. Capitalism with Derivatives: A Political Economy of Financial Derivatives, Capital and Class. Palgrave Macmillan, London.

Bugra, A., 1998. The Immoral Economy of Housing in Turkey. Int. J. Urban Reg. Res. 22, 303–307. https://doi.org/10.1111/1468-2427.00141.

Bugra, A., 1994. State and Business in Modern Turkey. State University of New York Press, New York.

Cahill, D., Beder, S., 2005. Regulating the Power Shift: The State, Capital and Electricity Privatisation in Australia. J. Aust. Polit. Econ. 55, 5–22.

Cakarel, E., House, J., 2004. IPP Investment in Turkey's Electric Power Industry (Working Paper No. 32). Stanford University Center for Environmental Science and Policy, Stanford.

Calvo, G.A., Izquierdo, A., Mejía, L.-F., 2008. Systemic Sudden Stops: The Relevance of Balance-Sheet Effects and Financial Integration. NBER Work. Pap. 14026. https://doi.org/10.3386/w14026.

Carchedi, G., 2008. Dialectics and Temporality in Marx's Mathematical Manuscripts. Sci. Soc. 72, 415–426.

Carvalho, F., 1984. Alternative Analyses of Short and Long Run in Post-Keynesian Economics. J. Post Keynes. Econ. 7, 214–234.

Castree, N., 2008a. Neoliberalising Nature: Processes, Effects, and Evaluations. Environ. Plan. A 40, 153–173. https://doi.org/10.1068/a39100.

Castree, N., 2008b. Neoliberalising Nature: The Logics of Deregulation and Reregulation. Environ. Plan. A 40, 131–152. https://doi.org/10.1068/a3999.

CBRT, 2014. Financial Stability Report (No. 19). CBRT (Central Bank of the Republic of Turkey), Ankara.

Celasun, M., 2002. 2001 Krizi Oncesi ve Sonrasi: Makroekonomik ve Mali Bir Degerlendirme. VI METU Int. Conf. Econ. 11-14 September, Ankara.

Celasun, M., Rodrik, D., 1989. Debt, Adjustment, and Growth: Turkey, in: Sachs, J.D., Collins, S.M. (Eds.), Developing Country Debt and Economic Performance, Volume 3: Country Studies – Indonesia, Korea, Philippines, Turkey. University of Chicago Press, by the National Bureau of Economic Research (NBER).

Cerutti, E., Dagher, J., Dell'Ariccia, G., 2015. Housing Finance and Real-Estate Booms: A Cross Country Perspective (IMF Discussion Note No. SDN/15/12). International Monetary Fund.

Chaudhry, K.A., 1993. The Myths of the Market and the Common History of Late Developers. Polit. Soc. 21, 245–274.

Chick, V., Dow, S., 2001. Formalism, Logic and Reality: A Keynesian Analysis. Camb. J. Econ. 25, 705–721.

Christophers, B., 2015. The Limits to Financialization. Dialogues Hum. Geogr. 5, 183–200. https://doi.org/10.1177/2043820615588153.

Cizre, Ü., Yeldan, E., 2005. The Turkish Encounter with Neo-Liberalism: Economics and Politics in the 2000/2001 Crises. Rev. Int. Polit. Econ. 12, 387–408. https://doi.org/10.2307/25124028.

Clark, E., 1988. The Rent Gap and Transformation of the Built Environment: Case Studies in Malmö 1860-1985. Geogr. Ann. Ser. B Hum. Geogr. 70, 241–254. https://doi.org/10.2307/490951.

Clark, J., 1993. Debt Reduction and Market Reentry under the Brady Plan. Fed. Reserve Bank N. Y. FRBNY Q. Rev., Winter 1993-1994 18, 38–62.

Coleman, J. 1968. The Methodological Study of Change, in Hubert M. Blalock (ed.) Methodology in Social Research, McGraw Hill, 105–131.

Correa, E., Vidal, G., 2012. Financialization and Global Financial Crisis in Latin American Countries. J. Econ. Issues 46, 541–548. http://dx.doi.org/10.2753/JEI0021-3624460229.

Correa, E., Vidal, G., Marshall, W., 2012. Financialisation in Mexico: Trajectory and Limits. J. Post Keynes. Econ. 35, 255–276.

Coşkun, Y., 2015. Türkiye'de Konut Finansmanı: Sorunlar ve Çözüm Önerileri. Türkiye Bankalar Birliği (TBB), Istanbul.

Coşkun, Y., Watkins, C., 2014. Macroeconomic Change, Housing Affordability and Public Policies: The Case of Turkey. Presented at the ENHR Conference, Scotland.

Crotty, J.R., 1990. Owner–Manager Conflict and Financial Theories of Investment Instability: A Critical Assessment of Keynes, Tobin, and Minsky. J. Post Keynes. Econ. 12, 519–542. https://doi.org/10.1080/01603477.1990.11489816.

Cutler, A. J. 1978. Problems of a General Theory of Capitalist Circulation, in: Cutler A. J., Hindess, B., Hirst, P., Hussein, A. (eds.), Marx's Capital and Capitalism Today. Routledge, London, pp 62–128.

Dagdeviren, H., 2009. Limits to Competition and Regulation in Privatized Electricity Markets. Ann. Public Coop. Econ. 80, 641–664. https://doi.org/10.1111/j.1467-8292.2009.00395.x.

Davidson, P., Weintraub, S., 1973. Money as Cause and Effect. Econ. J. 83, 1117–1132.

Demir, F., 2009a. Turkish Post-crisis Development Experience from a Comparative Perspective: Structural Break or Business as Usual?, in: Onis, Z., Senses, F. (Eds.), Turkey and The Global Economy: Neo-Liberal Restructuring and Integration in the Post-Crisis Era. Routledge, New York, pp. 11–33.

Demir, F., 2009b. Capital Market Imperfections and Financialization of Real Sectors in Emerging Markets: Private Investment and Cash Flow Relationship Revisited. World Dev. 37, 953–964.

Demir, F., 2004. A Failure Story: Politics and Financial Liberalization in Turkey, Revisiting the Revolving Door Hypothesis. World Dev. 32, 851–869.

Demir, F., Erdem, N., 2010. Labour Market Performance after Structural Adjustment in Developing Countries: The interesting but not so unique case of Turkey, in: Valencia, L.K., Hahn (Eds.), Employment and Labor Issues: Unemployment, Youth Employment and Child Labor. Nova Science Publishers, New York, pp. 1–55.

Demirguc-Kunt, A., Detragiache, E., 1998. The Determinants of Banking Crises in Developing and Developed Countries. IMF Staff Pap. 45.

Demirguc-Kunt, A., Detragiache, E., Gupta, P., 2000. Inside the Crisis: An Empirical Analysis of Banking Systems in Distress. Policy Res. Work. Pap. Ser. 2431, The World Bank.

Dos Santos, P.L., 2013. A Cause for Policy Concern: The Expansion of Household Credit in Middle-Income Economies. Int. Rev. Appl. Econ. 27, 316–338.

Dos Santos, P.L., 2011. Credit, Profitability and Instability: A Strictly Structural Approach (Discussion Paper No. 36). Research on Money and Finance.

Dos Santos, P. L., 2009. At the Heart of the Matter: Household Debt in Contemporary Banking and the International Crisis, Ekonomiaz, 7, 54–77.

Duménil, G., 1983. Beyond the Transformation Riddle: A Labour Theory of Value. Sci. Soc. 33, 427–450.

Duménil, G., Lévy, D., 2011. The Crisis of Neoliberalism. Harvard University Press, Cambridge.

Duménil, G., Lévy, D., 2004. Capital Resurgent: Roots of the Neoliberal Revolution. Harvard University Press, Cambridge.

Dymski, G.A., 2010. Why the Subprime Crisis is Different: A Minskyian Approach. Camb. J. Econ. 34, 239–255. https://doi.org/10.1093/cje/bep054.

Dymski, G.A., 2009a. The Global Financial Customer and the Spatiality of Exclusion after the 'End of Geography'. Camb. J. Reg. Econ. Soc. 2, 267–285. https://doi.org/10.1093/cjres/rsp011.

Dymski, G.A., 2009b. Racial Exclusion and the Political Economy of the Subprime Crisis (Discussion Paper No. 02). Research on Money and Finance.

EIA, 2017. Assumptions to the Annual Energy Outlook 2016. U.S. Energy Information Administration, Department of Energy, Washington, D.C.

Eichengreen, B., 2001. Capital Account Liberalization: What Do Cross-Country Studies Tell Us? World Bank Econ. Rev. 15, 341–365.

Eichengreen, B., Hausmann, R., 1999. Exchange Rates and Financial Fragility (Working Paper No. 7418). National Bureau of Economic Research. https://doi.org/10.3386/w7418.

EMRA, 2015. Electricity Market Distribution Segment Revenue Regulation, accessed from http://www.resmigazete.gov.tr/eskiler/2015/12/20151219-4.pdf).

Engelen, E., Ertürk, I., Froud, J., Johal, S., Leaver, A., Moran, M., Williams, K., 2012. Misrule of Experts? The Financial Crisis as Elite Debacle. Econ. Soc. 41, 360–382. https://doi.org/10.1080/03085147.2012.661634.

Engelen, E., Erturk, I., Froud, J., Leaver, A., Williams, K., 2010a. Reconceptualizing Financial Innovation: Frame, Conjuncture and Bricolage. Econ. Soc. 39, 33–63. https://doi.org/10.1080/03085140903424568.

Engelen, E., Konings, M., Fernandez, R., 2010b. Geographies of Financialization in Disarray: The Dutch Case in Comparative Perspective. Econ. Geogr. 86, 53–73. https://doi.org/10.1111/j.1944-8287.2009.01054.x.

Epstein, G.A. (Ed.), 2005. Financialization and the World Economy. Edward Elgar, Cheltenham.

Erdogdu, E., 2013. Essays on Electricity Market Reforms: A Cross-Country Applied Approach (PhD Thesis). University of Cambridge, Cambridge.

Ergunes, N., 2009. Global Integration of the Turkish Economy in the Era of Financialisation (Discussion Paper No. 8). Research on Money and Finance.

Erol, I., 2015. Türkiye'de Konut Balonu Var Mı? Konut Sektörü Kapitalizasyon Oranları Analizi, in: Özçelik, E., Taymaz, E. (Eds.), Türkiye Ekonomisinin Dünü, Bugünü, Yarını. Imge Kitabevi, Ankara, pp. 323–344.

Erol, I., Çetinkaya, Ö., 2009. Originating Long-Term Fixed-Rate Mortgages in Developing Economies: New Evidence from Turkey. METU Stud. Dev. 36, 325–362.

Erol, I., Patel, K., 2004. Housing Policy and Mortgage Finance in Turkey during the Late 1990s Inflationary Period. Int. Real Estate Rev. 7, 98–120.

Erol, I., Unal, U., 2015. Role of Construction Sector in Economic Growth: New Evidence from Turkey. MPRA Pap. 68263.

Erturk, I., 2003. Governance or Financialisation: The Turkish Case. Compet. Change 7, 185–204.

Erturk, I., Froud, J., Johal, S., Leaver, A., Williams, K., 2007. The Democratization of Finance? Promises, Outcomes and Conditions. Rev. Int. Polit. Econ. 14, 553–575. https://doi.org/10.1080/09692290701475312.

Erturk, I., Froud, J., Johal, S., Williams, K., 2004. Corporate Governance and Disappointment. Rev. Int. Polit. Econ. 11, 677–713. https://doi.org/10.1080/0969229042000279766.

ESMAP, 2015. Turkey's Energy Transition: Milestones and Challenges (No. ACS14951). Energy Sector Management Assistance Program, The World Bank Group, Washington, D.C.

EUAS, 2016. Annual Activity Report. EUAS (Turkish Electricity Generation Company), Ankara.

Faroqhi, S., 1984. Towns and Townsmen of Ottoman Anatolia: Trade, Crafts, and Food Production in an Urban Setting, 1520-1650, Cambridge Studies in Islamic Civilization. Cambridge University Press, New York.

Feldstein, M., 1999. A Self-Help Guide for Emerging Markets. Foreign Aff. 78.

Fine, B., 2013. Financialization From A Marxist Perspective. Int. J. Polit. Econ. 42, 47–66.

Fine, B., 2010. Locating Financialisation. Hist. Mater. 18, 97–116.

Fine, B., 2008. Rethinking the Rethink: The World Bank and Privatization, in: Bayliss, K., Fine, B. (Eds.), Privatization and Alternative Public Sector Reform in Sub-Saharan Africa: Delivering on Electricity and Water. Palgrave Macmillan, Basingstoke, pp. 55–87.

Fine, B., 2001. Neither the Washington nor the post-Washington consensus: An Introduction, in: Fine, B., Lapavitsas, C., Pincus, J. (Eds.), Development Policy in the 21st Century: Beyond the Post-Washington Consensus. Routledge, London & New York, pp. 1–27.

Fine, B., 1994. Consumption in Contemporary Capitalism: Beyond Marx and Veblen – A Comment. Rev. Soc. Econ. 52, 391–396.

Fine, B., 1990. The Coal Question: Political Economy and Industrial Change from the Nineteenth Century to the Present Day. Routledge, London.

Fine, B. (Ed.), 1986. The Value dimension: Marx versus Ricardo and Sraffa, Economy and society paperbacks. Routledge & Kegan Paul, London & New York.

Fine, B., 1985. Banking Capital and the Theory of Interest. Sci. Soc. 49, 387–413.

Fine, B., 1982a. Theories of the Capitalist Economy. Holmes & Meier Publishers Inc.

Fine, B., 1982b. Landed Property and the Distinction Between Royalty and Rent. Land Econ. 58, 338–350. https://doi.org/10.2307/3145941.

Fine, B., 1980. On Marx's Theory of Agricultural rent: A Rejoinder. Econ. Soc. 9, 327–331. https://doi.org/10.1080/03085148008538600.

Fine, B., 1979. On Marx's Theory of Agricultural Rent. Econ. Soc. 8, 241–278. https://doi. org/10.1080/03085147900000009.

Fine, B., Dimakou, O., 2016. Macroeconomics: A Critical Companion, Political economy and development. Pluto Press, London.

Fine, B., Harris, L., 1979. Rereading Capital. Columbia University Press, New York.

Fine, B., Lapavitsas, C., Saad-Filho, A., 2004. Transforming the Transformation Problem: Why The "New Interpretation" is a Wrong Turning. Rev. Radic. Polit. Econ. 36, 3–19.

Fine, B., Leopold, E., 1993. The World of Consumption. Routledge, London & New York.

Fine, B., Saad-Filho, A., 2016. Thirteen Things You Need to Know About Neoliberalism. Crit. Sociol. 43, 685–706. https://doi.org/10.1177/0896920516655387.

Fine, B., Saad-Filho, A., 2010. Marx's Capital, 5th ed. Pluto Press, London & New York.

Foley, D., 1986. Understanding Capital: Marx's Economic Theory. Harvard University Press, Cambridge, Mass. & London.

Foley, D., 1982. The Value of Money, the Value of Labour Power and the Marxian Transformation Problem. Rev. Radic. Polit. Econ. 14, 37–47.

Foley, D., Duménil, G., 2008. Marxian Transformation Problem, in: Durlauf, S.N., Blume, L.E. (Eds.), The New Palgrave Dictionary of Economics. Palgrave Macmillan, Basingstoke.

Fracchia, J., Ryan, C., 1992. Historical Materialist Science, Crisis and Commitment, in: Bonefeld, W. (ed.) Open Marxism, vol: 2, Pluto, London.

Froud, J., Johal, S., Williams, K., 2002. Financialisation and The Coupon Pool. Cap. Cl. 26, 119–151. https://doi.org/10.1177/030981680207800106.

Gabor, D.V., 2012a. Managing Capital Accounts in Emerging Markets: Lessons from the Global Financial Crisis. J. Dev. Stud. 48, 714–731. https://doi.org/10.1080/00220388.2011.649257.

Gabor, D.V., 2012b. The Road to Financialization in Central and Eastern Europe: The Early Policies and Politics of Stabilizing Transition. Rev. Polit. Econ. 24, 227–249. https://doi.org/10.1080/09538259.2012.664333.

Gabor, D.V., 2010. (De)Financialization and Crisis in Eastern Europe. Compet. Change 14, 248–270.

Gabor, D.V., Ban, C., 2013. Fiscal Policy in Financialized Times: Investor Loyalty, Financialization and the Varieties of Capitalism. Cent. Law Policy Finance Boston Univ. February 4.

Gadanecz, B., 2004. The Syndicated Loan Market: Structure, Development and Implications. BIS Q. Rev. December 2004. https://ssrn.com/abstract=1967463.

Gerschenkron, A., 1962. Economic Backwardness in Historical Perspective: A Book of Essays. Harvard University Press, Cambridge MA.

Grabel, I., 2011. Not Your Grandfather's IMF: Global Crisis, 'Productive Incoherence' and Developmental Policy Space. Camb. J. Econ. 35, 805–830. https://doi.org/10.1093/cje/ber012.

Grabel, I., 1995. Speculation-led Economic Development: A Post-Keynesian Interpretation of Financial Liberalization Programmes in the Third World. Int. Rev. Appl. Econ. 9, 127–149. https://doi.org/10.1080/758538249.

Gros, D., Selcuki, C., 2013. The Changing Structure of Turkey's Trade and Industrial Competitiveness: Implications for the EU (Working Paper No. 3), Global Turkey in Europe. IPC Sabanci University.

Guney, E.S., 2005. Restructuring, Competition, And Regulation in the Turkish Electricity Industry. TEPAV, Ankara.

Gungen, A.R., 2012. Debt Management and Financialisation as Facets of State Restructuring: The Case of Turkey in the Post-1980 Period (PhD Thesis). Middle East Technical University, Ankara.

Haiven, M. 2014. Cultures of Financialization. Palgrave Macmillan, London.

Haldane, A.G., 2015. The Costs of Short-termism. Polit. Q. 86, 66–76. https://doi.org/10.1111/1467-923X.12233.

Hall, D., 2012. Re-municipalising Municipal Services in Europe (PSIRU Research Report). PSIRU (Public Services International Research Unit at University of Greenwich).

Hall, D., Thomas, S., Corral, V., 2009. Global Experience with Electricity Liberalisation (PSIRU Research Report). PSIRU (Public Services International Research Unit at University of Greenwich).

Hall, D., van Niekerk, S., Nguyen, J., Thomas, S., 2013. Energy Liberalisation, Privatisation and Public Ownership (PSIRU Research Report). PSIRU (Public Services International Research Unit at University of Greenwich).

Hall, P.A., Soskice, D., 2001. Varieties of Capitalism. Oxford University Press.

Harcourt, G.C., 2006. The Structure of Post-Keynesian Economics: The Core Contributions of the Pioneers. Cambridge University Press, Cambridge.

Harvey, D., 2012. Rebel Cities: From the Right to the City to the Urban Revolution. Verso, London.

Harvey, D., 2003. The New Imperialism. Oxford University Press, Oxford & New York.

Harvey, D., 2002. The Art of Rent: Globalisation, Monopoly and the Commodification of Culture. Social. Regist. 38, A World of Contradictions, 93–110.

Harvey, D., 1982. The Limits to Capital. Blackwell, Oxford.

Head, C., 2000. Financing of Private Hydropower Projects (World Bank Discussion Paper No. WDP 420). The World Bank, Washington, D.C.

Hein, E., 2009. A Post-Keynesian Perspective on "Financialisation." Macroecon. Policy Inst. IMK Hans Boeckler Found. Res. Rep. 1/2009.

Hein, E., van Treeck, T., 2008. "Financialisation" in Post-Keynesian Models of Distribution and Growth – A Systematic Review. Macroecon. Policy Inst. IMK Hans Boeckler Found. Work. Pap. 10/2008.

Hilferding, R., 1981. Finance Capital: A Study of the Latest Phase of Capitalist Development. Routledge & Kegan Paul, London.

IFC, 2015. Hydroelectric Power: A Guide for Developers and Investors. International Finance Corporation, World Bank Group, Washington, D.C.

Ilyenkov, E.V., 1977. Dialectical Logic: Essays on Its History and Theory. Progress Publishers, Moskow.

IMF, 2017. Turkey: Financial System Stability Assessment (IMF Country Report No. 17/35), Financial Sector Assessment Program. International Monetary Fund, Washington, D.C.

IMF, 2015. World Economic Outlook: Adjusting to Lower Commodity Prices. International Monetary Fund, Washington D.C.

IMF, 2012. Turkey: Financial System Stability Assessment (IMF Country Reports No. 12/261). International Monetary Fund, Washington, D.C.

Itō, M., Lapavitsas, C., 1999. Political Economy of Money and Finance. Palgrave Macmillan, Basingstoke.

Jessop, B., 2001. What Follows Fordism? On the Periodisation of Capitalism and Its Regulation, in: Albritton, R., Itoh, M. (Eds.), Phases of Capitalist Development: Booms, Crises, and Globalization. Palgrave, Basingstoke, pp. 282–299.

Jessop, B., 1997. Survey Article: The Regulation Approach. J. Polit. Philos. 5, 287–326. https://doi.org/10.1111/1467-9760.00036.

JICA, 1997. Feasibility Study on Coruh-Berta Hydroelectric Power development Project (No. 36). Japan International Cooperation Agency, funded by Republic of Turkey Ministry of Energy and Natural Resources General Directorate of Electrical Survey and Development Adninistrationof Turkey.

Joskow, P., 1976. Contributions of the Theory of Marginal Cost Pricing. Bell J. Econ. 7, 197–206.

Joskow, P., Schmalansee, R., 1986. Incentive Regulation for Electric Utilities. Yale J. Regul. 4, 1–49.

Kahn, A.E., 1988. The Economics of Regulation: Principles and Institutions. The MIT Press, Cambridge Massachusetts.

Kaldor, N., 1957. A Model of Economic Growth. Econ. J. 67, 591–624.

Kaldor, N., 1955. Alternative Theories of Distribution. Rev. Econ. Stud. 23, 83–100.

Kaltenbrunner, A., 2011. Currency Internationalisation and Exchange Rate Dynamics in Emerging Markets; A Post-Keynesian Analysis of Brazil (PhD Thesis). SOAS, University of London, London.

Kaltenbrunner, A., Karacimen, E., 2016. The Contested Nature of Financialization in Emerging Capitalist Economies, in: Subasat, T. (Ed.), The Great Financial Meltdown: Systemic, Conjunctural or Policy Created? Edward Elgar, Cheltenham, pp. 287–306.

Kaltenbrunner, A., Painceira, J.P., 2015. Developing Countries' Changing Nature of Financial Integration and New Forms of External Vulnerability: The Brazilian Experience. Camb. J. Econ. 39, 1281–1306. https://doi.org/10.1080/13563467.2017.1349089.

Kaplan, E., Rodrik, D., 2001. Did the Malaysian Capital Controls Work? NBER Work. Pap. 8142.

Karacimen, E., 2015. Interlinkages Between Credit, Debt and The Labour Market: Evidence From Turkey. Camb. J. Econ. 39, 751–767.

Karacimen, E., 2014. Financialization in Turkey: The Case of Consumer Debt. J. Balk. East. Stud. 16, 161–180.

Karacimen, E., 2013. Political Economy of Consumer Debt in Developing Countries: Evidence from Turkey (PhD Thesis). SOAS, University of London, London.

Karahan, H., Toptas, M., 2013. Pricing Electric Power under a Hybrid Wholesale Mechanism: Evaluating the Turkish Electricity Market. Int. J. Energy Econ. Policy 3, 221–228.

Karatepe, İ.D., 2016. The State, Islamists, Discourses, and Bourgeoisie: The Construction Industry in Turkey. Res. Policy Turk. 1, 46–62. https://doi.org/10.1080/23760818.2015.1099781.

Karwowski, E., 2015. The Finance-Mining Nexus in South Africa: How Mining Companies Use the South African Equity Market To Speculate. J. South. Afr. Stud. 41, 9–28.

Kay, J., Vickers, J., 1988. Regulatory Reform in Britain. Econ. Policy 7, 185–252.

Keleş, R., 1990. Housing Policy in Turkey, in: Shidlo, G. (Ed.), Housing Policy in Developing Countries. Routledge, London.

Keleş, R., 1972. 100 Soruda Türkiye'de Şehirleşme, Konut ve Gecekondu. Gercek Yayinevi, Istanbul.

Kessides, I., 2004. Reforming Infrastructure: Privatization, Regulation, and Competition (World Bank Policy Research Report No. 28985). World Bank.

Khan, K. A., Paul, S., Islam, K. A., Islam, B. 2012. Modeling of a Biomass Energy based (BPL) Generating Power Plant and its Features in comparison with other Generating Plants, International Proceedings of Chemical, Biological and Environmental Engineering, 44, Singapore.

Knetter, M.M., 1989. Price Discrimination by U.S. and German Exporters. Am. Econ. Rev. 79, 198–210.

Kornai, J., 2000. What the Change of System from Socialism to Capitalism Does and Does Not Mean. J. Econ. Perspect. 14, 27–42.

Kornai, J., 1986. The Soft Budget Constraint. Kyklos 39, 3–30. https://doi.org/10.1111/j.1467-6435.1986.tb01252.x.

KPMG, 2017. Macro Trends in Turkish and Global Economy (No. 5). KPMG Turkey.

Kregel, J.A., 1978. Post-Keynesian Theory: Income Distribution. Challenge 21, 37–43. https://doi.org/10.1080/05775132.1978.11470449.

Kregel, J.A., 1976. Economic Methodology in the Face of Uncertainty: The Modelling Methods of Keynes and the Post-Keynesians. Econ. J. 86, 209–225.

Krippner, G.R., 2005. The Financialization of the American Economy. Socio-Econ. Rev. 3, 173–208. https://doi.org/10.1093/SER/mwi008.

Kurz, H., 1978. Rent Theory in a Multisectoral Model. Oxf. Econ. Pap., New Series 30, 16–37.

Kuyucu, T., Unsal, O., 2010. "Urban Transformation" as State-led Property Transfer: An Analysis of Two Cases of Urban Renewal in Istanbul. Urban Stud. 47, 1479–1499.

Kuznets, S., 1952. Proportion of Capital Formation to National Product. Am. Econ. Rev., Papers and Proceedings of the Sixty-fourth Annual Meeting of the American Economic Association 42, 507–526.

Langley, P., 2008. Financialization and the Consumer Credit Boom. Compet. Change 12, 133–147.

Langley, P., 2004. In the Eye of the 'Perfect Storm': The Final Salary Pensions Crisis and Financialisation of Anglo-American Capitalism. New Polit. Econ. 9, 539–558. https://doi.org/10.1080/1356346042000311164.

Lapavitsas, C., 2013. Profiting Without Producing: How Finance Exploits Us All. Verso, London.

Lapavitsas, C., 2009. Financialised Capitalism: Crisis and Financial Expropriation. Hist. Mater. 17, 114–148.

Lapavitsas, C., 1997. Two Approaches to the Concept of Interest-Bearing Capital. Int. J. Polit. Econ., Issues in Marxian Theory of Money and Credit 27, 85–106.

Lapavitsas, C., Dos Santos, P.L., 2008. Globalization and Contemporary Banking: On the Impact of New Technology. Contrib. Polit. Econ. 27, 31–56. https://doi.org/10.1093/cpe/bzn005.

Lavoie, M., 1992. Foundations of Post-Keynesian Economic Analysis. Edward Elgar Publishing Ltd.

Lavoie, M., 1984. The Endogenous Flow of Credit and the Post-Keynesian Theory of Money. J. Econ. Issues 18, 771–797.

Lavoie, M., Godley, W., 2001. Kaleckian Models of Growth in a Coherent Stock-Flow Monetary Framework: A Kaldorian View. J. Post Keynes. Econ. 24, 277–311.

Lazonick, W., O'Sullivan, M., 2000. Maximizing Shareholder Value: A New Ideology for Corporate Governance. Econ. Soc. 29, 13–35. https://doi.org/10.1080/030851400360541.

Levy-Orlik, N., 2012. Effects on Financialization on the Structure of production and Nonfinancial Private Enterprises: The Case of Mexico. J. Post Keynes. Econ. 35, 235–254.

Leyshon, A., Thrift, N. 1997. Money/Space: Geographies of Monetary Transformation. Routledge, London.

Lindo, D., 2013. Political Economy of Financial Derivatives: A Theoretical Analysis of the Evolution of Banking and Its Role in Derivatives Markets (PhD Thesis). SOAS, University of London, London.

Lipietz, A., 1982. The "So-Called Transformation Problem" Revisited. J. Econ. Theory 26, 59–88.

Lipietz, A., Vale, M., 1988. Accumulation, Crises, and Ways Out: Some Methodological Reflections on the Concept of "Regulation." Int. J. Polit. Econ. 18, 10–43.

Littlechild, S., 1970. A Game Theoretic Approach to Public Utility Pricing 8, 162–166.

Marois, T., 2011. Emerging Market Bank Rescues in an Era of Finance-led Neoliberalism: A Comparison of Mexico and Turkey. Rev. Int. Polit. Econ. 18, 168–196. https://doi.org/10.1080/09692290903475474.

Marx, K., 1981. Capital: A Critique of Political Economy, Pelican Marx library. Penguin, Harmondsworth.

Mazzucato, M., Semieniuk, G., 2016. Financing Renewable Energy: Who is Financing What and Why It Matters (SPRU Working Paper Series No. SWPS 2016-12 (June)). SPRU (Science Policy Research Unit) at the University of Sussex.

McKinnon, R.I., 1973. Money and Capital in Economic Development. Washington Brookings Institution Press.

McMillan, M., Rodrik, D., Verduzco-Gallo, I., 2014. Globalization, Structural Change, and Productivity Growth, with an Update on Africa. World Dev. 63, 11–32.

Michell, J., Toporowski, J., 2014. Critical Observations on Financialization and the Financial Process. Int. J. Polit. Econ. 42, 67–82.

Milonakis, D., 1997. The Dynamics of History: Structure and Agency in Historical Evolution. Sci. Soc. 61, 303–329.

Milonakis, D., 1995. Commodity Production and Price Formation Before Capitalism: A Value Theoretic Approach. J. Peasant Stud. 22, 327–355.

Milonakis, D., Fine, B., 2009. From Political Economy to Economics: Method, The Social and The Historical in the Evolution of Economic Theory. Routledge, London & New York.

Milor, V., 1990. The Genesis of Planning in Turkey. New Perspect. Turk. 4, 1–30. https://doi.org/10.15184/S0896663460000194.

Ministry of Energy and Natural Resources, 2015. Five Year Strategic Plan (2015-2019). Ankara.

Mohun, S., 1994. A Re(in)statement of the Labour Theory of Value. Camb. J. Econ. 18.

Montgomerie, J., Büdenbender, M., 2015. Round the Houses: Homeownership and Filures of Asset-Based Welfare in the United Kingdom. New Polit. Econ. 20, 386–405. https://doi.org/10.1080/13563467.2014.951429.

Moseley, F., 2015. Money and Totality: A Macro-monetary Interpretation of Marx's Logic in Capital and the End of the "Transformation Problem," Historical materialism book series. Brill.

Moseley, F., 2000. The "New Solution" to the Transformation Problem: A Sympathetic Critique. Rev. Radic. Polit. Econ. 32, 282–316.

Moseley, F., 1993. Marx's Method in "Capital"; A reexamination. Humanities press, Atlantic Highlands NJ.

Murray, P., 1988. Marx's Theory of Scientific Knowledge. Humanities Press, Atlantic Highlands.

Nagayama, H., 2007. Effects of Regulatory Reforms in the Electricity Supply Industry on Electricity Prices in Developing Countries. Energy Policy 35, 3440–3462.

Nesvetailova, A., Palan, R., 2013. Minsky in the Shadows. Rev. Radic. Polit. Econ. 45, 349–368. https://doi.org/10.1177/0486613412470090.

Newberry, D., 2001. Privatization, Restructuring, and Regulation of Network Utilities. The MIT Press, London.

Newbery, D., 1995. Power Markets and Market Power. Energy J. 16, 39–66.

Ng, F., Kaminski, B., 2006. Turkey's Evolving Trade Integration into Pan-European Markets (SSRN Scholarly Paper No. ID 917479). Social Science Research Network, Rochester, NY.

Ofori, G., 1990. The Construction Industry: Aspects of Its Economics and Management. Singapore University Press, Singapore.

Oguz, S., 2009. The Response of the Turkish State to the 2008 Crisis: A Further Step towards Neoliberal Authoritarian Statism. Presented at the 3rd International Research Workshop in Political Economy (IIPPE), Ankara.

Ollman, B., 2003. Dance of the Dialectic: Steps in Marx's Method. University of Illinois Press.

Onaran, O., 2009. Wage Share, Globalization and Crisis: The case of the Manufacturing Industry in Korea, Mexico and Turkey. Int. Rev. Appl. Econ. 23, 113–134.

Onaran, O., 2006. Speculation-led Growth and Fragility in Turkey: Does EU Make a Difference or "Can It Happen Again"? Vienna Univ. Econ. Bus. Dep. Econ. Work. Pap. Ser. 93.

Onaran, O., Boesch, V., 2014. The Effect of Globalization on the Distribution of Taxes and Social Expenditures in Europe: Do Welfare State Regimes Matter? Environ. Plan. A 46, 373–397.

Onaran, O., Galanis, G., 2012. Income Distribution and Growth: A Global Model. ILO Work. Pap., Conditions of Work and Employment Series 40.

Onaran, O., Stockhammer, E., 2005. Two Different Export-Oriented Growth Strategies: Accumulation and Distribution in Turkey and South Korea. Emerg. Mark. Finance Trade 41, 65–89.

Onaran, O., Stockhammer, E., Grafl, L., 2011. Financialisation, Income Distribution and Aggregate Demand in the USA. Camb. J. Econ. 35, 637–661. https://doi.org/10.1093/cje/beq045.

Oncu, A., 1988. The Politics of the Urban Land Market in Turkey: 1950-1980. Int. J. Urban Reg. Res. 12, 38–64.

Onis, Z., 2006. Varieties and Crises of Neoliberal Globalisation: Argentina, Turkey and The IMF. Third World Q. 27, 239–263.

Onis, Z., Senses, F., 2009. Turkey and the Global Economy: Neoliberal Restructuring and Integration in the Post-Crisis Era. Routledge, Oxon.

Orhangazi, Ö., 2020. Türkiye Ekonomisinin Yapısı: Sorunlar, Kırılganlıklar, Kriz Dinamikleri. İmge Kitabevi Yayınları, Ankara.

Orhangazi, Ö., 2008. Financialisation and Capital Accumulation in the Non-financial Corporate Sector: A Theoretical and Empirical Investigation on the US Economy: 1973–2003. Camb. J. Econ. 32, 863–886. https://doi.org/10.1093/cje/ben009.

Painceira, J.P., 2012. Financialisation, Reserve Accumulation, and Central Banking in Emerging Economies: Banks in Brazil and Korea (Discussion Paper No. 38). Research on Money and Finance.

Painceira, J.P., 2009. Developing Countries in the Era of Financialisation: From Deficit Accumulation to Reserve Accumulation (Discussion Paper No. 4). Research on Money and Finance.

Palley, T.I., 2013. Financialization: The Economics of Finance Capital Domination. Palgrave Macmillan, London.

Palma, J.G., 2012. How the Full Opening of the Capital Account to Highly Liquid Financial Markets Led Latin America to Two and a Half Cycles of "Mania, Panic and Crash." Camb. Work. Pap. Econ. CWPE CWPE 1201. https://doi.org/10.17863/CAM.5252.

Papadatos, D., 2009. Central Banking in Contemporary Capitalism: Inflation Targeting and Financial Crises (Discussion Paper No. 5). Research on Money and Finance.

Pargal, S., Banerjee, S.G., 2014. More Power to India: The Challenge of Electricity Distribution. World Bank, Washington, D.C.

Peck, J., Theodore, N., 2007. Variegated Capitalism. Prog. Hum. Geogr. 31, 731–772. https://doi.org/10.1177/0309132507083505.

Peiris, S.J., 2010. Foreign Participation in Emerging Markets' Local Currency Bond Markets. IMF Work. Pap. 10/88.

Perelman, M., 1999. Marx, Devalorisation, and the Theory of Value. Camb. J. Econ. 23, 719–728.

Pollitt, M., 2007. Evaluating the Evidence on Electricity Reform: Lessons for the South East Europe (SEE) Market (Working Paper). ESRC Electricity Policy Research Group and Judge Business School, University of Cambridge.

Pond, R., 2006. Liberalisation, Privatisation and Regulation in the UK Electricity (PIQUE Research Report). PIQUE (privatisation of Public Services and the Impact on Quality, Employment and Productivity).

Powell, J., 2013. Subordinate Financialisation: A Study of Mexico and its Non-financial Corporations (PhD Thesis). SOAS, University of London, London.

Rethel, L., 2010. Financialization and the Malaysian Political Economy. Globalizations 7, 489–506.

Reuten, G., 2003. On "Becoming Necessary" in an Organic Systematic Dialectic: The Case of Creeping Inflation, in: Albritton, R., Simoulidis, J. (Eds.), New Dialectics and Political Economy. Palgrave Macmillan, London & New York, pp. 42–59.

Robertson, M., 2014. The Financialisation of British Housing: A Systems of Provision Approach (PhD Thesis). SOAS, University of London, London.

Rodrik, D., 2009. The Turkish Economy After The Crisis. Turk. Econ. Assoc. 9.

Rodrik, D., 2006. The Social Cost of Foreign Exchange Reserves. Int. Econ. J. 20, 253–266.

Rodrik, D., 1998. Why Do More Open Economies Have Bigger Governments? J. Polit. Econ. 106, 997–1032.

Rodrik, D., Velasco, A., 1999. Short-Term Capital Flows (NBER Working Papers No. 7364). National Bureau of Economic Research, Inc.

Rosdolsky, R., 1977. The Making of Marx's Capital. Pluto Press, London.

Saad-Filho, A., 2002. The Value of Marx: Political Economy for Contemporary Capitalism. Routledge, London & New York.

Saad-Filho, A., 1997. Concrete and Abstract Labour in Marx's Theory of Value. Rev. Polit. Econ. 9, 457–477.

Samuelson, P.A., 1992. Marx on Rent: A Failure to Transform Correctly. J. Hist. Econ. Thought 14, 143–167. https://doi.org/10.1017/S1053837200004971.

Sarioglu-Erdogdu, P., Balamir, M., Pellenbarg, P.H., Terpstra, P.R.A., 2012. Position of Owner Occupancy in Turkey and the Netherlands: A Descriptive Study. METU J. Fac. Archit. 29, 157–180.

Sawyer, M., 2013. What is Financialization? Int. J. Polit. Econ. 42, 5–18.

Saygili, S., Cihan, C., Yalcin, C., Hamsici, T., 2010. Türkiye İmalat Sanayiin İthalat Yapısı (Working Paper No. 10/02). Central Bank of the Republic of Turkey, Ankara.

Schaberg, M., 1999. Globalization and the Erosion of National Financial Systems: Is Declining Autonomy Inevitable? Edward Elgar Publishing Ltd., Cheltenham.

Sengul, S., 2015. Political Economy of Financialisation in Developing Countries: A Study of Industrial Restructuring in Turkey (PhD Thesis). SOAS, University of London, London.

Şengül, T., 2003. On the Trajectory of Urbanisation in Turkey: An attempt at periodisation. Int. Dev. Plan. Rev. 25, 153–168. https://doi.org/10.3828/idpr.25.2.3.

Senses, F., 1989. The Nature and Main Characteristics of Recent Turkish Growth in Exports of Manufactures. Dev. Econ. 27, 19–33. https://doi.org/10.1111/j.1746-1049.1989.tb00145.x.

Shamsavari, A., 1991. Dialectic and Social Theory: The Logic of "Capital." Merlin Books, Braunton, Devon.

Shaw, E.S., 1973. Financial Deepening in Economic Development. Oxford University Press, New York.

Smith, N., 1987. Gentrification and the Rent Gap. Ann. Assoc. Am. Geogr. 77, 462–465.

Smith, N., 1979. Toward a Theory of Gentrification: A Back to the City Movement by Capital, not People. J. Am. Plann. Assoc. 45, 538–548.

Smith, T., 2003. Systematic and Historical Dialectics: Towards a Marxian Theory of Globalization, in: Albritton, R., Simoulidis, J. (Eds.), New Dialectics and Political Economy. Palgrave Macmillan, London & New York, pp. 24–41.

Smith, T., 1998. Value Theory and Dialectics. Sci. Soc. 62, 460–470.

Sozen, Z., Kucuk, M.A., 1999. Secondary Subcontracting in the Turkish Construction Industry. Constr. Manag. Econ. 17, 215–220.

Steiner, F., 2000. Regulation, Industry Structure and Performance in the Electricity Supply Industry (OECD Economics Department Working Paper Series No. 238). OECD.

Stockhammer, E., 2012. Financialization, Income Distribution and the Crisis. Investig. Económica 71, 39–70.

Stockhammer, E., 2005. Shareholder Value Orientation and The Investment-Profit Puzzle. J. Post Keynes. Econ. 28, 193–215.

Stockhammer, E., 2004. Financialisation and The Slowdown of Accumulation. Camb. J. Econ. 28, 719–741. https://doi.org/10.1093/cje/beh032.

Stockhammer, E., Onaran, O., 2013. Wage-led Growth: Theory, Evidence, Policy. Rev. Keynes. Econ. 1, 61–78.

Strassman, W.P., 1978. Housing and Building Technology in Developing Countries. Michigan State University International Business and Economic Studies, East Lansing.

Strassmann, W.P., 1970. The Construction Sector in Economic Development. Scott. J. Polit. Econ. 17, 391–409. https://doi.org/10.1111/j.1467-9485.1970.tb00715.x.

Streeck, W., 2011. Taking Capitalism Seriously: Towards an Institutionalist Approach to Contemporary Political economy. Socio-Econ. Rev. 9, 137–167. https://doi.org/10.1093/ser/mwq028.

Swyngedouw, E., 2005. Dispossessing H2O: the Contested Terrain of Water Privatization. Capital. Nat. Social. 16, 81–98. https://doi.org/10.1080/1045575052000335384.

Tavasci, D., Toporowski, J. (Eds.), 2010. Minsky, Crisis and Development. Palgrave Macmillan, London.

Taymaz, E., Kilicaslan, Y., 2005. Determninants of Subcontracting and Regional Development: An Empirical Study on Turkish Textile and Engineering Industries. Reg. Stud. 39, 633–645.

Taymaz, E., Voyvoda, E., 2009. Industrial Restructuring and Technological Capabilities in Turkey, in: Onis, Z., Senses, F. (Eds.), Turkey and The Global Economy: Neo-Liberal Restructuring and Integration in the Post-Crisis Era. Routledge, New York.

Taymaz, E., Voyvoda, E., Yilmaz, K., 2008. Turkiye Imalat Sanayiinde Yapisal Dönüsüm ve Teknolojik Degisme Dinamikleri (ERC Working Paper No. 0804). ERC – Economic Research Center, Middle East Technical University.

Taymaz, E., Yilmaz, K., 2008. Integration with the Global Economy: The Case of Turkish Automobile and Consumer Electronics Industries (Koç University-TUSIAD Economic Research Forum Working Paper). Koc University-TUSIAD Economic Research Forum.

TEDAS Report (2012) accessed on 14/07/2017 from https://www.sayistay.gov.tr/tr/Upload/62643830/files/raporlar/genel_raporlar/kit_genel/Kamu%20%C4%B0%C5%9Fletmeleri%202012%20Y%C4%B1l%C4%B1%20Genel%20Raporu.pdf

TEIAS and TUBITAK MAM Report (2013), accessed from https://teias.gov.tr/sites/default/files/2017-06/10Y%C4%B1ll%C4%B1kTalepTahminleriRaporu2016%282%29.pdf.

Tekeli, I., 1982. Turkiye'de Kentlesme Yazilari. Turhan Kitabevi, Ankara.

Thomas, S., 2009. Energy Planning in Brazil (PSIRU Research Report). PSIRU (Public Services International Research Unit at University of Greenwich).

Thomas, S., 2004. Electricity Liberalisation: The Beginning of the End (Research Report). PSIRU (Public Services International Research Unit at University of Greenwich).

TMMOB, The Chamber of Electrical Engineers, 2012. Report on Privatisation of Electricity Distribution (No. 42nd Energy Study Group). TMMOB (The Union of Chambers of Turkish Engineers and Architects), The Chamber of Electrical Engineers, Ankara.

Topal, A., Celik, O., Yalman, G., 2015. Case Study Paper Relating Financialisation of the Built Environment to Changing Urban Politics, Social Geographies, Material Flows and Environmental Improvement/Degradation in Ankara (FESSUD Working Paper Series No. 116). FESSUD.

Toporowski, J., 2016. From Marx to the Keynesian Revolution: The Key Role of Finance. J. Econ. Lit. 5, (Forthcoming).

Toporowski, J., 2010. The Wisdom of Property and the Politics of the Middle Classes. Mon. Rev. 62, 10–15.

Toporowski, J., 2009. The Economics and Culture of Financial Inflation. Compet. Change 13, 145–156.

Toporowski, J., 2007. On Rhetoric and Being Realistic about the Monetary Policy of Developing Countries. J. Econ. Methodol. 14, 47–55. https://doi.org/10.1080/13501780601170057.

Toporowski, J., 2000. The End of Finance: Capital Market Inflation, Financial Derivatives and Pension Fund Capitalism. Routledge, London.

Tori, D., Onaran, O., 2015. The Effects of Financialization on Investment: Evidence from Firm-Level Data for the UK. Greenwich Polit. Econ. Res. Cent. Work. Pap. 17.

Turel, A., 2010. Development and the Present State of Housing Production by Housebuilding Cooperatives in Turkey. Pap. Present. Camb. Cent. Hous. Plan. Res. Conf. 16-17 September.

Turel, A., Koc, H., 2015. Housing Production under Less-Regulated Market Conditions in Turkey. J. Hous. Built Environ. 30, 53–68.

Turhan, I., 2008. Housing Sector in Turkey: Challenges and Opportunities, in: 17th Annual International Conference, The American Real Estate and Urban Economics Association. Presented at the Deputy Governor of the Central Bank of the the Republic of Turkey, Istanbul.

Turkish Competition Authority, 2015. Elektrik Toptan Satis ve Perakende Satis Sektor Arastirmasi (Investigation Report). Turkish Competition Authority, Ankara.

Turkish Court of Accounts, 2004. Report on Energy (No. 5088/1). Turkish Court of Accounts, Ankara.

Turkyilmaz, O., 2015. Ocak 2015 Itibariyla Turkiye'nin Enerji Gorunumu Raporu (Bulletin No. February 2015). TMMOB (The Union of Chambers of Turkish Engineers and Architects), The Chamber of Mechanical Engineers, Ankara.

Unal, H., Demirguc-Kunt, A., Leung, K.-W., 1993. The Brady Plan, The 1989 Mexican Debt Reduction Agreement, and Bank Stock Returns in the United States and Japan (World Bank Policy, Research Working Papers No. WPS 1012), Debt and International Finance. World Bank, Washington, D.C.

UNCTAD, 2014. World Investment Report, Investing in the SDGs: An Action Plan. United Nations Conference on Trade and Development, Switzerland.

Vagliasindi, M., 2013. Revisiting Public-Private Partnerships in the Power Sector (World Bank Studies No. 76183). World Bank.

Van der Tak, H., 1966. The Economic Choice between Hydroelectric and Thermal Power Developments, World Bank Staff Occassional Papers Number One. World Bank, Washington, D.C.

Van Treeck, T., 2009. The Macroeconomics of "Financialisation" and the Deeper Origins of the World Economic Crisis. Hans Bockler Found. Macroecon. Policy Inst. IMK Hans Boeckler Found. Work. Pap. 9.

Van Waeyenberge, E., 2015. Crisis? What crisis? The World Bank and Housing Finance for the Poor. SOAS Dep. Econ. Work. Pap. Ser. 191.

Vasudevan, R., 2009a. Dollar Hegemony, Financialization, and the Credit Crisis. Rev. Radic. Polit. Econ. 41, 291–304.

Vasudevan, R., 2009b. The Credit Crisis: Is the International Role of the Dollar at Stake? Mon. Rev. 60, 24–35.

Voyvoda, E., Yeldan, E., 2001. Patterns of Productivity Growth and the Wage Cycle in Turkish Manufacturing. Int. Rev. Appl. Econ. 15, 375–396.

Weeks, J., 1983. On the Issue of Capitalist Circulation and the Concepts Appropriate to its Analysis. Sci. Soc. 47, 214–225.

Weeks, J., 1979. The Process of Accumulation and the "Profit-Squeeze" Hypothesis. Sci. Soc. 43, 259–280.

World Bank, 2015. Financing for Development, Annual Report. World Bank, Washington, D.C.

World Bank, 2013. Towards a Sustainable Energy Future For All: Directions for the World Banl Group's Energy Sector (No. 79597), World Bank, Washington D.C.

World Bank, 2009. Housing Finance Policy in Emerging Markets (No. 49052). World Bank, Washington, D.C.

World Bank, 2006. Thirty Years of World Bank Shelter Lending – What have we learned? (No. 36217). World Bank, Washington, D.C.

World Bank, 1993. Housing: Enabling Markets to Work (No. 11820). World Bank, Washington, D.C.

World Bank, 1984. Issues and Strategies in Developing Countries (No. 13531). World Bank, Washington, D.C.

World Bank, 1957. Cost of Capital in the Choice Between Hydro and Thermal Power (No. EC 53), Central Economics Staff Series. World Bank, Washington, D.C.

Wray, L.R., 2008. Lessons from the Subprime Meltdown. Challenge 51, 40–68.

Yeldan, E., 2011. Macroeconomics of Growth and Employment: The Case of Turkey (Working paper). ILO.

Yeldan, E., 2007. Patterns of Adjustment under the Age of Finance: The Case of Turkey as a Peripheral Agent of Neoliberal Globalization (Working Paper No. 126). Political Economy Research Institute, University of Massachusetts at Amherst.

Yeldan, E., 2006. Neoliberal Global Remedies: From Speculative-Led Growth to IMF-Led Crisis in Turkey. Rev. Radic. Polit. Econ. 38, 193–213. https://doi.org/10.1177/0486613405285423.

Yeldan, E., 2002. Behind the 2000/2001 Turkish Crisis: Stability, Credibility, and Governance, for Whom? IDEAs Conf. International Money and Developing Countries: Theoretical and Policy Issues in the Current Context, Chennai.

Yeldan, E., 1995. Surplus Creation and Extraction Under Structural Adjustment: Turkey, 1980-1992. Rev. Radic. Polit. Econ. 27, 38–72. https://doi.org/10.1177/048661349502700202.

Yenturk, N., 1999. Short-term Capital Inflows and Their Impact on Macroeconomic Structure: Turkey in the 1990s. Dev. Econ. 37, 89–113.

Yirmibesoglu, F., 2008. Emlak Komisyoncularının Mekânsal Dağılım Süreci ve İstanbul'da Konut Piyasası. ITU Derg. Seri Mimar. Plan. Tasarim 7, 128–140.

Yorukoglu, M., Cufadar, A., 2008. Capital Flows to Turkey: Financial Implications and Policy Responses (BIS Papers No. 44), Financial Globalisation and Emerging Market Capital Flows. Bank for International Settlements, Geneva.

Index

abstract labour   20–24, 31, 37

accumulation   9, 11–13, 26–28, 33, 35–38, 42–45, 47–53, 56–58, 63–79, 85–90, 92–93, 96–98, 102, 105–108, 116, 118, 130–132, 137, 154, 191, 193, 200–210, 216–217, 225, 234, 245–249, 253–254

aggregate demand   4, 9, 12, 42–48, 51–58, 76, 100, 147, 237

agricultural rent   13, 194, 200–206, 209, 224, 249, 252

asset price inflation   37, 47, 51, 55–57, 65, 76, 79, 192–240

Breton Woods   88

Cambridge theories of distribution   41–42, 44–45, 57

capital flows   3, 36, 60, 79–90, 92–93, 96, 102–103, 114, 117–121, 125, 246

capital markets   3, 6, 37, 39–40, 49–50, 55–58, 61–65, 75–78, 83–86, 92, 96–97, 102, 136, 192, 214, 242

capital-intensive   13, 97, 99–100, 125–126, 128, 130–132, 135, 138, 141, 166, 177, 190, 193, 196, 241, 246–247, 252

carry-trade   11, 80, 89–90, 93, 99, 102, 131–132

circuit of capital   11, 24, 26, 33–34, 37, 41, 57–58, 66, 74–76, 79, 134, 136–138, 185, 188, 191, 209, 214, 215, 239, 244–248

circuitist   41, 53–54, 57

commodification   11–12, 23, 37–38, 136, 189, 193, 201, 232–233, 239, 241, 243–247, 250

commodity relations   8–11, 21, 23, 134, 136–137, 188, 191, 245

contingencies   9, 11, 16, 24, 72, 239

contradiction   14, 16–17, 21, 27, 249

countertendencies   11, 15, 23–24, 27–29, 32, 72, 74, 166, 239, 249

coupon pool   60–61, 102, 108

crowding-out   7, 12, 39, 76, 79, 81, 90–91

economies of scale   12, 37, 59, 66, 81, 105, 144–146, 193, 195–196, 199–211, 214, 227, 242, 251

electricity provision   9–12, 34–38, 75, 95, 134–139, 141, 143–191, 244–247

emerging economies   78–86, 91, 98, 120, 245

energy sector   1–3, 5, 8, 10, 13–14, 38, 92, 94, 127, 133, 135, 137, 140, 142, 146–147, 151, 154, 163, 166, 168, 170, 177–178, 180, 189–190, 194–195, 210, 213, 221, 223, 228, 230, 242, 247, 251, 253

Essence   11, 15–16, 18, 20–24, 46

exchange rate stabilisation   103

export-orientation   7, 66, 99–100, 131–131, 217

financial expropriation   54, 70–71, 76

financial liberalisation   3, 11, 81, 83, 85, 100–101, 104, 109, 151, 188, 246

financialisation   1, 3–13, 28, 37–95, 120, 130, 132–137, 177, 180–181, 191, 232, 236–246, 249–251

fixed investment   39, 69, 79, 91, 94–96, 102, 127–128, 132, 170–180, 187, 205–206, 208, 212–213, 219

Fordist   59, 63–64, 66

formal logic   20–21

global financial crisis   71, 81, 96, 114, 118, 120, 125, 191–193, 246

Great Depression   69, 106

Hegel, Hegelian   16–19

housebuilding   13, 193, 211, 216–224, 227, 230, 240–242, 245, 249–250

Housing Development Administration   6, 13, 194, 209, 214, 217–219, 242, 245

housing provision   12–13, 95, 107, 122, 170, 191–249

hydroelectric power   12, 147, 149, 158–159, 166, 168–170, 190, 223, 250

Ilyenkov   14, 18–19, 22

indebtedness   4, 37, 42, 47–48, 52–57, 65, 86–88, 98–103, 112, 120–122, 125, 132, 183, 192, 237, 253

industrialisation   100, 106, 211, 215

Kaldor   42–44, 252

Kalecki   39, 41–42, 44–45, 47, 55–56

Keynes, Keynesian   39–48, 52–53, 57–59, 66, 69–70, 76, 249

labour productivity   27–29, 32, 45, 64, 71, 81, 101, 130–131, 146, 190, 198, 211, 241, 246, 251–252
labour shedding   99, 101, 191
labour theory of value   30–31
labour-intensive   13, 64, 97, 99–100, 125–126, 130–132, 190, 195–196, 216, 221, 227–228, 241, 246–247, 252
land supply   197, 218–219, 224, 230, 241
longue durée   60

manufacturing sector   7, 11–12, 49, 91, 93, 97, 99–100, 102, 108–109, 125–132, 146, 177, 180, 211–213, 246–251
marketisation   135, 188
Marx, Marxian   10–31, 34, 37–41, 50, 53–54, 57, 63, 68, 70–73, 75–77, 131, 194–195, 200–206, 209, 245, 247
materialism   11, 17, 19–20
methodology   9, 13–14, 20–21, 23, 29, 137, 146
Minsky   53, 80, 86, 192
mode of production   15, 23, 27, 35–36, 201, 208, 248
mortgage   5–6, 53–56, 75–79, 122–123, 191–193, 199, 209, 214, 218–219, 225, 232–234, 237, 239, 245, 250

neoliberalism   40, 59, 68, 70
new dialectic   16

periodisation   58–59, 63–64, 76, 95
Ponzi-financing   54, 56–57, 102–103, 192
Post-Washington Consensus   140
price cap   144, 157, 159
privatisation   37, 12, 92, 134–146, 149–155, 157–168, 176–177, 182, 186, 188–190, 233
profitability   13, 27, 48–49, 52–53, 60, 65–70, 78, 91, 93, 96, 99, 108, 111, 120–121, 132–134, 138, 146, 165, 190, 193–195, 199, 221–224, 230, 232, 241–242, 246, 251
profit-led   51, 65–66
provision goods   9–11, 36–38, 41, 245, 248
public debt   89–90, 93, 100, 102, 109

real estate   1, 4–5, 39, 85, 192, 214, 219, 221, 224, 236, 242, 249–250
Regulation approach   63–66
re-nationalisation   142–145
rent theory   200–210

rentier   6, 47, 50, 73, 75, 92, 108
restructuring   6, 11–12, 71, 74–75, 84, 99, 108–110, 120, 127–128, 130–133, 145, 166, 181, 190, 200, 208–209, 214, 224, 242, 245–246, 251
revenue cap   144, 157, 159

securitisation   9, 53–54, 56, 111, 113, 134, 136, 177, 188–191, 194, 214, 224–225, 244
shareholder value   42, 47–50, 57, 65–67, 76, 79, 180–184
short-termism   135, 188–189, 246
simple-abstract   15, 29, 32, 72, 239
social housing   196, 216, 224–225, 243
social provision   1, 33, 233
social reproduction   22–23, 26–30, 33, 36, 63, 248
structural change   3–4, 7, 49, 97, 99, 129, 131, 246
structures of provision   195
systematic dialectics   11, 16–17
systems of provision   10–11, 33–38, 240, 248

technical change   25, 27, 36, 43, 48, 69, 126–127, 166, 188, 199, 203–204
tendencies   9, 11, 15, 23–24, 27–29, 32, 34, 72, 74, 177, 239, 249
The Brady Plan   81–84
TOKI   6, 13, 175, 194, 209–210, 214, 217–225, 242, 245
totality   16, 22, 24, 26
transmission losses   160–163, 189–190
Tri-partite Class Regime   68–69, 76
Turkish Court of Accounts   154, 161, 163, 175, 220, 274

value of labour power   10–11, 15, 29–38, 58, 64, 77, 100, 133, 191, 239, 248–249
Varieties of Capitalism   6, 41, 66, 76
vertically integrated   134, 138, 140, 145, 149, 253

wage goods   10, 26–27, 34, 36–38, 41, 75, 77, 100, 138, 193, 232, 239–240, 244, 248
wage share   32, 37, 44, 47, 50–52, 54, 64, 69–70, 92–93, 101
wage-led   51–52, 65–66
Washington Consensus   83–84, 138, 140

CPSIA information can be obtained
at www.ICGtesting.com
Printed in the USA
JSHW022219150522
25891JS00001B/2